CATALONIA, A SELF-PORTRAIT

Catalonia,
a Self-Portrait

Edited and Translated from the Catalan by

Josep Miquel Sobrer

Indiana University Press
Bloomington & Indianapolis

© 1992 by Indiana University Press

Introduction, Translation, and Notes
© 1992 by Josep Miquel Sobrer

The paper used in this publication meets the minimum requirements of
American National Standard for Information Sciences—Permanence of Paper
for Printed Library Materials, ANSI Z39.48-1984.

∞™

Manufactured in the United States of America

Library of Congress Cataloging-in-Publication Data

Catalonia, a self-portrait / edited and translated from the Catalan by
Josep Miquel Sobrer.
    p.   cm.
    Includes bibliographical references and index.
    ISBN 0-253-35290-8 (alk. paper). — ISBN 0-253-28883-5 (pbk. :
alk. paper)
    1. Catalonia (Spain)—Civilization.   2. National characteristics,
Catalan. I. Sobrer, Josep Miquel.
DP302.C62C33   1992
946'.7—dc20   91-4050

1 2 3 4 5 96 95 94 93 92

For my brother Gonçal

CONTENTS

Preface and Acknowledgments

Catalonia, a Self-Portrait is an anthology made up of a number of texts translated by the editor from their original Catalan. These texts are grouped in three parts; the editor's introduction explains this grouping. All the texts are presented in continuous form; by this I mean that even though some texts are fragments of larger works, any division or fragmentation within them comes from the original, and so do all the footnotes contained therein.

A number of materials accompanying the texts help to integrate this anthology:

A map of Catalonia and a plan of the city of Barcelona. The map shows as many of the towns and landforms mentioned in the anthology as size and legibility allow, while the plan is simplified for the sake of clarity; it shows only the main streets. Ideally there should be only one map, encompassing both city and country. The plan of Barcelona ought to grow in detail and show the tiniest streets in the old city and even the buildings on them; the map of Catalonia ought to grow in scope and reach out to include Madrid if not Paris, Buenos Aires, New York, and Yakri in Indonesia—for these are all of importance to our story. The mapmaker, Suzanne Hull, and I struggled to find a middle ground. We also decided not to mark political frontiers, for we wanted to show a dynamic Catalonia reaching out to the world rather than closing itself in.

An introduction. This overview sets out the guiding ideas of the book and explains the reasons for the procedures followed. It also states the general and theoretical principles of the work.

Explanatory headnotes. Preceding each piece, these notes clarify details and expand on some of the issues only alluded to in the introduction. They also outline profiles of the authors and give a complete bibliographical reference for each selection.

A bibliography. This list contains full references to works mentioned or alluded to in the introduction and headnotes. I have added to the references a selected list of works in English that may satisfy the readers' further curiosity.

An index of proper names and terms. This list, which seeks to give readers the kind of background that an educated Catalan audience would have, should be used as a reference tool to complement the introduction and headnotes. The index includes the names of historical personalities referred to by authors in this anthology; the names or initials of political parties, labor organizations, and other political institutions; and key terms in the history and literature of Catalonia. Catalan personalities are given at least their birthplace and vital dates; only dates are given for non-Catalans mentioned. All names of Catalans have been left in their original Catalan forms; when personalities mentioned may be known by the Spanish forms of their first names, the alternates are given in parentheses.

Grateful acknowledgment is made to the following persons and organizations for granting permission to translate and publish the materials for this anthology:

Senyor Sebastià Borràs of Editorial Selecta for Joan Amades's "Les pedres i el culte als morts" in his *Folklore de Catalunya*, vol. 3 (Barcelona: Selecta, 1969), and for Carles Soldevila's "L'Art d'ensenyar Barcelona" in his *Obres completes* (Barcelona: Selecta, 1967).

Senyor Pere Calders for his "Els catalans pel món" and "Invasió subtil" in his *Invasió subtil i altres contes* (Barcelona: Edicions 62, 1978).

Edicions Destino of Barcelona for Jaume Vicens i Vives's "Els catalans i el Minotaure" in his *Notícia de Catalunya*, 3d ed. (Barcelona: Destino, 1962) and for Josep Pla's "Antoni Gaudí" in his *Homenots*, 1st series (Barcelona: Destino, 1969).

Senyor Josep Espriu i Castelló for Salvador Espriu's "Teoria de Crisant" and "El país moribund" in his *Narracions*, 5th ed. (Barcelona: Edicions 62, 1974).

Senyor Joan Fuster for his "Maragall i Unamuno, cara a cara" in his *Obres completes*, vol. 4 (Barcelona: Edicions 62, 1975).

Senyor Emili Giralt i Raventós of the Institut d'Estudis Catalans for Mercè Rodoreda's "Estiu" and "Aquella paret, aquella mimosa" in her *Tots els contes* (Barcelona: Edicions 62, 1979).

Senyor Quim Monzó for selections from his *El dia del Senyor* and his *ZZZZZZZZ* (Barcelona: Quaderns Crema, 1984 and 1987).

Senyor Josep Palau i Fabre for "Picasso i Catalunya" from his *Doble assaig sobre Picasso* (Barcelona: Selecta, 1964).

Senyor Baltasar Porcel for "Succinta explicació de Catalunya per a castellans" from his *Debat català* (Barcelona: Selecta, 1973).

Senyora Montserrat Roig for a selection from her *Els catalans als camps nazis* (Barcelona: Edicions 62, 1977).

Senyor Jaume VallcorbaPlana for J. V. Foix's "Presentacions" of Dalí, Miró, and Carbonell, and "Quatre colors aparien el món," all in his *Obres completes,* vol. 2 (Barcelona: Edicions 62, 1979).

These works have been translated with the help of a grant from the Dirección General del Libro y Bibliotecas of Spain's Ministerio de Cultura.

The translations from the Catalan by J. M. Sobrer have also received a grant from the Institució de les Lletres Catalanes of the Generalitat de Catalunya.

The text is decorated with a bird-and-leaves motif from a 1902 title design by the *modernista* Alexandre de Riquer i Anglada, and with a vase-and-flowers motif drawn by the *noucentista* Enric Cristòfor Ricart Giralt for a 1919 edition of poems by Millàs Raurell.

The preparation of this book was made further possible by the granting of a sabbatical leave during the spring semester of 1989 to its editor, who hereby expresses his thanks to the Dean of the Faculties' Office of Indiana University.

A grant-in-aid from the Office of Research and the Graduate School of Indiana University funded the preparation of the maps.

My thanks to all.

In addition to the writers or their representatives and the individuals from those offices mentioned above, I would like to express my recognition to all the friends and colleagues who have helped me in the preparation of this work.

Professors Willis Barnstone and Mark Musa were the first in a long list of colleagues who encouraged the development of this project and lent it crucial initial support. Further help came from Professors Luis Beltrán, Gabriel Berns, Edward Friedman, Anthony Kerrigan, and surely others.

I would like to thank especially Frances Wyers for her willingness to share her vast knowledge of modern Spanish literature and for her sensible readings and sound English ear; Arthur Brakel for his prompt and salutary reading of the Amades piece; Maryellen Bieder for her acute comments on the Rodoreda stories; David Pace for finding dear time to ponder over my introduction; and Suzanne Hull for her smart mapmaking.

xii

I must make particular mention of Lisa Ress, who became the first reader of this book and its honorary editor, convening into order the astray constructions of many drafts. I am greatly indebted to her stylistic *seny,* and also a little to her *rauxa.*

And finally, and although not directly involved with the preparation of this book, I want to express my appreciation to my brother Gonçal, who throughout the years, from Catalonia, has been a model international publicist of our country's culture. To him this book is lovingly and deservedly dedicated.

Josep Miquel Sobrer
Bloomington, December 31, 1990

CATALONIA, A SELF-PORTRAIT

Places of Interest		Streets & Squares	
1	Arc de Triomf (Arch of Triumph)	**A**	Carrer Sant Pau
2	Saló de Sant Joan	**B**	Carrer Hospital
3	Santa Maria del Mar	**C**	Carrer Carme
4	Llotja	**D**	Carrer Valldonzella
5	Monument a Colom	**E**	Carrer Elisabets
	(Columbus Monument)	**F**	Carrer Bonsuccés
6	Drassanes (shipyards)	**G**	Carrer Santa Anna
7	Murs de Santa Madrona (Ramparts)	**H**	Plaça (del Portal) de l'Angel
8	Sant Pau del Camp	**I**	Carrer Portaferrissa
9	Mercat de Sant Antoni	**J**	Carrer Boters
10	Hospital de la Santa Creu	**K**	Carrer Petritxol
11	Casa de Convalescència	**L**	Carrer Boqueria
12	Església de Betlem	**M**	Carrer d'Avinyó
13	Virreina	**N**	Plaça Reial
14	Liceu	**O**	Plaça Sant Jaume
15	Casa la Ciutat	**P**	Plaça del Rei
16	Palau de la Generalitat	**Q**	Carrer Vigatans
17	Catedral	**R**	Carrer Canvis Nous
18	Tinell (old Royal Palace)	**S**	Passeig de Picasso
19	Palau Reial (Royal Palace)	**T**	Rambla del Prat
20	Palau de la Música	**U**	(Josepets) Plaça Lesseps
21	University	**V**	Carrer Craywinckel
22	La Sagrada Família	**W**	Plaça Bonanova
23	La Pedrera (Casa Milà)		
24	Pedralbes (Monastery)		

PEDRALBES

Passeig Bonanova

C. El Pedró

W

SARRIÀ

Ronda General Mitre

Via Carlos III

Via Augusta

Carrer Pàdua

V

Avinguda Tibidabo

to Tibidabo

Avinguda República Argentina

Park Güell

HORTA

N

SANT GERVASI

U

Travessera de Dalt

Carrer Sangossa

T

GRÀCIA

Travessera de Gràcia

LES CORTS

Avinguda Diagonal

de Sants

Hospital de la Santa Creu i Sant Pau

Avinguda Josep Tarradellas

Carrer Urgell

Carrer Muntaner

Avinguda Diagonal

de Gràcia

C. Provença

Auda. de Gaudí

SANTS

E   I   X   A   M   P   L   E

23

de Sant Joan

22

Avinguda de Roma

Carrer Aragó

Passeig

Carrer Corts (Gran Via)

21

Carrer Corts   (Gran Via)

Plaça d'Espanya

Avinguda Exposició

C. Sepúlveda

C. Floridablanca

9

Ronda

D

Ronda

Plaça Catalunya

Ronda

Passeig de Sant Joan

Plaça de les Glòries Catalunes

Ronda

FORT PIUS

Auda. de Meridiana

POBLE SEC

Carrer Marquès del Duero (Paral·lel)

Ronda

E = F
= G
B   C   12   San blu
10   13
J   H
L   19
K   P
17 18
14   O
M   16
N   15

BARRI GÒTIC

20

Via Laietana

1

2

POBLE NOU

DISTRICT 5è
BARRI XINÈS

A

8

de la Rambla

Q   C. Princesa

R   3
4

S

Parc de la Ciutadella

Teatre Grec

Carrer Nou

CUITAT VELLA

Montjüic

7
6   5

Passeig de Colom

Barcelona
Map of the Major Streets

Port

BARCELONETA

MEDITERRANEAN SEA

Catalonia

Montpellier•

PYRENEES

Perpinyà
Prada
Montlluís• Prats de
Gràus• Mollò 1
Prats de
Andorra
Sapeira•
Talàrn•
Tragó•
Sant Pere de Roda
Peralada
Figueres•
Cotlliure
Núria•
Aranyonet•
Ripoll•
Olot A
Jonqueres•
Siurana
Empúries
L'Escala
Mieres•
Campdorà •Verges
C
Sant Feliu
D de Pallerols
Girona
Palafrugell
Vic•
Vilatorta•Sant Hilari
Su•
Sallent•
Santpedor•
Castellterçol•
Sacalm
Llofriu
Palamós
B
Balaguer•
Calaf•
Manresa
Puiggraciós
Santa Cristina d'Aro
Sant Feliu de Guixols
Lleida
2
Tàrrega•
Caldes• L'Ametlla
Tossa
Collbató•
4 Terrassa
E
Arenys de Mar
Sabadell•
Argentona•
L'Espluga•
Martorell•
Montcada•
Poblet•
Santa Coloma
Badalona
Valls•
de Cervelló•
3
Barcelona
Caspe•
La Selva•
Cerdanyola•
Prat de Llobregat
El Vendrell•
Sitges•
5
Reus•
Vilanova i la Geltrú
Riudoms•
Torredembarra
G
Mora
Prat de Comte•
Miravet•
Tarragona
Horta de
Sant Joan 7
Tortosa

MEDITERRANEAN SEA

Castelló de la Plana•

Pollença•

MINORCA

València•

SA DRAGONERA•
Andratx•
Palma•

Felanitx•

MAJORCA

Gandia•
Dénia•

EIVISSA

Alacant•

0   25   50   75   100   125 km

Mountains	Regions
1 Canigó	**A** Garrotxa
2 Montseny	**B** Empordà
3 Serra de Collserola	**C** Cabrerès
4 Montserrat	**D** Lluçanès
5 Costes del Garraf	**E** Vallès
6 Serra de Prades	**F** Priorat
7 Mountains of Pàndols	**G** Terra Alta
8 Puig Major	

JOSEP MIQUEL SOBRER

Introduction

Two kinds of experiences prompted this book: inquiries from friends and acquaintances and my reactions to a number of scholarly works touching on its subject matter. During the many years I have lived in the United States, quite often, as people learn that I am a Catalan and devote a considerable amount of my scholarly time to the literature and language of Catalonia, I have been asked what this Catalonia is, and who or what is a Catalan. At the same time, when reading works by literary scholars, linguists, historians, and anthropologists about Catalonia, I have felt that the very objectivity of the foreign scholarly view meant a kind of clinical distortion, for no vision of any human group or of any individual is quite complete from a single perspective, less so from a distant one. And so I conceived the idea of preparing a book to satisfy a general curiosity and to balance a certain coldness of vision about Catalonia, and immediately I realized that I should not *write* that book but rather let my compatriots speak from within their country, within their own roles, in their own voices. Underlying these motives was a third one, of a more theoretical nature: the wish to present as direct an image as possible of the cultural humus upon which the writers I selected grow like so many trees. Implicit here is my belief that culture can only be considered ecologically. Students of literature have often remarked on sources for and influences on writers; "intertextuality" is an inevitable term in today's critical speech. But an artist's work goes beyond the influence of artists in the same field: writers also look at painters, sculptors listen to music, dancers dance in architects' buildings, and they all vie for the same public, a public brought together by a sense of community. It is this sense of community, at once nourishing the artists and benefiting from them, that I have tried to capture here, convinced as I am that a small, clearly "critical" society such as Catalonia is ideal for an undertaking of this nature, an undertaking that might be utopian for a larger society like Spain or France.

So the basic idea was to gather in one volume a collection of writings that would amount to a self-portrait of my country; hence the title of this book. Probably no artist since El Greco has failed to paint or draw a self-portrait. One's self is of course always a fascinating topic for one's own exploration, but beyond a more or less noble narcissism, we must admit that artists' self-portraits have an authority that renders them unforgettable. For a self-portrait always looks for an inner truth, a kernel of individuality beyond the commonplace and superficial, and it shuns the flattery that makes official commissioned portraits unreliable if not downright sycophantic. Achieving such a view was my goal for this book.

Having set myself to choosing the pieces that would form such a volume, I found myself confronted with the ungrateful task of having to select just a few from among a great variety of possibilities. I have drawn my selections from Catalan-language originals, even though Spanish is also a language of today's Catalonia and the question of language-identification is crucial in the political self-representations of Catalans (McDonogh).* My reasons are two: I wanted to publicize the work done in a less-known language and, more important, I felt that the definition of Catalonia ought to be left to those who, by writing in the traditional language of the region, represent a self-determined, "Catalanist" attitude and portray historical and traditional values; the viewpoint of those who think Catalonia is no more than a region within Spain is served well enough by the de facto political situation of the country. Even considering only those texts written in Catalan, the pool available to me loomed imposingly large. I opted also for centering myself on the twentieth century, with an eye to providing enough background for an overall view of the present situation, and decided on a number of prose genres, from the scholarly article to the parable, from the short biography to the newspaper column, from folklore to fiction, from chronicle to prose poem. The criteria that guided me were

---

*Names in parentheses refer to recent discussions of topics mentioned. Because I have in mind general arguments rather than questions of detail, no page reference is given. For pertinent information on the references, see the bibliography at the end of this book.

mainly two: I wanted pieces that would offer clear explanations of some aspect of Catalan culture, but pieces that would also make for interesting reading; and I wanted to include works by as many respected authors as possible—twentieth-century Catalan classics, as it were. After research and consultation, after some debate with myself and with fellow Catalanists, after some initial choices that had to be discarded, and given the constraints gently imposed on me by the publisher, I came up with the pieces that comprise this anthology and set myself the task of translating them for what I hope will make informative and enjoyable reading.

Catalonia, a Self-Portrait is divided into three parts: Place, Time, and People. These headings are to be taken loosely, for none of the categories named in these titles make sense without the others. Generally, however, the selections for the first part deal with geography (but also with a sense of belonging in the culture), those for the second deal with history (but also with allegory), and those for the third are basically biographical (but also symbolical). As none of the selections were originally written with an international audience in mind, basic clarifications for each piece appear as explanatory headnotes. In addition, readers may appreciate being provided beforehand with background information rather than having to resort to a system of burdensome notes that might be confused with the notes that some of the authors saw fit to include. The rest of this introduction will be devoted to such general background information.

PLACE

Any knowledge of history reveals that precise political borders are always to a greater or lesser degree fictitious. Whatever unites or separates human formations is complex and changing enough to make frontiers not only porous but also shifting. The map of Catalonia (page 00) shows no political borders in order to illustrate my conviction that the kind of human conglomerate we call a nation is a network of interdependent communities rather than a discrete geographical area.

The official borders of Catalonia have changed through the centuries and are bound to change again. But even at this moment it is difficult to point out the exact perimeters of Catalonia. There are at least two diverging notions of what Catalonia is: one narrow and one broad. This anthology will not pronounce itself in favor of one or the other but rather leave it imprecise, as imprecision seems to have suited the writers themselves.

The narrow version of Catalonia coincides with the autonomous region called Catalunya in present-day Spain. Referred to by historians as the Principality of Catalonia, it occupies 3,193,000 hectares, or 31,930 square kilometers, according to the Institut Cartogràfic de Catalunya and the Instituto Nacional de Estadística. It is situated at the northeast triangle of the Iberian Peninsula formed by the Mediterranean coast and the eastern end of the Pyrenees range.

A broader view of Catalonia claims that what really constitutes the country is the geographical area in which Catalan is spoken. Most Catalans feel this linguistic yardstick to be a better gauge than any spatial consideration, because mountains and plains and woods, even fields and rivers, cannot be said to belong to any country or have any nationality; countries are made by people united in their culture. According to the linguistic criterion, then, we should speak of a Greater Catalonia or, as the common phrase goes, *Països Catalans,* "Catalan Countries." The Països Catalans spread out under four different national states: (1) in Spain, the above-mentioned Principality of Catalonia, the autonomous regions of Valencia and the Balearics (the latter comprising the islands of Majorca, Minorca, Ibiza, and Formentera), and a zone of eastern Aragon where Catalan is spoken (called *la franja de Ponent,* "the Western strip"); (2) the independent Pyrenean Principality of Andorra; (3) in France, the old counties of Rosselló (Roussillon in French), Capcir, Conflent, Vallespir, and part of Cerdanya that comprise the French Department of Pyrénées-Orientales (note that the official French terminology seeks to deny any mark of autochthonous identity for the regions); and (4) in Italy, the city of Alguer (Alghero) on the island of Sardinia.

The exact delimitation of Catalonia as a nation is impossible and so, consequently, is the number of its inhabitants. Catalonia proper, according to the 1989 *Europa World Year Book,* is inhabited by 6,099,319 citizens. The total number of inhabitants of Spain's Catalan-speaking regions is, according to the same source, 9,473,098; perhaps only some seven million of them can be said to be speakers of Catalan, as immigration into Catalonia has been heavy and linguistic assimilation incomplete.

Catalan is a Romance language, and to untrained ears it sounds like something between Spanish and French, with a touch of Portuguese. It is not a creole made up by a blending of these languages, however; it is an indigenous language derived directly from Latin. Educated Spanish and

French speakers are able to understand a fair amount of written Catalan, just as they can make out a text in Portuguese or Italian. But spoken Catalan is quite impenetrable to foreigners, for it has a phonology all its own. In syntax and vocabulary it comes close to the Romance languages spoken to the north, particularly Provençal, for during Roman times these two areas were exposed to similar patterns of colonization. In morphology, however, Catalan comes closer to Spanish. Since most of "greater Catalonia" has been ruled by a centralist, Castilian-dominated Spain, the language has felt the heavy influence of Castilian, and frequent rulings against Catalan's public use have led to the emergence of significant dialectal forms within the language and a low literacy rate among native speakers in their language. The present government, through its Department de Política Lingüística, seeks to remedy these ills (Woolard).

Claims for a Catalan sense of self have often referred back to the land, to *la terra catalana,* and the modern revival of Catalan nationalism has been imbued since the 1830s with an ecological sense, an idealized view of the terrain that the lack of political independence has made more acute. Catalonia originated in the eighth century in the eastern Pyrenees, but that core soon expanded down the coast to Barcelona. From there the Balearics, and in particular the main island of Majorca, are seen as a natural extension of the country, since from the medieval period Catalans have considered themselves people of the Mediterranean, seafarers and merchants (Bisson). The Romantic period brought a revival of the image of the mountains as bastions of purity and authenticity and began to breach the notion, still found in some authors, of two Catalonias: a wild area in the mountains and a commercial zone on the littoral (Elliott). The mountain of Montserrat, which rises on Catalonia's central plain, has become the site for the Catalans' foremost religious shrine. A geological anomaly, the imposing granite formation of Montserrat establishes a symbolic link between coast and hinterland. The Black Madonna who is venerated on the mountain became the patron saint of Catalonia—and made the name Montserrat popular for countless Catalan women.

Whatever the country may be, its human geography is dominated by Barcelona, the most populous city on the Mediterranean coast, with 1,703,744 inhabitants in 1989 (according to *Europa;* the total for the Barcelona province was 4,734,291), and the economic and cultural capital of Catalonia and the Països Catalans. With its port, its well-preserved medieval core, its *modernista* legacy, and its temperate climate, Barcelona is an appealing tourist attraction as well as a cultural center and dynamic capital.

The history of Catalonia goes back to the Middle Ages, when a new nation and a new language emerged from the collapsed power of the Roman Empire and the new order of the Germanic tribes settled in the province. After some two hundred years, the language, Catalan, was to consolidate into a literary medium not very different from its present-day form; the nation, however, had a much less clear fate. A factual overview of that history would touch on the following events.

In 801 Louis the Pious, who was to succeed Charlemagne in 814, conquered Barcelona from the Moors and established a Marca Hispanica, leaving a handful of feudal counts to rule that buffer zone created between his empire and the Arabs. The Marca Hispanica, a name that goes back to the Roman term for the Iberian Peninsula, Hispania, is the origin of Catalonia. The Romanized local population spoke a Latin that had evolved into Catalan by this time, a language akin to those of the southern half of present-day France, such as Provençal. Etymologists have been unable to agree on the origin of the name Catalunya, which, Latinized as Catalonia, has entered the English language.

In 878 Wifred the Hairy, count of Barcelona, united all the Marca counties under his rule and declared his independence from the French. This union marks the rise of the house of Barcelona, whose medieval emblem, four red bars over gold—in heraldic terms, four pallets of gules over or—is to this day the emblem of Catalonia and of all the kingdoms ruled at one time or other by the house of Barcelona. According to a romantic legend, Count Wifred, eager to leave his new country an emblem, dipped four fingers into his open battle wound and, with a dying gasp, drew four bloody lines on his golden shield.

In 1137 Ramon Berenguer IV, ninth count of Barcelona, married Petronila, daughter of Ramiro II, king of Aragon, and succeeded his father-in-law. Catalonia and Aragon became dynastically united, forming what is unofficially called the Crown of Aragon. Later conquests by James I of the kingdoms of Majorca (1229) and Valencia (1238) enlarged the Aragonese Crown; the two new kingdoms and the old counties make up the core of what is today referred to as Països Catalans. A number of Mediterranean possessions—Montpellier, Sicily, Sardinia, the Duchy of Athens—were tied to the Crown at some time or other; this expansionism has prompted some historians to speak of a Catalan empire in the Mediterranean (Shneidman), a view dismissed by others (Hillgarth). The fourteenth-century chronicler Ramon Muntaner is the main source for a notion of a medieval Catalan empire. A good portion of his chronicle describes the exploits of the largely Catalan *almogàvers* (mercenary shock troops) in the Byzantine Empire. The diverse national identifications of Catalans appear in the terminology used by Muntaner: the Greeks refer to the almogàvers as Franks, while they themselves rally to the battle cry of "Aragó!"; Muntaner insists on their use of the Catalan language.

With Martin I, the Humanist, the Barcelona dynasty died in 1410. Two years later a compromise was reached in the Aragonese town of Caspe, and Ferdinand of Antequera was elected to succeed Martin as king of Aragon. Ferdinand was a member of the Castilian family of the Trastámaras; this family was to be in power in both of the main clusters of kingdoms in Spain—Castile and Aragon—until the Habsburgs.

Ferdinand I's grandnephew, Ferdinand II (V of Spain), married Isabella of Castile in 1479; they are known as the Catholic monarchs. Though married to each other, each monarch ruled one of the two kingdoms, which were federated rather than united, preserving their own laws and organization. The dynastic union they achieved is nevertheless the origin of present-day Spain. Since their daughter, Joan the Mad, was thought unfit to reign, both crowns went to a Habsburg, Charles, who was Charles I of Castile and Aragon but would soon become Charles V of the Holy Roman Empire.

When the Count-Duke of Olivares, the favorite minister of Philip IV (Charles I's great-grandson), attempted to recruit Aragonese and Catalans for the war in Flanders, the Catalans rose in protest and the so-called War of the Reapers ensued, from 1640 to 1652; a result of the war was that part of Catalonia, the Pyrenean regions of Roussillon, Cerdanya, and so forth, were ceded to the French Crown (Elliott).

The Habsburg dynasty came to an end with the death of Philip IV's son, Charles II, in 1700. Charles II changed his will during the last months of his life; in the new document the French Bourbon Philip of Anjou replaced Charles of Austria as heir to the Spanish crown. The change provoked a civil war: the War of Succession. By and large, though not unanimously, the Catalans sided with Charles. But Philip V's forces overcame the pro-Habsburgs in 1714 and the victorious monarchy proceeded to unite the two crowns of Spain into a modern state in the French fashion. A decree known as Nueva Planta issued in 1717 eliminated the historic rights of the

Aragonese and Catalans as it restructured all of Spain. The Nueva Planta excluded the Catalan language from use in the courts and legal documents; this was the first of the political persecutions against it.

The capitulation of Barcelona at the end of the War of Succession on September 11, 1714, gave rise to Catalonia's "national" day; Catalans still celebrate their struggle for sovereignty on this date, *l'onze de setembre*. That date may represent the closest modern Catalonia has been to real political independence.

The Bourbon order of the eighteenth century evolved into the political upheavals of the nineteenth. Early in the century King Charles IV of Spain (whose family gave the Aragonese Francisco de Goya one of his most famous portrait subjects) was forced to abdicate in favor of his son Ferdinand. He in turn soon abdicated in favor of Joseph Bonaparte, Napoleon's brother. The Spanish people, including the Catalans, rose against the French monarchy and its internal allies, the *afrancesados,* and for five years Spain suffered what is known as the War of Independence (*Guerra del francès* in Catalan), the horrors of which were also depicted by Goya. The war ended in a French defeat and the return of Ferdinand to the throne. The king, nicknamed *el Deseado,* "the Yearned-for," soon brought about a reign of conservative repression followed by the three Carlist Wars, which were sparked by the fact that his appointed successor was female, Isabella II.

Having emerged as the most economically advanced of the Spanish provinces during the eighteenth century, Catalonia entered Spanish politics during the nineteenth as the country reorganized itself against Joseph I and in the absence of Ferdinand VII. So in Catalonia a Junta Superior del Principat de Catalunya was organized as its first democratic government; but this autochthonous organ was soon integrated into general Spanish rule. Centuries of political periphery for Catalonia meant that its autonomic aspirations could not be concretized. The political ambivalence of Catalonia—its doubts about whether it should strive for independence or for increased political power within a unified Spain—continues to this day.

The Bourbon monarchy also continues, for King Juan Carlos is a distant heir of Philip V's; today's king, however, has sworn to uphold a democratic constitution and does not govern. There have been three interruptions to monarchic rule in modern Spain: the first Republic (1868–1875), the second Republic (1931–1939), and the dictatorship of General Francisco Franco (1939–1975), who came to power after the military uprising of July 18, 1936, which led to the Civil War (1936–1939).

During the rule of the Habsburgs Catalonia was governed by a
viceroy; during that of the Bourbons and Franco, by a captain general or
civil governor, normally a non-Catalan appointed in Madrid. The main
organ of local authority during those times was, with varying degrees of
power, the Diputació del General, or Generalitat, a representative assem-
bly first created by the Corts held in Barcelona-Vilafranca-Cervera in
1358–1359. The Bourbons split the Generalitat into four provincial *diputacions.* Today the Generalitat is the autonomous administration of Catalonia,
a body not unlike the state governments in the United States.

The modern Generalitat is the successor to the revival effected
in 1914 by Enric Prat de la Riba, who united the diputacions of the four
Catalan provinces (Barcelona, Tarragona, Lleida, and Girona) into one
governing body, the Mancomunitat de Catalunya. The Mancomunitat was
the culmination of the movement for autonomy in Catalan politics. The
country benefited from the prosperous turn-of-the-century period and,
aided by Spain's neutrality during World War I, saw a great upsurge in
Catalan cultural production. In the arts the flamboyant art nouveau style,
known locally as *modernisme,* was followed by the neoclassical revival,
noucentisme. Modernisme left its brilliant mark on the architecture of Barcelona and other towns, principally in the then recent enlargement of the
city known as the Eixample. Under Prat de la Riba, noucentisme, a movement whose ideologue was the philosopher Eugeni d'Ors, reached its peak.
Also under Prat the Catalan language was "normalized"—that is, organized linguistically to accord both with its medieval literary background
and with the demands for grammatical coherence characteristic of the
twentieth century. The linguist who undertook this task was Pompeu
Fabra, whom Prat called back to Barcelona from his post as professor of
engineering in Bilbao to head the Secció Filològica of the newly created
Institut d'Estudis Catalans. Fabra elaborated a set of Normes Ortogrà-
fiques, which were approved by the institute in 1913, and prepared a
normative *Diccionari General de la Llengua Catalana,* published in 1932.

Social unrest and violence have also marked the first third of
this century in Catalonia; at times repression followed with more cruelty
than that of the events that prompted it. Catalonia had become the first
industrialized region in modern Spain. The massive working class created
there by the textile industry had to struggle for improvements in its working conditions and social situation. Inspired mainly by the anarchist leader
Mikhail Bakunin, the ideals of libertarian communism inflamed most of
the Catalan workers. The Confederación Nacional del Trabajo (CNT) was
established in 1911, but anarchist reaction against capitalist exploitation

10 and the role played in it by the Catholic Church had already sparked the riots and church burnings of the "Tragic Week," July 26–August 1, 1909 (Ullman). Leftists organized themselves around a number of political parties known by their initials and mentioned in some of the essays that follow. The Federación Anarquista Ibérica (FAI), the political arm of the CNT, was established in Valencia in 1927. A Catalanist Esquerra Republicana de Catalunya (ERC, or Esquerra) was founded in 1931 by Francesc Macià, who was president of the Generalitat. A number of communist parties united to form the Partit Socialista Unificat de Catalunya (PSUC) in 1936, the year the Civil War began.

The disasters of the Civil War were many for Catalonia. Conservative and radical Catalanists would fall on opposite sides, but all were equally repressed by the fervid anti-Catalanist Franco, the winner of the war. The communist Left was split between the Trotskyites (parties such as the Partit Obrer d'Unificació Marxista [POUM]) and the Stalinists; the clashes between the latter and both the Trotskyites and anarchists erupted in the "events of May 1937," a civil war within the Civil War described by George Orwell in *Homage to Catalonia*. The end of the war signified a massive exile for Catalans; many of those who crossed the border were to find a worse fate at the hands of the Nazis. Among them, the last president of the Republican Generalitat de Catalunya, Lluís Companys, was captured by Gestapo agents in France and handed over to Spanish authorities, who executed him in 1940.

The forty years of the Franco dictatorship brought cultural as well as political repression. Little by little, however, Catalan cultural life reemerged, along with a widespread sentiment for the autonomy of Catalonia. Shortly after Franco's death in 1975, a provisional Generalitat was reestablished and its president in exile, Josep Tarradellas, was called back from France to head it (October 24, 1977). In 1979 the Spanish Cortes, or Parliament, approved a statute granting autonomy to the region. All of Spain joined the European Economic Community in 1986. In 1990 Catalan was accepted as an official language in the EEC.

PEOPLE

Some of the greatest names in the arts of the Western world during the twentieth century have been Catalan. The architect Antoni

Gaudí is one of the acknowledged innovators in his field; Gaudí springs
from the artistic blooming of modernisme but also transcends it by the
originality of his work, if not merely by the sheer scale of his main project,
the Sagrada Família. The painters Salvador Dalí, Joan Miró, and the
younger Tàpies command a world audience and hold preeminent places in
the development of modern painting; the sculptors Arístides Maillol, Manuel (Manolo) Martínez i Hugué, Pau Gargallo, and Juli Gonzàlez, although less known, have been quite influential. In music such composers
as Enric Granados, Isaac Albéniz, and Frederic Mompou, the cellist Pablo
Casals, and singers such as Victoria de los Angeles, Montserrat Caballé,
and Josep (or José) Carreras have commanded the attention of audiences
around the world. That they all come from a small and stateless country,
Catalonia, with little public support for the arts is astounding in itself,
perhaps indicating that Catalonia—for whatever reasons—has poured its
energies toward creative expression rather than its own political independence.

But these important figures do not exist in isolation. For one
thing, the list ought to be completed with the roster of writers. Catalan
literature has been in existence for more than eight hundred years, but I
would not hesitate to consider the period represented most saliently in this
anthology, from the 1920s to the 1970s, its most brilliant era, a true
golden age for Catalan letters. Catalonia's writers, of course—and in particular those who opted to use the Catalan language over the more widely
studied Spanish—are little known beyond the orbit of the country. They
deserve greater fame, for their achievements are in no way inferior to their
colleagues' in the other arts. There is a living connection among the arts,
and the exploration of that connection is one of the purposes of this book.

I hope the present anthology will bring to the attention of
English speakers the craft of the most notable prose writers of twentieth-
century Catalonia, and for this reason I have combined essayists, poets, and
fiction writers. A few words about names may be pertinent at this point.
The names of all Catalans mentioned are given in their original Catalan,
although some of them have also used the Spanish equivalents of their first
names (Jaume, for example, corresponds to the Spanish Jaime, Josep to
José, and so on). In the pieces translated here, the authors' names appear
as they do in the original books from which their essays and stories are
taken; in my headnotes and index, however, I have provided each author's
full name. In the Catalan tradition, similar to the Spanish one, everybody
has two surnames, the first corresponding to one's father and the second to
one's mother. These names are often united by the conjunction *i,* "and,"

so that, for example, the full name of the anthologist is Josep-Miquel Sobrer i Barea. As in my case, many writers shorten or vary their names professionally, generally preferring their first surname.

Ultimately this anthology ought to give its readers not only widespread information about Catalonia and the Catalan area but also a feeling for the spirit of Catalans. I see our culture as a sedate yet playfully imaginative enterprise, both frustrated and enriched by the political dependency of the country. But mostly I hope I have provided readers with sufficient materials, and sufficient editorial restraint, to let them view the portrait themselves.

I.

Place

A Note on Soldevila's
"The Art of Showing Barcelona"

Carles Soldevila wrote this essay as a pamphlet for the World's Fair held in Barcelona in 1929. The fair was the second such event in the city; there had been one in 1888, and like its predecessor the 1929 fair contributed notably to the monumental development of Barcelona. This exposition was held in the new parklike grounds on Montjuïc, the mountain rising over the port and associated since medieval times with the Jews, hence its name.

The city, now doubled in population, has of course changed since 1929, and it might be an amusing exercise for readers who visit it to compare present-day Barcelona with the image of the city presented by Soldevila. His advice for visitors and their hosts maintains its appropriateness, and the core of the city's architectural treasures presented here has undergone few changes.

The German pavilion for the 1929 fair has been reconstructed; it was the work of Mies van der Rohe, who also introduced there his famous design for the armless Barcelona chair. Soldevila wrote his essay before the exposition opened, however, and makes no mention of this or other developments, much as he enjoys the gardens surrounding the pavilions that were begun in the 1920s.

As a writer, Soldevila is a member of the generation known as

noucentista. The word derives from the Catalan for nine hundred, *noucents,*
16   a reference to the new century. The *noucentistes,* whose most renowned
publicist was the philosopher Eugeni d'Ors, took hold of Catalonia's intellectual life in alliance with the conservative Catalanist party led by Enric
Prat de la Riba. Being the generation to follow the *modernistes* (the Catalan
word for the turn-of-the-century artistic movement which in the visual arts
is known mostly as art nouveau), the noucentistes detested their predecessors' artistic expression. Soldevila is particularly acerbic in his decrying of
modernista monuments, particularly those by Antoni Gaudí and Josep Maria Jujol. Gaudí's famous apartment house, the Casa Milà, called popularly
La Pedrera, "The Stone Quarry," is considered a regrettable eccentricity.
The overstated abandon of art nouveau was felt as the antithesis of the
noucentista ideal of classical simplicity; Soldevila, for example, shows himself candidly proud of Catalonia's ties to Greek colonization. Ironically,
Barcelona's main attraction nowadays is its modernista legacy, and the city
is known throughout the world as Gaudí's city.

Carles Soldevila i Zubiburu (Barcelona 1892–1967), a novel-
ist, playwright, essayist, and translator, brought a cosmopolitan sophistica-
tion to the Catalan stage of the 1930s. His first play, *Civilitzats tanmateix*
(Civilized nevertheless), enjoyed such a success that Luigi Pirandello was
prompted to translate it into Italian. His essay on taste and manners presented here is only disguised as a tourist pamphlet.

My translation is taken from Soldevila's *Obres completes,* published in Barcelona by Editorial Selecta (1967).

CARLES SOLDEVILA

The Art of Showing Barcelona

PRELIMINARY WORDS

Everybody is writing orientation guides for foreigners coming to Barcelona; you can find dozens of them, in all sizes and colors.

But no one takes care to guide the Barcelonese in their own
city. This seems to me an injustice, and most imprudent.

Barcelona is becoming an important tourist center. Any one of
us can be put in the position of having to escort friends from Berlin, customers from Paris, acquaintances from Rome. Where shall we begin? What
is of interest? What monuments are worth our while? Which aspects of the
city are fashionable? Which are picturesque?

All these questions will find *an answer* in this essay. An answer
that does not aspire to being *the answer*. Rather, the author has attempted
to awaken in the consciousness of those Barcelonese who read him the idea
that to show their native city may become a kind of artistic endeavor.
Those persons whose hobby or whose social duty it is to serve as guides
may, by measuring effects and combining contrasts, by underscoring or
understating impressions with their commentaries, *create* a city much more
interesting than the one we see every day in the course of our affairs.

With this notion in mind, the guide's métier becomes a noble
trade, with some similarities to those of painters and poets, producers and
stage directors.

Even if the help this booklet offers you does not quite have the power to elevate you to those sublime categories, it will spare you not a few blunders. This fact alone is, let us admit it, priceless.

THE ARRIVAL

A telegram. A telegram addressed to you: "Arriving tomorrow with wife and daughter 12:50 express. Greetings. Otto Kaufmann."

"And here they are!" you exclaim with a mixture of satisfaction and nervousness. Satisfaction, because the Kaufmann family is very pleasant, treated you very well when you visited Berlin, has rendered you admirable services; nervousness, because you foresee the weight and complexity of the duties of hospitality.

Keep calm! Do not panic. If the Kaufmanns impressed you during your visit to Berlin, you will impress them during their visit to Barcelona. Otherwise, what would be the point, doggone it, in my writing the manual that you are now holding?

The first step is to assure for the Kaufmanns adequate lodgings. Unless your domicile lends itself to the intense practice of hospitality, you will have no other solution but to hunt for hotels and pensions in order to solve the problem. An arduous, difficult problem, almost insoluble! Never mind. Your triumph will be the more appreciated the more difficulties you will have had to overcome.

Let us suppose that after a long pilgrimage, after having exerted your influence and tipped the appropriate people, you have secured rooms for the Kaufmanns in the category and the location they require.

At this point you should take a precaution: check the exact arrival time of the supposed 12:50 express in the latest timetable. Travelers often give an inexact or erroneous time. You must know the exact time so that, five minutes before, you can show up at the station platform all dressed up and with a smile on your lips.

Here's the train! Do not rush. Do not behave like some Barcelonese, neophytes in the art of welcoming travelers; do not start hurrying down the platform. Stop when you are level with the steps of the first car. Or else you'll run the risk of letting the Kaufmann family slip to your rear guard, toward the exit. That would be a blunder. Stop, therefore, at the foot of the first step and keep your eyes sharp so as to catch the

Kaufmann features. It is better to find them preparing to follow the porter bearing their luggage than to miss them.

There they are! Amid the mass of arriving passengers you have spotted the blond hair of Daddy Kaufmann and at once the no less blond braids of Alice, his daughter. O.K. You may move. Now you may run to meet them. Greet them all and, if you must kiss someone, kiss, but do not impede circulation, nor lose sight of the porter, who, indifferent to all these effusions—he's seen so many!—keeps walking, walking toward the door with the Kaufmann baggage. There can be nothing more unpleasant than finding oneself outside the station next to the bus stop without a clue as to where the suitcases went. Avoid such moments of anguish; even if it is not your responsibility, the newcomers will blame the friend who went to welcome them, the local, the indigenous. They'll look at the friend as if to say, "Well! Is this the way you run a welcoming party? Do you want us to come to Barcelona with no more clothes than those we have on?"

You will not find yourself in this vexing situation. As you pay a compliment to Frau Kaufmann and exchange a pleasantry with her daughter, you will lead them on behind the impassive porter. As soon as you are outside the building you'll search for the shuttle bus to the Metropol Hotel, where you have reserved rooms for the Kaufmanns. Should the bus be too crowded or should you simply feel grand, check the luggage with the hotel employee and take the Kaufmanns in a taxi. But watch out! For the same money you can find them a decent taxi, even a pretty one (it is no longer difficult: two or three companies today offer perfect material). As you give the driver the hotel's address, tell the chauffeur which route to take. It is worth the while! With the best of intentions he might take you the most direct but not the most decorative or pleasant way. "Go through the park, follow the Saló de Sant Joan, the Rondes, Plaça Catalunya."

The first impression may not be decisive, but it is highly important. After a long journey, as one's perhaps sleepless eyes make the effort to grasp the traits of the unknown city, it is quite restful to be able to say, Oh, what delightful gardens!"

"The Arch of Triumph," you'll say, pointing out the red brick mass.

"Ah, yes, it's large."

"Large, indeed. It was built in 1888 for the first Universal Exposition."

You have assumed your role as a cicerone. Do not wallow in it too much. Be parsimonious in your indications and comments; try not to dazzle your guests with torrents of information. Avoid the naiveté of giving five-minute summaries of the life and miracles of each monument, of each building, of each avenue. Do not force them to break their necks turning to the right and to the left. Keep calm!

Have you ever watched youngsters fly a kite? If they are experts they give it no more string than it wants. And the kite rises, rises. Well: treat the Kaufmanns as you would treat a family of kites. Give them slack when they call for it; do not force their curiosity but follow it closely.

"What bustle! One can see Barcelona is a big city. How many inhabitants?"

"One million; it is safe to assume that we are over one million," you answer, with no boasting in your tone.

Some Barcelonese tend to exaggerate. From a million they slip into a million and a half, and it's a miracle that they do not get to two million. They are wrong, not only from a statistical point of view but from a psychological one as well. The Kaufmanns will not swallow such a fib, whether in Barcelona or in Seville, where they would be better prepared for such deglutitions.

Think that the Kaufmanns, being German, are fond of studies and love exactitude. They come saturated with Baedeker. You may explain to them that since that work's last edition Barcelona has doubled its population. It will be harder to convince them that it has tripled.

By now you are at the hotel. Remain there just the time necessary to put them in contact with the reception desk and ensure that their rooms have been reserved. The Kaufmanns want to change and wash. (If not, you will lose nothing in assuming so.)

"When would you like me to come for you? Tell me in all frankness. After lunch? Tomorrow morning? I am at your disposal."

They are tired, they need rest. You have completed your preliminary day.

FIRST DAY. MORNING

Where shall we start? A problem! Having conceived our role of cicerone as full of noble responsibilities, we cannot help but spend a doubting moment before we take our first steps.

Shall we take the Kaufmanns directly to the fair, since it's the World's Fair that brought them to Barcelona? Shall we give them a tour of the whole city, so that they may form a general opinion, and reserve the fair for tomorrow?

There is no doubt that to pose this problem neatly we must keep in mind a number of factors: the temperament and disposition of the Kaufmanns, the weather, the number of days your friends have resolved to devote to Barcelona.

If these factors do not make it too onerous, I would advise you to begin with a tour half by automobile, half on foot. Nothing interests the average citizen more—and even the unaverage—than the features of a new city. I always thought it absurd, tolerable only to specialists or fanatics, to arrive in a city and, the general layout unexplored, lock oneself up in a museum or visit a Romanesque cloister. European cities are all quite alike, but their museums and cathedrals are even more alike. And the very differences that separate some museums and some cathedrals from other museums and other cathedrals are the streets, the shops, the faces of people; there those differences find an obvious and eloquent explanation. First the living city, unclassified, unlabeled; first people on the go, conversing, gesturing; the flow of vehicles, café terraces, the scenery.

Which does not imply that, while on your general exploration, you should skip all the monuments that present themselves to you. No. I imagine, say, moving since ten in the morning in a convertible or semi-convertible automobile, the temperature and the disposition of your guests allowing. You have followed the Passeig de Gràcia. When you reach LA PEDRERA you give them a resigned smile and point.

"What's that?" the Kaufmanns will intone as a chorus.

"We're not yet quite sure," you may tell them. "The building has been in existence for more than twenty years, and yet we Barcelonese do not quite know what to make of it."

"But . . . it surely must serve some purpose?"

"Of course. It's destined for human habitation. People live within; there are flats for rent. It is really meant to be an apartment house. But is it?"

"It's outré."

"It's the work of an architect of unquestionable genius but with a highly personal taste. Let us, if you will, take a look at another of his works, LA SAGRADA FAMILIA, a cathedral still under construction. And let us be done with this unavoidable chapter."

And the automobile takes you there. On the way, under questioning from the Kaufmanns, you will have to explain that Barcelona has had the misfortune to have a good part of its Eixample built to follow the beat of the so-called modernism. Toward the end of the nineteenth century, it abandoned the moderate norms of neoclassicism that had given birth to the Marianao and Planàs Palaces and the house called El Cano and so on and got entangled in the creation of an original architecture without precedent, and often without grace. You tell them this nicely, without pedantry, without a shadow of disdain for previous generations, the way one deplores a blemish in one's own family

And all of a sudden you will have before you the bell towers of the new cathedral. Get out of the car and walk around a bit, to the nativity facade. The Kaufmanns (after all, they are German) might find some virtue in that enormous attempt to fluidize stone. Don't approve of their judgment, but don't contradict it openly either. Let them slide on their own down the slopes of architectural expressionism. If you were to escort a French family you would surely encounter a clear revolt against Gaudí's style. Then it would be quite appropriate to let them know that the present generations find small delight in it, generally.

Return to the Passeig de Gràcia and follow Diagonal Avenue to its upper limits. You will go through a beautiful and magnificent development that does honor to Barcelona. As you go by, point out the Royal Palace; make some discreet comment on its construction. Foreigners require trustworthy information.

It's been a while now since you have been able to see the pavilions of the fair and the gardens of Montjuïc from the car. Point them out. They will make an excellent appetizer.

Then, following Pearson Avenue, you arrive at PEDRALBES. A quick look at the monastery founded by Queen Elisenda de Montcada. Its cloisters are beautiful, but if you do not want to fatigue your foreigners you may skip them, go back to the car, and drive down to Plaça Bonanova, following the passeig of the same name.

Remember that our plan is to give a fast and superficial view of the city, a film in which panoramic vistas will alternate with significant close-ups. To begin with: no tiresome insistence, no meticulous detailing. The row of mansions alongside the road creates an excellent effect. If the taste of the architects is sometimes at fault, the number of the villas and the exuberance of the gardens that surround them will nevertheless charm the spirit. The great convents—Pious Fathers, Jesuits—weigh positively on the scales. Bonanova! Visiting its parish church is not required. Its worth is minimal, and to get an idea of Barcelonese devotion in its most popular aspect, your hand holds other trumps. Believe me, turn on Carrer Muntaner, and as you cast your glances to right and left, do not stop until you reach Carrer Corts.

Follow that to the Plaça Espanya. The monumental fountain

erected there is an inexplicable mistake. All consultants favored a low fountain, something along the lines of the Madrid fountain to Cibele. For some
mysterious reason the oversize project of Senyor Jujol, the author of several
infra-Gaudinian buildings, won the day. To make matters worse, a bunch of
sculptures laden with symbolisms, the work of Miquel Blay. This gentleman, who had already threatened us with a monument to Pi i Margall,
decided not to let us off this time. Since he did not take the republican, he
took the monarchic way and has planted here samples of his heavy-handed
baroque. Now it's done! Do not carry on with explanations to your guests.
Make them look up the Avenue of the Exposition. But don't let them go in
yet. Your duty is to show them Barcelona. They will see the fair on their
own, at their own pace.

Follow the Carrer Marquès del Duero.

"You see, Herr Kaufmann, a popular neighborhood. We are
coming close to the Parallel, our little Montmartre. Theaters, cafés, music
halls. To our left, between the street we are now on and the Rambla, lies
the Fifth District. Some, given to hyperbole, call it Barri Xinès, "China-
town." Exaggerations. Along these lines, in Hamburg you have something
much more impressive. What has happened is that this district has become
fashionable. Recently Francis Carco devoted half a book to it; Paul Morand
had made it the background for one of his stories in *Ouvert la nuit.* Our
local authors have also exploited it. Well, if you are interested, we can take
a stroll through it. You and I alone, understand me.

Frau Kaufmann protests. Their daughter feigns distraction.

"These ramparts," you are now at Santa Madrona, "are the
remnants of those that encircled the city. Behind them stand the old shipyards, probably the only medieval shipyards that have survived almost intact. The sea used to reach this far but has receded. The Columbus
monument. Do you wish to go to the top? An elevator will take us to the
very feet of the great discoverer."

I would not dissuade you from undertaking this little ascension,
even though it is not indispensable. The spread of rooftops and the view of
the harbor will impress any tourist.

Whether you go up to the top or remain on the ground, you
may dismiss the automobile and walk up the Rambla. Oh yes! The Rambla
deserves particular attention. Do not go into, now or ever, a long-winded
exordium. All you need to say is "If you do not mind, we might now walk
about a little. This avenue that we are beginning to follow is one of the
most typical in Barcelona. It is lined by decaying edifices, it is quite irregular, traffic jams are frequent, but we Barcelonese are given to coming here
often. It's the heart of the old city."

24

That's it. Let the Rambla speak for itself. If the Kaufmanns have the sensitivity to understand it, they will understand it; but if they have a city councillor's soul that would like to see the Rambla as a boulevard, there's nothing you can do, and your comments will bear no other fruit than the consolidation of their boredom.

But let us not fall into pessimism. The Kaufmanns, as soon as they enter the middle Rambla, respond to it. What bustle! What vitality! So many shops, so many vehicles, so many people. And the flowers!

The flowers! My friend, a little gallantry: buy a bouquet of carnations for Frau Kaufmann and another one for Fräulein Alice.

Stop in front of LA VIRREINA. Don't fail to call attention to this majestic palace. The Betlem Church also calls for a moment of consideration. It is a beautiful baroque monument, the work of the Jesuits. Nothing lost in going in. Its interior is not lacking in grandeur, and besides, one goes in and comes out almost without realizing that one has left the Rambla.

And now, why don't you sit in the terrace of the Café de la Rambla or the Continental for an aperitif?

It's an idea. On a good day, toward one o'clock, the Rambla is contagiously splendid.

Perhaps one of the Kaufmanns, after taking in the spectacle, will feel the urge to write postcards. Do not be alarmed. This brand of graphomania infects an elevated percentage of tourists. There's no antidote for it. Rather than oppose it, you'll be better off to offer sensible help. Do not let the Kaufmanns buy the first postcards offered by an impertinent vendor. Take the time to hop into some nearby store and purchase a selection of two dozen postcards signed by Zerkowitz or Sans Ricart.

Half-past one. Lunch time. If your plans involve generous treats for the Kaufmanns, take them to the Colom or to that very Continental for a good meal. Otherwise let them go back to their hotel and you go home, after having agreed when to resume the tour in the afternoon.

AFTERNOON

Let me suggest the Gothic quarter, the cathedral area. I do not mean to claim that on your first afternoon you should feel obliged to make this visit. You could find an equally valid use of your time. I make suggestions; I do not give orders. Giving orders is for martial itineraries whose main aim is to make a soldier out of each tourist.

Even though the Kaufmanns, being Germans, are docile to discipline, one should not overdo things but rather allow them the sense of freedom and individualism that befits our latitudes.

O.K. Imagine that you are in front of the CATHEDRAL. You have reached it on foot through Plaça Nova and the Corríbia so that the facade suddenly stands before your eyes. Please alert them to the fact that this facade, certainly no eyesore, was built last century and, next to the rest of the monument, has the glacial look of mannerism; it lacks the secret lyricism that animates true Gothic.

Do not tarry. Climb the steps and enter the temple. Soon your sun-drenched eyes become used to the penumbra reigning in its interior. Soon the graceful columns of the nave appear with their weightless harmony and the apse windows surge softly with their celestial polychromy. Be silent as you observe whether these catalysts of the first order have their effect upon the sensibilities of the Kaufmanns. They will! They only fail with the most absolute imbeciles. When your friends turn their eyes toward you and signal that they are beginning to feel impressed, say nothing but "Beautiful, isn't it?"

Go around the nave, slowly. All in all there are very few interiors in the world that rival those of our see. We have been quite sober applauding our own things so that our pronouncement may now be trusted.

A sensible traveler, a poet, said that the harmony of this interior made him break out in tears. Do not demand from everyone such a sign of emotive plenitude; not everyone is a poet, not everyone has tears available. But if in any one place you are allowed to show a legitimate satisfaction and ancestral pride, that place is doubtless Barcelona's cathedral.

Go around the CLOISTERS; in spite of being unfinished, they are delicious.

To amuse the Kaufmanns, point out to them the geese swimming or about to swim in the pond. The medieval aftertaste of that spectacle is of great delicacy.

Do not forget to walk around the cathedral. SANT IU'S PORTAL and those of the PIETAT and SANTA LLUCIA deserve some minutes. The narrow street that follows the outside of the see is also full of character. Take advantage of the situation and peep through the grillwork gate of the archdeacon's house and, if you can, go in. An intelligent restoration makes for a pleasant visit to this building, which now houses the City Archives.

Carrer del Bisbe, or Bishop's Street. The Gothic, super-Gothic bridge. Give it a date. Confess that it is very recent work and suffers from an obvious pedagogical willfulness: a whole course in Gothic art may be found in it. Well, rush under it and enter the PALAU DE LA GENERALITAT.

Again you'll need all your subtlety so that the eyes of the visitors may distinguish what is old and worthy from what is modern and ill-conceived. The entrance courtyard and its staircase maintain their original nobility almost intact. Point out the vault and turn your back to a Renaissance door, recently built, that's on your left. Go up the stairs. Admire the delicacy of the columns, the fineness of their decorative sculptures, the variety and beauty of the gargoyles. Pay little attention to a symbolic triptych very recently affixed to one of the walls. When you get to the courtyard of the orange trees, make an attempt to distract your friends' minds from the two nouveau riche street lamps on either side, and the Valencia or Seville tile work that covers the planters and that, with its excessive luminosity, diminishes the golden dignity of the stone; eliminate the fountain with the Saint George's figure that crowns it. Well, eliminate mentally all that gets in the way. And then leave. The Hall of Saint George's: I am not *forbidding* you to visit it, but I advise you to give it no more than two minutes. A quick viewing does a lot for it.

As to the other rooms and halls, let them not take your time or your effort. Cross Plaça Sant Jaume's and enter the CASA LA CIUTAT, or Town Hall. An overview from its courtyard to the old Gothic facade that is now hidden by the great nineteenth-century pastiche. Then take the new stairs to your right. A handsome set of stairs, don't you see? It is proof that Catalonia is still producing architects who can imitate gracefully. Point it out. It would be a pity to let the Kaufmanns leave with the idea that our race exhausted its artistic talent with fourteenth-century works and has none left to apply to the present.

The Gothic gallery has also improved since they removed the glass panes. Visit the Saló de Cent. Solemn, magnificent; almost nothing out of place. It would be a good spot to talk to the Kaufmanns about the prosperity of our old municipal institutions. But if you can't sing this tune properly, you'll be better off not attempting it. Try and visit the impressive hall just decorated by J. M. Sert, here making a powerful mural comment on Muntaner's chronicle.

As you come out of the Saló de Cent take the new and comely black marble staircase to your right and don't neglect a glance at the Gothic facade of Carrer Ciutat. It is an excellent sample of our civil architecture.

You will soon be on Carrer Paradís, toward the top of the old Mount Taber. Go into the Centre Excursionista de Catalunya and admire the columns from the Temple of Hercules, a remnant of the Roman colony. And proceed immediately to the Plaça del Rei to see another column of the same family and to breathe for an instant between the walls of Santa Agata and those of the old Royal Palace. Do not visit either.

And to bring to a close this archaeological promenade, follow Carrer Mercaders, with its Gothic houses and lordly courtyards: take note of the Dalmases courtyard, which is not Gothic but baroque—don't make a goof here—and end up at Santa Maria del Mar. Go in!

You have another important card in your hand. This temple is a wonder. Only on rare occasions has the Gothic style been able to bring together so much sobriety with so much elegance.

I think the Kaufmanns will take notice. At any rate, the sun is setting. One should not force even the purest beauty. Call it a day and rush your guests by taxi to tea at Casa Llibre. It will cost you a bit, but you'll make a great impression. This tearoom's soft, French comfort will contrast nicely with the grave and harmonious visions that have just filled your retinas. As they sip their tea (he might have beer; that's fine), the Kaufmanns, as they drink, and eat some pastries, bread, butter, and marmalade, will find that Barcelona is a complete city.

Having had tea, you may leave them to their own initiatives. There is a time when even foreigners wish to be en famille and even to get lost roaming the confusion of unknown streets.

SECOND DAY. TIBIDABO AND VALLVIDRERA

I refer to the second day of your tour with the Kaufmanns, not to their second day in Barcelona.

If the weather is good, a climb to Tibidabo is recommended for this leg. Toward noon, get on streetcar 22 or 23; do not take a taxi. The open upper deck in those vehicles makes for a peerless viewing spot. From there the Passeig de Gràcia gains notably; the perspectives of Carrer de Corts and Diagonal—which you will make the Kaufmanns remark with barely a word, simply with a meaningful twist of the head—give it grandeur. The arrival in Gràcia is a disaster; may the gardens now under construction minimize its ugliness. On the other hand, the first part of Carrer Salmeron is quite honorable; beyond the Rambla del Prat it decays indecorously. Tell the Kaufmanns that the narrowing of that street is temporary, that it will have disappeared before the fair is over. This may be an excessive fit of optimism, but not inopportune.

Josepets. A run-down square but not unpleasant.

República Argentina Avenue. Its recent renovation lends it a certain tone. As you arrive at the handsome opening of Vallcarca, do not fail to call it to the Kaufmanns' attention. The spread of houses climbing from the bottom of the valley all the way to the hilltops, toward the highway to Horta, toward the pine groves on the hill to the south, presents a pleasing candor.

Finally, following Craywinckel, a street which every citizen spells a different way more or less related to the real spelling, you reach Tibidabo Avenue. The blue streetcar will take you to the lower station, along a line of mansions that, if nothing else, is a witness to power and sybaritic living.

As you ascend by funicular—need we say it?—you will look to right and left in order to grasp the successive revelations of the panorama, and once at the top you will savor them in good order and comfort. The Pyrenees! The Montseny! The Montserrat! The eastern coast with its line of towns, the western shore with El Prat and the Llobregat River behind! The Vallès so near!

I have never been lucky enough to see Majorca from the top of Collcerola. It doesn't matter: tradition will have you affirm that on a clear day one can see the island's Puig Major, and you cannot betray this very suggestive tradition.

Pay little attention to the disturbing church and ignore the deplorable raree-show housed under the terrace. We do not mean to call them out of place, but they are not the kind of thing fit for the Kaufmanns, or for you. You'll do better inviting them to climb the gigantic mechanical tower or even to ride in the captive airplane. These are childish diversions, if you will, but proper ones for any dignified tourist. Should Frau Kaufmann resist such elevations, do not insist; father and daughter may enjoy them while you keep the mother company. Should only the daughter desire to experience the elation of going up in the tower or flying with no danger, it's your duty to accompany her.

You may lunch at the mountaintop restaurant or at the Hotel Florida. The cuisine may be better in the first. Conveniences and setting are definitely more complete in the second; the dining room offers a splendid view.

You have lunched. After a brief digestive rest, if the season allows it, if mother and daughter Kaufmann are wearing adequate shoes and Herr Kaufmann is not fatigued—make sure that you get these details right!—you may propose to walk to Vallvidrera (you can always hop onto the blue streetcar). It is downhill and not a very long way. In Vallvidrera take the funicular and then the so-called Sarrià train that will take you to Plaça Catalunya. We might as well show off this new underground station that has cost us so many millions of pesetas! The terminal is superb, and the overground bit of railroad between Vallvidrera and Sarrià and then between Sarrià and Carrer Muntaner has pleasant and even graceful aspects. Have no doubt that one of Barcelona's least arguable assets is its environs; for this reason I have insisted on your touring them.

What time is it? Six in the afternoon? Let us say six. Take your group out for tea at the Maison Dorée or perhaps to a café, a true café, lively, crowded, such as the Or del Rin, which bears a Germanic name to boot.

After that, suggest hopping into the Coliseu to end their day. They will see the most sumptuous theater in Barcelona—after the Liceu, of course!

THIRD DAY. CIUTADELLA PARK. MUSEUM. BARCELONETA. LLOTJA. PORT. SANT PAU DEL CAMP

Yes, you must visit the park. Its gardens are not going to stun any well-traveled European, but they lend their charm to Barcelona. The avenue of the lindens and the waterfall plaza, the Plaça d'Armes and the monument to General Prim are things that do honor to a city.

On the other hand, do not insist they see the zoological collection. The Kaufmanns are from the north, from the land of magnificent Tiergärten. Along these lines you will be unable to show them anything new.

Nor am I in favor of your imposing on them a detailed visit to the archaeological museum. Unless they are true aficionados or have the systematic bent to follow a program no matter how boring, do not force them to follow the numismatic or the arms collections, or even the textile, though it is one of the best in the world. They would get tired. As a good stage master you will simply take them to see our medieval paintings, a really important collection in our art history; the glass collection, particularly the Cabot legacy, which proves that our glass rivals the famous ones from Venice and Murano (it is often mistaken for those); and the ceramic collection with the triumph of its old Catalan plates, and the Manisses, Teruel, and Paterna earthenware—the latter show a remarkable oriental influence. Review quickly the objects brought over from the diggings at Empúries and the statue of Aesculapius presiding over the gallery; it is tangible proof that Catalonia was colonized by the Greeks and that we are the relatives of Socrates and Phidias. This is a fact to our honor. The Kaufmanns will surely appreciate it.

Your ace will be the visit to the Romanesque frescoes brought over from the ancient churches in the Pyrenees and now mounted on the wall and vaults that replicate their structures. A sure hit. A unique sensation.

Tell them—it's always pleasant—that the Americans lusted after that treasure and had begun, with skillful maneuvering, to take it. Attentive scholars and artists were able to stop that sad drain. Only one of those frescoes has crossed the ocean and is on exhibit at the museum in New York. The rest are here.

Go back out in the sunshine. The halls in this museum are somewhat damp and could give you a chill.

Proceed to the Llotja to visit the most superb of our Gothic halls. Take a look at the neoclassical building surrounding it. I wish its excellent architecture had been able to create a school.

Now let a taxi take you to Barceloneta. If it's the swimming season, sit for a while at the terrace of Sant Sebastià. You could even take your lunch there. Not a bad idea.

"Waiter!"

While they set your table, between bites, you can admire one of the liveliest spectacles that a city may offer: bathers of both sexes playing with the waves.

The sea breeze is pleasant; take your time. Let the Kaufmanns become imbued with this light that is unfamiliar to them, let them store as much of it as they can so as to break down the gray mists awaiting them back in their homeland.

And when you think you have achieved this noble objective, pay the bill and proceed to sail in a *golondrina*. The short passage will suffice to give the Kaufmanns an idea of our harbor. Remember they have seen colossal ones—the one in Hamburg, perhaps the one in Amsterdam or in Antwerp—and that ours in Barcelona cannot impress them to any extreme. They might even have arrived here still dazzled by the unique spectacle of Marseilles's Vieux Port.

At any rate, limit yourself to the golondrina's short tour. That will be enough.

Having landed, you will be taken by car to the venerable church of Sant Pau del Camp, Saint Paul-in-the-Fields. A small church, but unforgettable. Its visit is a must. In the midst of a populous, irregular, noisy neighborhood, the facade of this temple, the oldest in Barcelona, has a surprising effect. After going around the church—soon done—visit the cloister to the right. What severe delight! What a burst of primitive faith! In its smallness, how strong!

Back to the car and then to the entrance to the Hospital de la Santa Creu. That will give your guests a less pure, less complex sensation, but one worthy nevertheless of recollection. The Gothic remnants are mixed with baroque additions within an atmosphere of melancholy that probably emerges from a sense of the sick within or from the delicate shadows cast by the trees.

Consider going into the courtyard of the Casa de Convalescència, a well-proportioned rectangle enriched by friezes of eighteenth-century tiles.

When you have done this, I dare give you no more advice. It's been a full day. Sit down for tea; the emotions of art and tourism burn up one's energies. And too, the Kaufmanns appear to enjoy their food.

FOURTH DAY. MONTSERRAT

Take them to Montserrat. Do not hesitate. Do not stop to consider if they would be more impressed by Sitges or by Santa Cristina, Vic or Poblet. All these make for excellent visits, the second and the last especially recommended, but if you only have time for one outing, give it to Montserrat.

After all, it is a universally famous shrine, and the geology supporting it, even though it has become all too familiar, never fails to provoke a deep response in foreigners. Even artistic spirits, less given to allowing simple rarity to move them, feel the spell of the innumerable gray pinnacles of our mountain.

If your means allow it, take the car. The approach is shorter and infinitely more pleasant. Besides, it will allow you to leave toward eleven, so that you can be almost sure it is to be a nice day. On the way you may stop at SANT CUGAT and visit the monastery with its formidable cloister and, coming back, the church of SANT MIQUEL in Terrassa, a small Romanesque wonder.

More: you'll traverse twice and in opposing directions the range of Collserola. Do not disregard this chance, close as the range is to the city. As you climb to the top in the morning, every road turn will seem to you a lightning of joy: country houses, hills, groves, blue sea. At dusk when you return, the lights of Barcelona will wink at you lovingly at each curve. *Féerique*! Wonderful! This will be the moment, if you cannot hold back any longer, in which to utter all the corny phrases stored in your heart. The Kaufmanns will tolerate them with little difficulty and might even contribute one of their own.

The woods of l'Arrabassada are nevertheless admirable.

In Montserrat, after the necessary visit to the shrine, you will inevitably take the funicular to Sant Joan. If at all possible, lunch there. It will be a below average meal, but surely no worse than the one served in the monastery's restaurant, where, alas, you would be further deprived of a nice view.

As you lunch, if you haven't told them yet, you may remind the Kaufmanns that our Montserrat may have inspired the Monsalvat where Parsifal, the Germanic hero, was born. It's a risky and fragile hypothesis. Fear not; it's as good as any other, it's cute, and all those who have been to Montserrat are initiated into a kind of Masonic order that defends it lustily. For counterbalance you might evoke the very Montserratian legend of beautiful Riquilda, the Count's daughter seduced by Friar Garí, and tell them of the penance this character had to do to expiate his crime.

The present church in Montserrat is built on the ruins of the older one burned by the French, which in turn was built over the remains of a modest Romanesque chapel. Surely that old chapel must have produced a shiver of faith and poetry more than the present basilica. Tell the Kaufmanns.

Tell them too that the monumental Via Crucis along the path to the cave (where you should really go) is of rather unequal worth. Some monuments are fine, some medium; the bad ones are in abundance.

Buy postcards. There is at least one skillful collection.

In the afternoon do not forget to go over to the Monk's Lookout and take in, between two cypresses, the panorama it offers. A stark, sharp, magnificent orography. The valley where the Llobregat meanders among hillocks exudes a majestic melancholy. Be respectful of the Kaufmann family's silence.

If you forgo the visit to the Romanesque churches in Terrassa, you'll have time to wait for the sunset and hear the *Salve* sung by the altar boys' choir. You decide, as you investigate your friends' wishes.

Whatever your decision, as you reach the hotel's door you may take leave of the Kaufmanns. You have given them a good day and they will be thankful.

THE NIGHTS. LICEU. PALAU DE LA MUSICA. OLYMPIA

You will have observed that the activities I proposed for the guidance of the Kaufmanns did not include any night program. I did not forget. I suppressed it on purpose. I supposed that after the several visits I recommended for the daylight hours, they, or you, or both parties would be more inclined to devote the night to rest than to vigil.

But on one hand we must take into consideration the possibility that the Kaufmanns belong to that race of heroic tourists who leave home with the intention of reaching total exhaustion, and on the other we must foresee the possibility of their extending their sojourn in Barcelona so as to have the time for night life without over stress.

In both cases you ought to know the night offerings in Barcelona. Legend has it that they are infinite and more or less infernal. But I have no intention of acting as a Virgil for ill-intentioned Dantes; I shall simply help you to entertain an honest and responsible family.

So, one of the first numbers I recommend is the soiree at the Liceu. Behind a modest, unpretentious facade, our theater hides one of the most beautiful halls in Europe. You may be sure of it. Do not boast about it, for vanity makes any cicerone unbearable, but be aware of it.

Elegant proportions, grandeur, excellent acoustics. If you are lucky to catch a full-house day with passable artists, your friends will admire a magnificent spectacle and will learn that in our latitudes there is *also* a refined worldly tradition. Not a negligible aspect. Believe me. The Kaufmanns may discover a less picturesque and exotic Barcelona than they had imagined. It will hurt no one if they leave with the impression that a good dose of normality and quality has replaced local color.

As you leave the Liceu, step into the Maison Dorée or Casa Llibre or the Ritz for a late supper.

You could allow another evening to hear a concert in the Palau de la Música Catalana. Shoot for a first-class concert; it would involve, ideally, a performance by the Orfeó Català, a choral group of exquisite quality that should be appreciated with little difficulty. Only a good program will help dissipate the bad impression that the building will have on your tourists. All Barcelonese are by now convinced that this so-called palace is a disaster. Do not apologize. Do not protest; limit yourself to pointing out that you took them to that temple because of its cult, not for the beauty of its architecture.

I also recommend a soiree at the Olympia, especially if the show is an equestrian circus. Olympia is a big hall, a *kolossal* hall, and may impress the Germans and those who are not German.

If you did not go to the Coliseum some afternoon, go there one evening. The Tivoli theater may also be worthwhile, if they present an operetta or a zarzuela with some dignity.

And there might be a night session at the pool of the Club Natació Barcelona.

Then again, I would not recommend that you be tempted by any of the numerous huts that imprudently bear the name of theaters. Take the Kaufmanns to experience our theater only if they show true curiosity, and try to find a day on which, for whatever reason, you suspect the hall to be animated. In any case, do not overburden their goodwill, and should you sense that two acts suffice, do not keep them for four. To hear comedy in an unknown language is not an exercise to be kept up for long.

SUGGESTIONS FOR ANOTHER DAY

Allow me to insist that these itineraries do not mean to be taken literally. They are suggestions, reminders; not dogmas.

As soon as you run out of monuments and essential vistas, following one option or another becomes a highly personal matter. To formulate detailed guidelines without knowing the Kaufmanns (or the Duponts, or the Wallaces, or the Cárdenas, or the Toscaninis) whom you have to lead is like prescribing medicines without knowing the patient.

A few traits of curiosity are common to all tourists. They will all want to have seen some things, even if they did not draw any delight from their contemplation. These are the things more or less explored during the previous days.

At this point I shall suggest items to combine in further outings according to the temperament of the Kaufmanns, which with a little psychology you surely know by now.

Let me suggest the Labyrinth, in Horta. These delicious gardens, owned by the Marquès d'Alfaràs, are more valuable than is normally imagined. Foreign journals have reproduced them in detail; there are few like them in this corner of Europe.

Let me suggest a good soccer match at the CAMP DE LES CORTS. (I will say nothing about the Montjuïc stadium; doubtless, if it is in working order, you won't need to seek other sporting thrills.)

Let me suggest a walk through the streets inside Barcelona (Portaferrissa, Petritxol, Boqueria), which furnish a vigorous picture of vitality, plethora, mercantile unctuousness. Jules Romains, the unanimist poet who lived for a few months in our city, placed our Boqueria among the most personal and characteristic streets in Europe, next to the London Strand and Marseilles's Cannebière.

Of course, this kind of sensation is only appreciated by trained palates. It is difficult for it to have an exceptional value for a middle-of-the-road family. Keep this in mind.

In the same category we may place those streets in the Fifth District, the red-light district, to which we have already alluded: the Carrer Nou de la Rambla and its tributaries, Carrer Sant Pau, and so on. Certain foreigners will enjoy walking through them, not simply for what they'll see there, really, but by the fiction they will be able to imagine behind each bar door, inside each murky staircase, around each heavily made-up prostitute or each drunken sailor.

We should feel neither indignation nor enthusiasm. Barcelona has these quarters, more or less the equivalent of those in other cosmopolitan port cities in the world. It is as foolish to make them into the very essence of the city as it is to deny them in a spurt of patriotic moralism.

MONTJUÏC, WITH AND WITHOUT THE FAIR

We have willfully abstained from referring to the World's Fair. Who can fail to visit it while it lasts, and even after it closes?

But for the time being we are unable to make any recommendations for the visit or visits to the fair, for the powerful reason that we still don't know what kind of interest it will hold. Besides, one normally visits fairs thoroughly and methodically, without taking time to choose. Those who have undertaken a trip to visit a fair will not easily resign themselves to skipping any of its sections or its palaces. Even if it requires a constant trot, the Kaufmanns will look at all the exhibits.

Of the permanent elements on Montjuïc, the exposition mountain, some are essential: the Laribal park and the pergolas descending toward the Font del Gat; this fountain, in its delicious location among high tree clumps; the overlooking platform at the end of the main avenue, with its views over the harbor; and the square presided over by a statue of Saint George which today is occupied, partially and provisionally, by a palace, on the side looking toward Prat. An exquisite vista!

Add to that, if the strength has not failed you, the funicular ride starting at Marquès del Duero Avenue. The restaurant terrace, near the upper stop, offers an interesting perspective.

Finally, now and ever, while it lasts, the "typical Spanish village" must inescapably be visited. All together, it offers foreigners such a complete and emotive idea of the rest of the Iberian Peninsula that it would not be surprising for some to feel no need to penetrate farther.

GOOD-BYE

Whether you follow the program I have suggested or design your own with these elements, there will be a day when the Kaufmanns will tell you: "We must go home. We've been away too long."

Even if such a statement gives you a slight feeling of deliverance, you will take care not to show it.

"So soon? Do not be cruel! Stay for two more days. We shall take a trip to Santa Cristina, to Tarragona. You'll see how interesting it is."

But their minds are made up and, fatally, the hour of leave taking arrives. You have given them enough and there is no need to add anything else. They might ask you out to dinner.

When you are at the train station, among the beautiful frenzy of those arriving and those departing, in the middle of the conversation that will be somewhat heated because of the nervousness inevitable in all partings, show them a last gesture of courtesy. Call the florist, buy two bunches of carnations, and give them to Frau and Fräulein Kaufmann.

Their fragrant redness will, much better than ordinary sealing wax, seal the pact of your friendship.

The train starts to move.

"Thanks for everything! We leave most appreciative! We will never forget Barcelona!"

Such words are sincere. You know, you feel it. A great melancholy satisfaction spurts from the bottom of your being and films your eyes. The train disappears behind the first curve. All your efforts now seem worthwhile.

A Note on Amades's
"Stones and the Cult of the Dead"

 The following pages are a small sample of Joan Amades's monumental *Folklore de Catalunya*. Amades spent a lifetime gathering folktales and anecdotes, which he recorded with Sisyphean determination. His explanations of the funeral properties of rocks, chosen for this anthology, demonstrate the mind of a man devoted to his country's nonwritten history. Modern anthropologists may find Amades's method primitive, in particular with reference to our folklorist's notion of primitive cultures and the rosiness with which he views the ancient past; yet Amades manages to tell his legends with a conviction that brings them to life.

No two essayists could be more different than the urbane and selective Soldevila and the humble but relentless Amades. Their essays represent two extremes in Catalan intellectuality. I have already referred to Soldevila's leanings toward the *noucentista* school, which I imagine would consider Amades an example of retrograde antiquity. Yet Soldevila and Amades share a delight in the monuments of their country and capital city, and partake of the conviction that Catalonia is a direct cultural descendant of Greece. This conviction, which could be termed Mediterraneanism, is quite frequent among modern views of Catalonia.

In these pages by Amades we sense the oldness of Catalonia and, in an almost surrealist way, see the emergence of ancient forces and emotions under today's buildings and streets. Amades's stones give the reader a very physical sense of place. The maps and index provide most explanations needed, but I should clarify here the reference to a profession that has now disappeared but was still alive when Amades wrote: the *sereno*. The sereno was the watchman who patrolled neighborhoods at night, in part to deter crime and in part to help latecomers get into their homes. Most people in Barcelona lived in apartment buildings that locked their main doors at ten every night; since those doors had locks that required large and heavy keys which neighbors could not or would not carry with them at all times, latecoming citizens would clap and get the night watchman to let them in with the key he kept on his clamorous ring. The spread of more efficient locks and smaller keys in the 1960s eliminated the profession.

Joan Amades i Gelat (Barcelona 1890–1959), Catalonia's preeminent folklorist, was commissioned by UNESCO to prepare the bibliographical corpus of Catalan folklore. He is the author of two monumental collections: *Costumari català* (Customs of Catalonia), published between 1950 and 1956, and *Folklore de Catalunya,* published posthumously.

The work translated here is the opening essay in part 2, "Les pedres" (The stones), in his "Mitologia popular," included in volume 3 of his *Folklore de Catalunya* and published originally in the Biblioteca Perenne of Editorial Selecta in Barcelona (1969).

JOAN AMADES

Stones and the Cult of the Dead

Stones may well be the natural element most easily grasped by illiterates, the starkest and least poetic of them all; yet stones, for all their simplicity and dryness, play a more decisive role than one would assume in present-day customs and beliefs. Most of today's uses for and beliefs about stones have distant origins, constituting a survival of primitive cultural stages. From prehistory we know that the longest period in the incalculable life of human beings belongs to the Stone Age, when stones were among the materials most used in the production of utensils, few and elementary as they were during those times.

Stones have been objects of worship since the childhood of humanity. The primitive mind considered stones to be the containers of spirits, of benevolent geniuses with a will of their own. Whatever use primitive people derived from a stone was not the result of its materiality but the effect of the empathy and goodwill of the genius within.

The passage of time has made people forget the great advantages we once derived from stone tools, but we never forgot their sanctity. Primitive axes were eventually attributed virtues that evoked the respect and veneration they once enjoyed, not simply an appreciation of their usefulness. The Greeks called them *keraunites* from the place-name Keraunos, meaning "lightning." They gave them a divine or otherworldly origin, brought about by Lightning and its daughters. The universality of such a belief is remarkable; it can be found in cultures with no Hellenic influences, even in more backward ones. Our folk even today speak of *pedres de llamp,* or lightning stones, a name that is more or less common to a number of languages and is used by diverse peoples who, like us, perpetuate that Greek belief.

Proof of the appreciation and consideration felt for prehistoric axes was exemplified by Galba. When he was elevated to the throne of the Roman Empire, Galba considered his finding some lightning stones in a pond in the Cantabrian province a great omen.

An inventory of valuable objects belonging to the unhappy Prince Charles of Viana lists a lightning stone. Saint Isidore of Seville challenged the virtues attributed to axes and criticized the esteem in which they were held. The Council of Toledo forbade their worship. Yet the cult of primitive axes is alive today, although in disguise. Their appreciation and veneration has suffered the corrosion of millennia as well as the influence of innumerable layers of civilization. In many spots they are kept as a family relic handed down from parents to children and would not be parted with for any money in the world, since people would feel they were selling off one of their own.

The preservation of a lightning stone in the household as the object of a family tradition and the resistance to losing it recall the times when one believed that the genius living inside the stone was the spirit of some ancestor, a spirit protector of the family, or indeed its founder, who, next to the hearth where these stones are normally kept, guarded the family's continuity and prosperity. To get rid of the stone, then, would have the same effect as choosing to get rid of the head of the household.

The idea of death worried primitive folk most deeply and influenced their notions and customs. Our ancestors (just like folk who today are in the most rudimentary states of cultural development) believed that upon dying the spirit of the dead lived on within the body of some animal, a bole, or any other object. It seems, however, that spirits preferred to house themselves in stones, perhaps because stones let them be closer to the living, whose company and warmth the dead needed.

Each stone contained a spirit or a soul, and prehistoric burials, in the eyes of primitive folk, gathered multitudes of souls to keep the deceased company so they would not feel alone and provoke, in their need for company, the death of some relative. Even today we can see traces of those beliefs; people say among other things that one dead calls for another.

Our folk believe that one should not kick stones encountered along one's way because that would disturb the souls in purgatory, and who knows whether that stone is not the soul of some relative who wanted to see us as we went by? People also say that, when one trips on a stone, a soul in purgatory was thinking of us and asking for help or remembrance. The habit of casting a stone whenever one walks by a place where tradition claims a crime was committed or an accident took a person's life persists as a tribute to the deceased. We offer that person in effect the soul contained in the stone so as to avoid being taken away to our death, should whoever died there violently feel the desire for company.

The top of Mount Catllar in the vicinity of Ripoll, just in front of the Hermitage of Our Lady, had until recently a heap of rocks that, according to tradition, was the tomb of a faithless woman who, having offended the Mother of God, fell dead at that spot; whoever climbed that mountain was obliged to throw a stone onto that heap. In the outskirts of Tortosa at the foot of Mount Baset, there is a pile of stones known as Potra del Pino; according to popular belief, it is the tomb of a terrible cervine wolf, a fearful dragon, or a three-headed fox ready to emerge and devour any traveler who does not add a stone to the heap. On the north slopes of Montserrat somewhat below the cave called Alfons stand great piles of rocks known as Pallers dels Regira-rocs, "Haystacks of the Rock-tossers." The Regira-rocs were a family of giants who terrorized the local country-side. One year when the wheat crop failed they stole the wheat of the nearby villages and killed all who protested. The heavens punished them by turning their haystacks into ruins under which the thieves lie buried. Some claim they lie on the bottom of the Pouerons cave not far away. They say that from time to time one can hear them moaning from the depths. In the Ribera del Sió, by Aranyonet, there are some stone haystacks similar to those of the Regira-rocs; these are the burial grounds of a wealthy land-owner who denied straw to a poor man dying of cold during a harsh winter. As people go by these mounds they throw in a stone.

Legend has it that long ago the Ribagorça was practically unin-habited, for it was so barren and roadless. To get it populated the king delivered a sum of money to a very virtuous monk named Benet Larraz to build roads and permit traffic to pass. It happened, however, that after some time an epidemic laid waste to the region and the monk decided to devote the allotted monies to improving people's health. The king did not share his views and ordered the monk hanged for his disobedience. The monk requested one grace: that thirty years hence someone should stab his arm, and if it emitted blood he would be interred near the one road he had started. In due time people saw from the ground over his grave a hand emerging holding a parchment, a reminder of the royal grace. The monk was exhumed; when they stabbed his arm, it bled. He was then buried in the crypt of the church in the hamlet of Sapeira, which lies by the road the monk had opened. A venthole opens right on the roadside over the crypt; it was the habit of travelers to throw a stone forward from the venthole with a prayer for the monk who had started the road they were enjoying. Significantly, the name of the hamlet, Sapeira, means "the stone," perhaps as a reminder of this legend or in remembrance of a deeply primitive practice native to that spot and the origin of its name.

It was also the general custom to cast a stone to the bottom of precipices, a habit relating to a tradition that assumed travelers might tumble to their deaths. In popular wisdom, stone casting was a tribute to death.

Around Sant Hilari there is a spot that once inspired great dread. A courageous young woman decided to approach it by night holding a dead man's head. Once on the spot, she drove a nail into a stone. Her clothes were caught on some brambles. She felt that dread was dragging her back, and she fell down the bluff. The place is now known as Fossa de la Minyona, "Maiden's Tomb."

The deepest abyss in the mountain heights of Núria is known as Salt del Sastre, "Tailor's Leap." The tailor was a smuggler who, to flee the guards, threw himself down the bluff and reached the bottom unscathed. He tried the feat a second time to win a bet and killed himself.

Salt de la Núvia, "Bride's Leap," in Puiggraciós recalls a bride whose parents had married her off to a man she did not love. Walking by a bluff, she feigned a nature call, got away from the wedding procession, and threw herself into the void. The same tradition appears about Coll de Pixanúvies, "Pass of the Pissing Brides," in the Guilleries and Pixaenlaire, "Piss-in-the-Air," in the Cabrerès. Pas de la Mala Dona, "Bad Woman's Pass," in the Costes del Garraf refers to a married woman who, in order to marry another man, pushed her husband, who was blind, off the promontory by the sea. The same legend is told of Mare de Déu del Far and of some cliffs next to the shrines of Mare de Déu de la Salut in the Garrotxa near Sant Feliu de Pallerols. In these versions, however, the husband, foreseeing his wife's intentions, moved out of the way and it was she who fell into the void.

A hair-raising cliff in the Prades Mountains in the Priorat is known as Salt de la Reina Mora, "Moorish Queen's Leap." According to legend, the queen from Siurana's castle jumped to her death when the

Catalans took her fortress by surprise. Legend has it she was bathing and the Catalans gave her no time to dress. Something similar is said of another cliff and castle near Siurana, Sant Salvador, on the mountains of Verdera in the Pyrenean ridge of Sant Pere de Roda.

The relationship between name and legend is rarely arbitrary, and an inquiry into the original meaning of the term *Siurana* can make our topic more interesting. Intriguingly, one may see by the two cliffs near Siurana in Empordà an etched horseshoe believed to glow afire on midsummer's night. In old times on that night, the spot was visited by local folk. Into all these precipices and even into others people would throw stones as they went by, devoting the stones to the memory of the victims fallen to their deaths.

Essentially the ceremony of throwing a stone to the bottom of an abyss is the culmination of a very primitive liturgy whose symbolism implies the offering of a spirit or soul to keep another spirit company so that the dead may be benevolent and tolerant with the practitioner. But in the original belief the offering was addressed to a divinity, genius, or spirit, with power over the spot the travelers crossed. That divinity could demand a soul for tribute, our soul. It was not the spirit of just whoever had the misfortune of falling when traversing the difficult passage, as tradition claims, and to whom we were to devote a prayer in the form of a stone in a voluntary and spontaneous gesture, but rather a higher spirit, a genius, a major divinity, ruler of the mountain, imposing a tribute that could turn costly to those who refused to render it.

It is highly remarkable that all the prehistoric monuments we have studied and analyzed so far have a funeral content. They might have had other meanings, but the funeral one is undeniable. Dolmens, mounds, menhirs, and steles had all been burial sites; their diversity in shape may indicate differences in race, in epoch, or in the social category of the buried. In any case, their funeral content is clear. And so is the sacred character of those places, since they were the abodes of divinities who oversaw the interests of their own folk. For this reason burials took place at the edges of tribal lands at the time when there was no private property. Later, when land was divided and land ownership took hold, each family had its burial place at the boundaries of its estates. These spots would forestall the fury or the greed of neighbors or the malevolence of evil spirits, who could damage the cycle of cultivation, destroy the crops, or poison the cattle. The boundaries of states and properties assumed the character of temples, devoted to each tribe or each family. People brought offerings, made sacrifices, and surrounded those spots with everything believed to be necessary and pleasant to the spirits living inside the stones. For these reasons one finds, next to dolmens and menhirs, stone axes and other tools and objects built with soft materials that have no practical use, only a votive function. They were given to the dead or their spirits as an offering to the divinity rather than as a result of any stone cult per se.

The passage of time and the refinement of spiritual life led to the polishing of primitive stones. The rough menhir became the well-wrought funerary stele. Plain stones at first and polished steles later became synchronic idols. These are the first images at humanity's dawn. From their sites, which became shrines, they guard the well-being of their folk according to the sacrifices and offerings they received. These primitive funeral monuments, in renovated states and having lost their original pagan character, are today's markers and milestones. On those locations rise Christianity's crosses, which fix the boundaries between communities and attempt to erase their paganism. Milestones that partition private estates in some cases keep their primitive shape as a mound of rocks.

Today, in order to place a property marker the concerned parties, generally the owners of the two or more adjacent estates, dig a hole and fill it with pieces of broken glass or earthenware and coal. The pieces of glass or flowerpots are the vestiges of a ceremonial sacrifice and a possible reminder of the offering of a being to the patriarchal divinity locked in the stone. In today's customs we may find numerous traces of ancient human sacrifices which, by successive attenuations, have turned into the breaking of a pitcher, an earthen pot, or any other ceramic ware. A century ago, once the ceremony of the planting of the markers had been carried out, the intervening parties would celebrate with a meal, a sign that they profited from the sacrifice that had been made formerly to the genius. In fairly recent times in Castile, the town marshals would round up a few youths, take them willy-nilly to the spot where the ceremony was to take place, and having planted the marker, tie the boys and flog their exposed backsides. This custom was also practiced in some French locations, but we have found no trace of it in Catalonia. It unequivocally harkens back to human sacrifices. A legend speaks of a king's armorer whose nephew was the victim of a flogging as a testimonial for the planting of a marker. The armorer, considering that custom onerous and barbaric, complained about the king's sanctioning of it. His words reached the ears of Philip IV. The king called the armorer, who, having confessed that he had indeed criticized the king, was placed in jail and told that the advice of a mere knife sharpener was not needed for the governance of the state. Sometime later, on the outskirts of Madrid, new limits had to be set and markers placed. It was difficult for the marshals to find boys to serve as witnesses, since everybody hid their offspring as soon as they learned that such a ceremony was to take place. The marshals heard youthful cries in a nearby woods and found two boys at play. They grabbed them, took their clothes off, and, having tied them to the stone marker, flogged them royally; one of the boys kept on saying he was the king's son and the other his servant, but the floggers laughed and hit them harder. In the middle of the beating they heard a loud trotting of horses and soon saw a noble cavalcade led by the king, who was shocked at the spectacle—particularly when he recognized that one of the victims was indeed his son. Then he understood the armorer's truth, freed him at once, and abolished that barbaric custom.

In the Empordà region, when people set a milestone, they bury a black cat. They say today that such practice prevents damage to the locality during storms. Clearly this is a milder version of yesterday's floggings and yesteryear's human sacrifices.

Popular justice considers the removal of a marker one of the gravest of crimes, to be punished accordingly. The voice of tradition tells of a man in Prat de Comte who coveted a very large olive tree. The tree belonged to his neighbor but grew very close to his land. The envious farmer went out one extremely cold and dark winter night, pulled out the stone marking the partition between his estate and his neighbor's, and replanted it a little beyond the tree, so that the coveted olives would fall within his property. As soon as he had pulled the marker, the loosened stone fell on top of him and left him dead. As this happened far from the village in a secluded area, no one witnessed the event. The villagers found the delinquent missing but did not know what had befallen him. There was a rumor that a ghost haunted the scene of the crime, moaning and weeping dolorously. Dread took hold of the neighborhood and no one dared approach that spot by day or night. Fall and the olive harvest were approaching, and everybody complained that because of their fear they would lose the fruit from that area. Something had to be done. A very brave youth, known as Meix, agreed to go out one night in search of the ghost. As soon as the sky turned black, he heard the ghastly tones of a pitiful voice saying:

> Poor little me
> Poor little me
> I can't budge
> I can't leave
> This sad spot
> As I'm damned

By this stone.
Where shall I put it,
Where shall I leave it?
Until I solve it,
I'll have no rest.

When the youth recovered from his fright, he answered the ghost:

You return it
Where you found it,
You can plant it
Where you dug it.

And the ghost replied:

Poor little me
I can't be;
If you help me
I'll replace it.

The young man, who was brave, helped the ghost return the marker to its proper place. When they were done, the envious man thanked him, and at that very instant a demon appeared and took him away. The ghost was heard no more. The young man took the hoe used by the ill-fated neighbor to dig and pull the stone. He kept it forever after, as did his descendants. I have heard that some years back it was still displayed. You could see it at the house of the Meix in Prat del Comte; they would show it as a testimonial of the anecdote.

The Hermitage of Sant Pere del Romaní could be found in a desolate stretch near the old village of Santa Creu d'Olorda, a village that disappeared long ago, absorbed first into Sarrià and today into Barcelona itself. Its hermitage was abandoned except during its two or three yearly celebrations. At a certain point in the middle of the night, the inhabitants of the few scattered houses nearby heard the tolling of the bells of Sant Pere, not just once but many times, and not just one night but every night. One can imagine the alarm this produced in the area. Nobody dared come within one hour of the hermitage. No one could rest, out of anxiety and uncertainty about that mystery. One of the farm hands, called Xixa, was a well-traveled man who thought nothing of a seven-hour journey on foot. Xixa decided one night to go all alone, as no one would go with him, and find out who was ringing the bells of Sant Pere at such an hour. He hid inside the hermitage and waited for the bell to ring. The bell rang and he saw no one pulling the rope, but he heard a tremulous voice saying:

> This marker,
> This milestone
> Is my perdition.
> Who can help
> Save me?

And Xixa, from his hiding place, answered:

> I will lend you a hand
> If you grease my palm.

The voice replied:

> The glory of heaven
> Will be given
> To whoever shows me this favor.

Xixa left his corner and found himself before a skeleton, who told him he had removed a marker and until he returned it to its place he could not leave the area as long as the world would last. Xixa helped him replant the stone. Having finished, the skeleton shook hands with him and gave him a kiss. It was such a cold kiss that poor Xixa, as long as he lived, was unable to get rid of the spark of coldness it left. The handshake had been so enthusiastic that Xixa's own bones creaked and hurt thereafter. Having taken his leave, the skeleton flared up as if made of lint. When Xixa died, he went to heaven for that good deed.

Tales of this type, focusing on a sense of respect for stone markers and on harsh punishments even beyond death, are not exclusive to Catalonia; they are known in Asturias, in the Basque country, and in other places.

There are also some beliefs and traditions that lead to the conservation of stone markers and imbue the folk with a kind of awe that makes them look at the stones with both fear and respect.

Some believe that if one bangs one's head against a stone one hears singing inside it. It is quite remarkable that only the person who has hit the stone enjoys the pleasure. This belief recalls a sacrifice offered the genius, spirit, or soul living in the stone, which responds in gratitude only to the person who has made the offering, not to those who just happened to be there. In the very center of the portal in the outer walls of the monastery at Pedralbes there is a large rock. People say that those who strike it hard with their heads hear the angels singing from inside. In Callicant in the Vallès there was a megalithic monument, long disappeared, with the legend that upon banging it with one's head, one heard the crowing of a rooster, and it was thus named *call* (for *gall*, "cock"); *i*, "and"; *cant*, "song": Callicant. Along the old road from Collbató to Montserrat known as Les Voltes, there is a rock that supposedly signaled the limits of the town of Collbató. It is known as Roca dels Polls, "Rock of the Chicks," for, as the story goes, those who hit it with their heads hear inside the stone a great peeping of chicks. The folk say that the marker cross at Vila-real makes the head banger hear cock-a-doodle-do.

49

Many menhirs and stone markers are supposedly the key or the plug locking a copious subterranean river known as the Jordan in many places. It is said that if one pulled out the stone the river would overflow and flood the countryside. A number of dolmens are said to allow one's ear to hear the rumble of underground water. Once a careless fellow tried to remove the marker stone at Su, and as he set to his task he heard a very deep voice coming from the stone say:

A marker you want to pull
It will drown both Su and you.

It was the memory of the genius who had lived in the stone during humanity's childhood now protesting the sacrilege and profanation of its shrine and person.

There is memory of a circle dance being performed periodically around the *pedra fita*, "marker stone," that has given its name to the town of Perafita in the Lluçanès.

Workers who gather sand from riverbeds and beaches to use in construction make great piles, and as they leave the mounds to be picked up they place a stone atop each one to signal that the sand has been spoken for and no one should mess with it. In the areas with a scarcity of stone some people gather as many as they can from dry riverbeds and washes; they make piles and wait to have enough to justify a cartload. In the same manner they place atop each pile a larger stone or draw a cross with stones to signal their ownership. Woodmen use stones as signs when they cannot carry away or keep an eye on all the wood they have cut. Those who manufacture lime, plaster, or coal use the same method to mark their ownership over the stones and firewood when they must leave them unattended in the woods or wilderness. Itinerant merchants use stones to delineate the perimeter reserved for their stands and place a larger stone in its center.

The genius in the stone protects the home as well as the land.

There is a variety of the lightning stone known as witch's stone that keeps evil spirits and the evil eye from a household. The same meaning is attached to those rocks inexplicably placed on the roofs of houses. In old mountain homes one may still see, at both sides of the main door, two large, rough, unpolished stones; they are sometimes used as places to sit but may have the same mythical value we have been discussing. Primitive houses had no door; to protect the inside, people used a large rock, as it is still normal to use in caves and natural grottoes inhabited by humans. More than as a door or a key, the rock functioned as the guardian of the house, since it was equivalent to its own spirit. Some assert that the term *keystone* is a reminder of primitive times when there were no keys other than stones. The habit of anchoring open doors with stones might be a remnant of those distant and dark times. The same goes for the mysterious custom of keeping two or three pebbles on the crossbar behind the door. In the small country houses of the Terra Alta one finds large rocks that people use as seats; for all the scant comfort they offer, the folk are reluctant to replace them.

Stones guarded the house and its people, but one also sought their protection away from home. Shepherds kept lightning stones in their sacks and hung one from the neck of their bellwether, perhaps as the bell clapper. My mother always carried a tiny pebble in her pocket but did not know why. Whenever she misplaced it she would get upset and soon find a replacement. Her only comments were that it was good and that the stone could be of any kind.

The toponymic tradition in Barcelona speaks of the Pedró, "Large Rock," that gave the name to a whole neighborhood. Pedró had been the junction of two roads: one coming from the south gate—the Jews' Gate, today's Carrers Boqueria and Hospital—and another from the north gate, at the end of today's Baixada de la Presó. That road followed the city walls, passed in front of the west gate, opened to the Carrer del Bisbe, and continued toward today's Carrers Boters, Portaferrissa, and Carme. It eventually led south toward Tarragona.

There was another notable stone in Barcelona's old city near the portal of the Church of the Angels in the plaza by that name. As children we heard the story that a man was turned into a stone dog because he refused to attend mass and would mock the faithful from the church portal. Those who considered themselves especially knowledgeable about that figure, however, said it was no dog but a lion sculpted in memory of a parishioner named Lleó ("Lion") who financed important renovations of the building.

Petrification was often a punishment for evil deeds, normally against religion. Examples may be found in Barcelona itself. When the Corpus Christi procession was instituted, the heretics, witches, and warlocks of our city surrounded the cathedral and, as the host emerged, set to shrieking and ranting. One day a witch cast a stone. Later, as a punishment for their heresy, the pagans and sorcerers were turned to stone and condemned forever to see the passage of the procession from the cathedral walls. That horde is now the magnificent gargoyles around the see, most of which represent monsters and imaginary beings.

Last century, Barcelona mothers, especially those from working-class neighborhoods, used the dog from the Church of the Angels to threaten their rebellious children. In Girona, mothers scare their young ones with the stone man from Sant Domènec, who, according to folklore, had been petrified precisely for his delight in scaring children. Keep in mind that before Barcelona had its walls the road from its west portal, or Carrer Bisbe, proceeded toward the Collegiata of Santa Anna and on to the gulch later known as Valldonzella to end up at today's Creu Cuberta. This road, now transformed into the Carrers Santa Anna, Bonsuccés, and Elisabets, passed in front of the Church of the Angels. The dog before that church, then, may well be an ancient marker stone.

I am unfamiliar with Girona's topography and thus cannot judge if the man of Sant Domènec is similar to the dog of the Angels, but they are probably related. From time immemorial the characters used to scare children were personifications or divinizations of death. The Greeks had their Mormo, a child-eating female. The Romans had Cacus, the giant killed by Hercules, and Gorgo, a stone divinity represented in tombs who was thought to guard the burial site from profanation. The Romans also used the Lamia, a death divinity similar to the Greek Mormo in that she ate infants. Our Papu and the Castilian Coco are supposedly figurations of death. Even today mothers and nannies refer to the souls of Rosegacebes ("Gnaw-onions"), Esgarrapadones ("Claw-women"), and the "soul of the water pitcher jumping and dancing on the walls."

The *sereno*, used to this day as a bogeyman, the hero and ruler of the night—the time preferred by the dead and their skulls—is a blurred reminder of death. In his distant origins the true bogeyman for the children of downtown Barcelona was not the dog of the Angels or the stone that preceded it but the genius of death contained in the rock.

There had been a famous stone in Barcelona at the spot of today's Plaça de l'Angel. It was round and marked the confluence of the four quarters of the old city. It was therefore a marker or milestone. The northern edge of the Roman city began there, with one of its four gates, at the end of the Baixada de la Presó. It was the starting point of the most important of the historical roadways into Barcelona, quite likely of pre-Roman origin and adapted later for the Via Augusta, which left Rome, crossed Gaul, and reached Tarraco. It has become our Travessera. That round stone, documented in the fourteenth century, may have a much older origin, even a prehistorical one. Its nearness to a roadway and to the gate of a city contribute to its significance. Tradition tells us that at that spot rose the scaffolding for the gallows where the condemned were flogged. If this tradition is true, the scaffolding may have been a remnant of the primitive milestone later used again as a marker. Recall the abundance of stone pillars where delinquents were pilloried and malefactors punished. Tradition considers it the city's first stone, around which all the buildings emerged.

These pillars must have derived from milestones and ultimately from the tribe's genius or protective divinity. Sacrifices were carried out on those stones to keep their spirits happy and ensure their protection. So we have traditions of the caning of children when a marker is planted and, in milder form, pieces of broken ceramic or glass placed under markers, to say nothing of the punishing of criminals—all of which have replaced the ancient sacrificial slayings of prisoners of war and slaves. Those who considered themselves the descendants of the genius and in some way the children of a stone, which was the symbol of a clan's tutelary divinity, gathered around it. The stone was at once god, parent, and temple, since people have always sought to live near shrines. This mentality continued in Christianity and particularly in Latin cultures where towns have always grown around a religious building.

In an unconscious way the folk bring together the concepts of stone and death. This is shown by many archaic legends, which go back to the time when it was dogma to believe in souls stored inside stones. Over the old road from Campdorà to Jonqueres, near a crossroads, one can see the Pedra de l'Amortallat ("Stone of the Shrouded Man"); it is a flat slab with a hole in the middle. From this hole a man shrouded in white would come out and roam that stretch while saying in his cavernous voice:

> When I was alive
> I walked these mountains
> And now I am dead
> I walk these depths;
> As you follow my road
> Look behind you.

And, the story goes, travelers always found him behind them. Even if there were several travelers going in opposite directions, that macabre song rang in their ears. It was supposedly the soul of a warlock who delighted in frightening passersby. It kept people away until they had the stone blessed. The ghost disappeared after many prayers.

Warlocks are descendants of divinities and pagan priests. Their stories must have been much more abundant than they are today, but the legend is well known of a dead man wrapped in a white sheet holding a lighted candle who comes out at night singing:

> When I was alive
> I walked this river,
> Now that I am dead
> I walk this garden.

When we were children we talked about one such ghost patrolling the fields between the Sant Antoni market and the old road from Barcelona to Reus, following today's Carrers Floridablanca and Sepúlveda. That ghoul came out of a huge rock we used to visit after school; but we only observed it from afar, out of childish fear. The braver of the boys dared get somewhat closer.

It is said that when fear roamed the world, it issued from a rock in the shape of a fire horse, in the municipality of Mieres. It was called Fear's Rock.

High in the Pyrenees, especially toward Ribagorça and Aragon, deals are closed over a tablelike stone devoted to this function and normally placed by a road at the outskirts of the village. When the hired musicians left the village after playing for its patron-saint celebration, they went to that stone to be paid. The officials put the money on the stones and the musicians took it. To ensure music for the following year's celebration, the contract was extended at that time and place. Such contracts would be honored no matter what might happen. If the musicians, out of greed or whatever, decided to play for another town or refused to honor the pact, the folk say that the villagers could form a posse and safely take justice into their own hands. One such story claims that a posse killed some musicians with no legal consequences; but the musicians could do the same to the villagers who had fallen back on the contract. This was the custom at Graus and surrounding villages. The stone or its hidden genius was the witness. Word given in its presence was sacred and could not be broken without grave penalties.

Most of the stones alluded to are found near trails. Not because the stones were placed near the trail but because the trails would follow famous stone sites as the cult of stones is much older. The land adjacent to stones with estate-protecting and limit-guarding spirits was also held sacred and thus uncultivated so as to avoid any accidental chipping of the stone by the plow, which could hurt or anger its genius. Strips of untilled land grew along rows of markers, respected equally by the owners of the fields on both sides, since both feared the wrath of the genius as much as their neighbor's. Those uncultivated zones between fields became passageways so people would not disturb the crops. This is the origin of prehistoric trails.

The so-called oaths of Odin had the parties stand on both sides of a hollow rock and, through the hole, shake hands. Such deals were legal and even considered sacred.

The folk say that purification rites were practiced on hollow and hallowed stones. According to Serra i Pagès, we have conserved the tradition when we put a child suffering from hernia through a tree's opening on midsummer's night. Other than this we have no knowledge of any practices attached to the rather few hollow rocks in Catalonia.

A Note on Monzó's
"Barcelona Beat"

 Joaquim Monzó i Gómez, born in Barcelona in 1952, belongs to the first generation of writers in history who were able to make a living by using Catalan exclusively. Quim Monzó achieved popularity with his collections of short stories (a well-loved genre in Catalonia) and has also written two novels. One of Monzó's short-story collections, *Olivetti, Moulinex, Chaffoteaux et Maury*, winner of the Catalan Critics prize in 1981, has been translated into English as *O'Clock* by Mary Ann Newman (New York: Ballantine Books, 1986). He supplements his income by translating (mostly from English, the study of which he perfected during long sojourns in New York City) and by writing columns for the two Catalan dailies in Barcelona. The best of these columns he gathers in collections that are published as books, and from his first two books of this kind, *El dia del Senyor* and *Zzzzzzzz . . .* , I have selected, under my title "Barcelona Beat," the ten pieces presented here.

These short essays show the witty and urbane viewpoint of the writer on a number of topics but always with an eye to presenting a picture of Catalonia, and particularly of Barcelona, at once accurate and faithful to the Catalan ethos. Yet Monzó lives in times, like all times, of great complexity, and the speaking of Catalan or Castilian (which he, like many young Catalanists, calls Spanish), the song-and-dances of politicians, the metamorphoses of snobs, the efforts to re-Catalanize Catalonia's mass media, the pervasive discrimination of the centralist state, and the heartbeat of daily life inspire Monzó's lively criticism.

The introduction and the index of proper names should provide explanations for most of the topics and names brought up in what follows. Some references may remain obscure. That, for example, the Catalan king of Majorca, James, was also lord of Montpellier, which he inherited from his mother, or that Catalans felt much more enthusiasm about the 1992 Olympic Games in Barcelona than about the celebration of the five hundredth anniversary of the discovery of America (events summarized in the slogans "Barcelona '92" and "Quinto Centenario") may not be immediately apparent to American readers. Also the word *xarnego,* left untranslated, requires some clarification. Monzó uses this term quite unabashedly and lashes out at those who have been trying to appropriate it to wage populist demagogy. The word is of obscure etymology; the only hypothesis I know, which derives it from Castilian *nocharniego,* "night owl, lowlife," is not entirely satisfactory. In present usage it is a derogatory term describing immigrants from southern Spain, mainly from Murcia and Andalusia, and their descendants. Its American equivalent might be "Okie," although *xarnego* also carries with it a general meaning of boorishness and might thus be translated as "hick."

A great number of people from southern Spain, often unskilled laborers thrown out of their native regions by feudal economic policies, moved north and became the labor force of a more industrial Catalonia. During this century the rate of migration has been so high that these laborers could not be assimilated by the native population and ended up the victims of social discrimination. The industrial belt around Barcelona is mostly occupied by these *xarnegos,* who, speaking a different language and coming from culturally and economically deprived milieus, are often viewed with unjustified scorn.

At one time *xarnego* signified a person of a mixed marriage, a hybrid, and particularly someone with one parent born in France. Monzó goes back to this original notion of the word and ultimately makes a claim for the *xarnego* condition of all Catalans. His aim is to criticize politicians or public figures who for demagogic and self-advancing reasons make empty claims of solidarity with the downtrodden. The existence of a deprived, often discriminated against, non-Catalan working class in Catalonia is all too often used to discredit any Catalanist movement as elitist, bourgeois, and therefore undemocratic. Because the Spanish economy has shifted in the last decade and migration into Catalonia has decreased, cultural assimi-

lation is slowly advancing and claims of Catalanist elitism sound more and
more hollow, although one continues to hear them.

The first six essays are from *El dia del Senyor* (Barcelona:
Quaderns Crema, 1984), the other four from *Zzzzzzzz* . . . (Barcelona:
Quaderns Crema, 1987).

QUIM MONZÓ

Barcelona Beat

NAME LAUNDERING

Not long ago, Joan Fuster, in one of his articles in *El món*, mentioned Pablo Casals; when he saw the article in print he found they had changed the cellist's name to Pau. Fuster released his understandable wrath in a letter to the editor in which he explained why Casals is called Pablo and not Pau.

Fuster's letter was a model of reason. It is getting to be time to call things and people by their names. If Pablo Casals lived in this world with the name Pablo—and let us not forget that because he was living in exile no one could prevent him from using Pau—why should we now call him something else? Let's cut the cake here: plenty of *Cant dels ocells,* plenty of *Pessebre,* plenty of declarations of what is called Catalanicity at the U.N., but whenever he signed concerts, Casals used the name Pablo. Was that the way he wanted it? Fine. We all have the right to use the name we want. Eugenio Trias signs Eugenio whether he publishes his books in Catalan or in Spanish, and I do not think anybody should object.

Joan Miró always made it clear that his name was Joan, and as Joan he is known from Chile to Manchuria. Anyone who would now rebaptize him as John, Juan or Giovanni would be seen as an idiot. Likewise, Julio González was called Julio, not Juli; that name, he used to say, displeased him because the French—Paris was then the world capital of the visual arts—would confuse it with the feminine Julie. (As to González's fears, we should note that in the Anglo-Saxon world Joan could be seen as a woman's name. Miró, however, dismissed such idiotic excuses, which, by the way, would cause Joan Collins to change her name so as not to be taken for a man here—a mistake that could only stem, of course, from myopia.)

By the same principle José María Flotats—even though he now figures in the Generalitat's Centre Dramàtic—is José María and not Josep Maria, as he was known everywhere by the first form, principally on the billboards of the Comédie Française. I fail to see why, in Barcelona, Senyor Flotats should be called Josep Maria and, in Paris, José María (and not Joseph Marie, eh?). Likewise, José Carreras is the name the opera singer uses to sign his records and his performances throughout the world. Why, then, *Josep* Carreras whenever he sings at the Liceu? And José Guinovart likewise. If Senyor Guinovart finds it normal to be announced at the door of the gallery in New York as José Guinovart, I fail to see by what miracle, all of a sudden, his name should become Josep Guinovart here.

About ten years ago the great journalist Eugeni Xammar—interviewed by Montserrat Roig in *Serra d'Or*—said he found the attitude of young journalists who signed their names in Catalan, even though they wrote in the Barcelona press in Spanish, highly ridiculous.

Xammar did not see the key to the conundrum, which is the fabulous invention of *bilingüismo*. Casals, Flotats, Guinovart, González, and Carreras are Pau, Josep Maria, Josep, Juli, and Josep among us. But thanks to the magic of our bifid tongues, they become Pablo, José María, José, Julio, and José in any other place in the world. They do not become, however, Paul, Joseph-Marie, Joseph, Jules, or Julius. It is a pity that we are not granted a trilingualism decree or a quaterlingualism one, for you must admit that seeing the name Joe Guinovart on the window of a New York SoHo gallery or Joseph-Marie Flotats on the bill of the Comédie Française would be totally awesome.

THE MONUMENT TO PICASSO

Four months and a few days ago a monument was dedicated to Picasso on the promenade that bears his name. The Barcelona City Hall had charged Antoni Tàpies with this project. The monument consists of some iron beams painted white, chairs, ropes, a kind of sofa-mirror-armoire, and a scribbled bedsheet, all stuffed inside a glass cube measuring sixty-four cubic meters, on the transparent walls of which a sort of water curtain falls. Alícia Suárez and Mercè Vidal—in the *Serra d'Or* of last May—defined it as "an assemblage provoking a new contemplation as each component piece, by itself, could be the carrier of significations that multiply themselves in their interrelations."

The day before yesterday I read in the newspaper that by now "one of the glass panels has been completely cracked," that the cube "is covered with condensation and stained with calcium as a result of the constant water movement," that the water in the ponds around the work "is stagnant, with the ensuing health hazards," and that "papers, feathers, pieces of plastic, and leaves float on the water in which some tadpoles and minnows breed."

Last night after supper in the Barceloneta at Can Costa—which, by the way, has been cleaned to the point of resembling a nouveau riche living room—we went to take a look. True, the monument looks like a filthy shop window. One cannot even read that nice quotation, "A picture is not meant for interior decoration . . . ," which is the message painted on the sheet. One cannot even see the sheet, or the sofa-mirror, or the beams.

So as not to be accused of unconstructive criticism, let us propose a solution: adding truck-size windshield wipers, really big ones, activated day and night. Do not panic. If—as Suàrez & Vidal say in *Serra d'Or*—"the modernista furniture evokes turn-of-the-century Barcelona," if "the sheet is a quotidian element," and if "faced with the perenniality, with the permanence of the solid materials that befit a monument, Tàpies contrasts perishable, ephemeral, degradable materials, conventionally nonartistic," what could be more appropriate, degradable, conventionally nonartistic, and ephemeral than the practical windshield wipers which, besides, could symbolize future encounters along the highway? And with the addition of a little detergent to the falling water, the glass would shine ever clean. Surely the Netol corporation would donate the detergent in exchange for a little corner inside the cube where they could display their logo of a butler with a puffy face and broad smile.

Otherwise we can always discard the cube and replace it with a palm tree.

Antonio Figueruelo, a journalist born in Seu d'Urgell and now director general of Civil Protection, a branch of the Ministry of the Interior, declared this week to *El món:* "I read, understand, and even speak Catalan, but with the common folk. I don't like intellectual Catalan."

There we are. Now I understand why—in meetings, at restaurants, and during those radio and television interviews he granted when he was the Citizen's Protection delegate to the Barcelona City Hall—I have always heard Senyor Figueruelo answer in Spanish questions posed to him in Catalan. It turns out that he "even"—"even," wow, what an effort!—speaks Catalan! Why were you keeping so mum, eh, you rascal? Of course, he only does it "with the common folk." Why? Because he does not like "intellectual Catalan."

Could this be a new version of that statement by Adolfo Suárez according to which one could not teach nuclear physics in Catalan? Or could it be that Figueruelo does what Eugenio Trías does: boasts he speaks Catalan when he is in Madrid to pester the Madridians? In Catalonia, however, Trías does not speak Catalan. Why should he, when it would pester no one and, besides, make him appear provincial?

Figueruelo's case is different. He does not speak Catalan in Madrid. He speaks it "with the common folk." He must go to little towns equipped with his "common folk detector," and whenever he finds people of that kind, he starts to speak to them in Catalan. He talks about the weather, whether their tractors need a tune-up, about oxen and cows, of cabbages and kings. If the conversation starts to climb—"common folk" have been known to have such quirks—and veer toward weightier topics, Figueruelo changes quickly to Spanish. For he does not like "intellectual Catalan." That is why, in interviews for Catalan radio and television programs, he always answered in Spanish. They took place in Barcelona, and he did not speak about oxen and cows, isn't that so? We're not among the "common folk," man! When it is time to speak "intellectual," Spanish. Of course, he "even" speaks Catalan. Don't you think otherwise.

Figueruelo and Trías remind me of an acquaintance born in Barcelona, the daughter of Galician parents and a militant Spanish speaker, who says she knows how to speak Catalan.

"I *know* Catalan," she says in Spanish. "What happens is that I do not speak it."

HOOKERS UP, HARLOTS DOWN

They say Rodolf Guerra, a representative from the first and fifth districts in Barcelona, wants to rid the neighborhood of delinquents, prostitutes, and all those now called "marginals." Senyor Guerra wants to turn around the decay of his neighborhoods, clean the Rambla, and leave it tidy and shining. A couple of weeks ago he said "he will not tolerate any activities that may favor the extension of influence of the world of illegality, gambling dens, sex shops, and slot machines that are more and more widely used." In order to succeed he will increase the number of police patrols. Then, he says, he will kick out noisy musicians and con artists. And those who peddle political articles he will send to Ciutadella Park. And in some zones, so as to make it impossible to paint on the ground, he will alter the pavement.

He will also do away with prostitution. From September on the hookers will be forced to "remain in closed quarters or get out." "Our intention," says Senyor Guerra, "is to prevent them from exercising their activities on the street." This last statement has left us stunned: we have never seen a whore exercising her activities on the street. What Senyor Guerra surely means is that on the street they attract their customers so that later they can exercise their activities in some of the nearby rooming houses.

Well: the fact is they will be forced to move or work in enclosed places. Dictionary in hand, we can say that an enclosed place with strumpets is nothing less than a brothel. Fancy that; we are now faced with the resurrection of whorehouses! Senyor Guerra's notion is nothing short of magnificent. Given the proliferation of "relax" and massage parlors, the youth of this country have never gained a solid idea of what an honest-to-goodness whorehouse was, whorehouses like the ones described by our grandfathers, and of whose magnificence we have approximate notions thanks to Signor Fellini's *Roma* or Monsieur Malle's *Pretty Baby*. In New York, Mr. Koch's City Hall is bent on a similar enterprise: to clean up 42nd Street (which, given New York's large scale, can compare with the lower part of the Barcelona Rambla); and to do so they thought of nothing better than to send all the sexual commerce to the Lower East Side, a working-class neighborhood the streets of which are already the main drug market of the city.

As if, here, we seized the Rambla traffic and moved it to

Verdum. Senyor Guerra's solution is much more appetizing, and it explains, by the way, why the old Carassa building is being refurbished, that old bordello at the corner of Carrer Mirallers and Carrer Vigatans. They claim they are building a retirement home? Ha!

XARNEGOS

For quite some time the papers have been gathering statements from a number of ladies and gentlemen who declare that they "too" are *xarnegos*. "I am also a xarnego," said Joan-Manuel Serrat this summer after climbing the stairs of the Greek Theater. At the beginning of fall, from the counter at the Zig Zag, Maestro Ramon Barnils explained to me that last year in Girona *Señorito* Felipe González had the nerve to declare, at the height of the electoral campaign for municipal elections, that he too was a xarnego. Xarnego? A good-family Seville boy who has made a career in Madrid? I am the Pope of Rome.

Let us speak clearly: what are they trying to sell us? Why does Senyor Serrat (the son of a Catalan and an Aragonese) remind us constantly that he is a xarnego while I (the son of a Catalan and an Andalusian) have forgotten it for the last thirty-one years? I must be missing something. From today on I firmly resolve to waste no opportunity to state that "I am a xarnego too." Surely this will help me sell a few more books.

The best part is that as soon as you scratch a little, you find this type of xarnego—those of us who, unawares, thought ourselves Catalan—all over the place: Francesc Bellmunt i Moreno, Joan-Josep Isern i Márquez, Francesc Parcerisas i Vázquez, Xavier Lamuela. How dumb we have been, all of us, thinking we were Catalans simply because we felt we were, to a greater or lesser degree! (Even the minister of culture, Max Cahner i Garcia, is an unconfessed xarnego!)

At last the wool has been pulled from my eyes! So many years living just like a regular Catalan and I now see I have been a traitor for having adapted to this country. For the way things are going, being normal means living in saecula saeculorum estranged from where one lives, cursing and protesting and casting accusations of oppression. It may be true that the locals are the ones who should adapt to the ways of the newcomers, a proposal offered for sale along with the "new Catalan identity" and the "Catalonia with her legs spread." How wrong I was! As a good xarnego

I should have opted to collaborate with the cultural occupation army, a magnificent term coined by Josep Termes during the Critical Symposium on Catalan Culture. Mea culpa.

The one thing I do not understand is why precisely those who call themselves xarnegos every five minutes claim this country was made by waves of immigrants—therefore xarnegos—come from all over Europe and Africa. Iberians, Greeks, Romans, Goths, Jews, Arabs, Occitans, Italians, Spaniards, Africans from Maghreb and from the blackest of negritudes. In that case, every Catalan is, if you go back a few generations, a xarnego, be their name Puigdengoles, Bozzo, or Martínez. Why must we speak so much of xarnegos, then, if—as they say—we are all xarnegos? To be saying nothing and gaining time?

> Signed: Quim Monzó (i Gómez, i Garcia i Rodríguez i Vidal i López i Benavent i Rodríguez i. . . .)

THE NAMES OF THINGS

The other night at the counter of Pep's frankfurter place, Jordi Vendrell and I philosophized about the relativity of things, the fugacity of life, and the brevity of gin-and-tonics. The spot we had chosen is ideal: Pep's frankfurter bar on Carrer Espaseria, a bar where—just to give its name the lie, perhaps—they serve no hot dogs. But there you can eat rice dishes, omelets—salt or green garlic omelets—cod—in *samfaina* or garlic mousse—calamari, or fish that will make you hear the angels sing, the angels from the old cathedral in Barcelona, Santa Maria del Mar, in the protective shade of which Pep cooks for a number of down-and-out gourmets who would of course never accept that designation. (On the other hand, whenever you tell members of the gastronomic snobs' club that one eats very well at Pep's, this proliferating band will stare at you in disdain. Their loss. Screw them.)

And we talked—with Vendrell, who, since he m.c.'d Up&Down's video festival a few days ago, is the apple of the Barcelona jet set's eye—about the fact that in many highfalutin restaurants, for all their big names—and their prices—you eat much worse than you do in a frankfurter bar. Particularly in many of those which add the phrase *cuina de mercat*, "market cooking," to the name of the restaurant, as if one could have "bookstore cooking" or "hardware-store cooking" or "shoe-store cooking."

As we downed our respective dishes of cooked ham in sauce, we proceeded to reinvent the wheel. Our game consisted of finding examples proving the wise dictum that the name does not make the thing. In politics the trick is repeated constantly. Members of Convergència i Unió have the gall to define themselves as nationalists when they are only regionalists. Members of PSOE, who call themselves socialists, are to the right of the defunct UCD. And Esquerra Republicana? Is it much of an *esquerra* ("left")? And Alianza Popular? This "popular" thing, where did they get it from?

Having arrived at the fish course, it became clear that everything is fragile and mobile and that—more so each day—names define nothing; we baptize things so as to hide them under a coat of paint. Right now the Vatican has made public a document on sexual education which—once again—confuses sexuality with reproduction; a document which, instead of explaining how sexuality should be taught, explains how it should be dodged. But, oh yes: it is presented as a document "on sexual education" because that is the veneer they need these days to continue giving us their injections of moth-eaten morality. On the other hand, when Sánchez Dragó preaches this "new chastity" that he says he has learned from the Yankees, what he really does—horny and cynical as he is—is not to propound any sort of chastity but rather to create a little more suspense before one hops into bed.

A copy of this week's *El món* lay on the counter, open at the page where Joan Solà recalls Voltaire's saying: "Whenever a politician says 'yes,' he means 'we'll see'; when he says 'we'll see,' he means 'no'; and when he says 'no,' he is no politician. When a lady says 'no,' she means 'we'll see'; when she says 'we'll see,' she means 'yes'; and when she says 'yes,' she is no lady." And when Voltaire says "she is no lady," he means "she is a lady who doesn't mince words." And so ad infinitum.

MIRROR, MIRROR ON THE WALL

Some weeks ago, to celebrate Saint John's eve, TV3 shot a program on the squares and fountains of Montjuïc. Those were images presenting a notably pleasant and balanced city. On a daily basis, either in particular programs or on the news, the same TV3 offers us completely different images of Barcelona: chaotic, slummy, messy, ugly, interesting images. And not only of Barcelona; portraits of the most diverse Catalan cities appear daily on the little screen. Daily. This *daily* throws Barcelona and the other Catalan cities into *normality*. And, as it does so, makes all of us *normal*.

For the first time and in a regular way, then, we exist as "normal" on such a mass medium as television. Now, after months of continued airings, we can begin to think about the magnitude of this fact. On TVE we were strangers, as we did not follow with any fidelity the model offered us by the screen. We were strangers because we did not quite accord with the *normality* shown us. Whenever we went out for an aperitif we went to the Plaça Reial and not—as that *normality* showed us—to a beer hall near the Nuevos Ministerios in Madrid. What was *normal* was to have the new year heralded by the clock on Puerta del Sol in Madrid. Since this past New Year's, the twelve clocks TV3 reported are *normal*. *Normality* used to be Marisa Medina, Alfredo Amestoy, and Yale. *Normality* now is Angel Casas and Angels Barceló; and Susan Sontag speaking about Barcelona, cinema, Catalan culture, and cancer. By dint of sunbleaching our brains, and simply because the *normality* shown us was not ours, we had ended up believing we were not *normal*.

If they want to know what their faces look like, people need—even if only in the morning, before shaving—to take a look, to determine whether shaving is really necessary or whether we can wait one more day. Or whether our eyes are bloodshot. Or whether our wrinkles are improving in either quality or quantity.

A little time spent before the mirror is good not just for people. Also for cities. New York would be an extreme case. With the greatest of ease New Yorkers use New York as their pattern to measure the world. And perhaps without reaching that extreme, the rest of the big and mid-sized cities in the world, at the very least, do not turn up their noses at self-contemplation. Not that Barcelona or Catalonia would do so, turn up its nose: what used to happen (and continues to happen, for TV3 is only one of the many mirrors needed) is that we did not (and still do not) have enough mirrors. The small mirrors employed all focused on the faces of our neighbors, in part to keep them happy, in part to see what they looked like (lest they swung their big sticks once more), and in part to avoid being accused at the slightest opportunity of being provincial and localist.

When we have enough mirrors to see ourselves wholly, we will be surprised.

ORNITHOLOGY

In the latest issue of *Le Nouvel Observateur,* François Caviglioli published an article on the wave of Gallophobia current in Spain. The "envoyé spécial en Espagne" based almost all of his article on conversations held with Catalan intellectuals: Josep Ramoneda, Xavier Rubert de Ventós, Ricardo Bofill. And—perhaps not surprisingly—as he tried to condemn this wave of anti-Frenchism, he wrote an article that is a perfect specimen of the petulant ignorance attributed to the French.

To begin with, he explains that "le catalan est une langue romane primitive." Just like that.

To continue, he explains that it was from the Hotel Oriente on the Rambla—he wrote *Ramblas,* of course—that "George Orwell tirait sur les franquistes qui entrait dans Barcelona," clearly confusing the events of May 1937 with Franco's entry into Barcelona in January 1939.

Finally, he confuses either J. V. Foix or Jordi Sarsanedas—both having recently received France's Medal of Arts and Letters—with a member of Parliament. The author shows his indelicacy and lack of professionalism by forgetting the representative's name, even when the best part of his article is the anecdote explaining a feat of this unnamed or unnameable "member of Parliament."

The anecdote is this: to rid Barcelona's airport of starlings, the hero in question called some French ornithologists with experience in these matters. To oust the birds the ornithologists used the cassette tapes they normally used, tapes—made in France—reproducing some starlings' shrieks of terror before an approaching hawk. (Just as in Joan Rendé's story where a partridge's whistling is tape-recorded.) The trick, which had worked so well in all the French airports where it had been put to use, failed in Barcelona. Apparently, "quand les étourneaux catalans ont peur, ils le disent en catalan," a fact which enabled Caviglioli to conclude that "les oiseaux français n'ont pas réussi à imposer leur langage dans le ciel de Catalogne. Les oiseaux catalans continuent de pialler en catalan." Considering the ease with which the French made Catalan disappear among the humans living on the little piece of the Kingdom of Majorca they conquered in the seventeenth century, it is logical for Frenchmen to find the starlings' behavior curious and even surprising.

TO THE GOOSE STEP

The Advisory Council of the Generalitat de Catalunya published, in a book entitled *Ordenació legal del plurilingüisme als estats contemporanis,* the proceedings of a conference held in November 1982 while the cultural policy committee of Parliament debated the drafting of the linguistic normalization law. The conference consisted of four lectures that described the present situation in four multilingual states: Italy, Belgium, Canada, and Switzerland.

In the lecture referring to Belgium there is a highly interesting paragraph, at least for our corner of the continent. It is the one that deals with the use of languages in the armed forces.

To begin with, there is a law—of 30 July 1938—regulating the use of languages in the military, a law unthinkable among us. This law organizes the grouping of troops into linguistic units according to their native speech, be that Flemish, French, or German, so that training can be carried out completely in each soldier's native tongue. Furthermore, all officers are required to know the second official language of the state. And those officers in command of German-speaking units must of course know German.

How do they manage? In a very simple way: no one, absolutely no one, can pass the preliminary exam for the rank of officer if he or she does not know both French and Flemish—the native language in depth, the other sufficiently. The law of course ensures all the necessary dispositions so that training, orders, communiqués, commands, service relations, and administration are issued in the unit's language.

All this happens in Belgium, a highly civilized country in spite of its Queen Fabiola and King Baudouin. That Belgium is a highly civilized country can be demonstrated easily: were it not, it would never have managed to invent such beers as Ketje, Faro, Kreik, Triple Trappist, or the splendid Gueuze.

In the meanwhile, here, as the press has reported (some papers in tiny entries, the lower and more to the left on the page the better), some days ago, because of his studies, Jordi Buixadera, from Lleida, who had been drafted for military service, requested an extension. As they say, the paperwork required for the granting of an extension could not be simpler or more routine: basically, one must submit a certificate from the school one is attending, and that's that.

Something as simple as this has been unable to proceed because the certificate in this case was written in Catalan.

To top it all, many of those recycled flower people who are still
singing their tango for peace, love, and not war, consider that the only
problem worth debating here is whether there ought to be conscription or
not; they pay no heed to such banalities as whether the training is carried
out in Spanish or in Catalan. What comes out of so much pacifism? People
are conscripted, and they serve, in Spanish.

How far we are from the dark and dense perfection of Gueuze
beer!

ARTICLE

It has been at least a quarter century since we have seen so
many objects in the shape of other objects. All you need to do is stroll by
the home-accessory shops. Or by the modern gift shops, those shops that
began by selling original gadgets and *objets* but are becoming more and
more like traditional gift shops, those with ungrammatical signs—
"Gifts'n'Such," they read, ninety percent of the time—and showing porce-
lain statuettes representing shepherds, deer, and other diverse bucolic
characters painted in rose and blue pastel tones, and little imbecile desk
signs with phrases such as "The boss is always right."

This Christmas, as absolute or partial novelties, there have
been telephone receivers in the shape of automobiles or in the form of a
banana, an eggplant, a robot, a shoe, or Mickey Mouse. Lamps in the
shape of a camera, an umbrella, a banana, a palm tree, a mushroom. Salt
shakers in the shape of food cans or heads of garlic. Pepper mills in the
shape of mussels. Cigarette lighters in the shape of a hand grenade with
two detonators and a fuse, of a matchbox, a gun, a motorcycle, a can of
pop, a microphone, or a fire extinguisher. Notepads in the shape of a shirt
collar with its tie. Toilet-paper holders in the shape of an automobile or a
human hand. Containers in the shape of undershorts to hold pencils and
pens. Armchairs in the form of a tennis shoe. Erasers shaped like lemons,
watermelons, or strawberries. Clothes hangers in the shape of skis. Calcu-
lators in the shape of cars.

Some years ago, design schools required the reading of a book
by Bruno Munari, *Arte come mestiere*, which had been issued in Spanish by

Labor, translated and with an introduction by Juan-Eduardo Cirlot. Munari wrote his book during a time when the situation was similar to the one we experience today, but without the present intensity. He was shocked to find umbrella stands in the shape of a boot, clocks in the shape of a frying pan, brushes in the shape of a cat, ashtrays in the form of a woman's hand, cutting boards in the shape of a pig, chamber pots in the shape of a duck, lamps in the form of a bouquet of flowers, drills shaped like a pig's tail, pipes in the form of a bull's head or a shoe, piggy banks in the shape of a pear or an apple, picture frames in the form of a pocket watch, scissors in the shape of a bird. Munari ended up not knowing where to put the ashes of his cigarette because he could not discern the ashtray among that spread of objects looking like other objects.

His final advice was "Let us buy a pipe that is a pipe, let us light a lighter that is a lighter, a candlestick that is a candlestick, and let us smoke tobacco that is tobacco once it is inside the pipe-pipe. Next to a tray looking like a tray, on a table that is a table, and sitting on a chair that is a chair."

After the time of Munari's complaint there was a certain reduction in the number of disguised objects and a partial—nothing is ever absolute—return to pipe-pipes and lighter-lighters. But some ten years ago there began a slow, progressive, and sneaky renaissance of the object in the shape of another object. This Christmas has been the culminating point of the trend, up to now. Bruno Munari was shocked because he was a designer and a theoretician of design. Since we are not, we may look calmly at the phenomenon from the outside and see that these transmuted objects are nothing but the perfect accessories for a stage filled with, let us say, people who can barely fry an egg in the form of cooks in a "market cooking" restaurant, imbeciles in the form of modern professionals, good-for-nothings in the form of secretary-generals, regionalists in the form of nationalists, obvious right-wingers in the shape of social democrats, hatreds in the shape of satire, resentments in the form of objective criticism, despicable pamphlets in the shape of yuppie novels, Quinto Centenario in the form of Barcelona '92, slips of the tongue in the shape of improvisation, Finley- or Kas-brand soda in the form of tonic water, talcum powder disguised as flour, Madonna in *Material Girl* posing as Marilyn Monroe in *Gentlemen Prefer Blondes,* and reams of objects and persons transmuted into other articles.

A Note on Rodoreda's
"Two Stories"

Two banal anecdotes inspired these short stories about life in Barcelona: a disgruntled husband's summer night fantasy about a pretty young woman, and a story of love between a housemaid and a soldier. These last two figures, called *la minyona i el soldat* in Catalan, constitute traditional items in folklore and song as icons of the perennial renovation of the ritual of mating; the fantasy of sexual and ecological freedom in the other story gives an idea of the sense of entrapment big cities can instill in their inhabitants. Rodoreda's artistry elevates these commonplaces to a delicate portrait of life in the city.

Many of the blocks of apartment houses in Barcelona, particularly in the nineteenth-century extension of the city known as Eixample, are built with a hollow center, which the first-floor apartment dwellers can use as gardens; the humbler apartments on the upper floors enjoy the view of such gardens from their enclosed *galeries,* or rear balconies. One such balcony is prominent in "Summer," the fist story.

Mercè Rodoreda i Gurguí (Barcelona 1909–Girona 1983) emerged as Catalonia's most influential fiction writer after the Spanish Civil War. Her career began in Barcelona before the war and continued in her Geneva exile until she returned to her native city to devote herself to her writing. She is best known for her novel *La plaça del Diamant* (which, among other languages, has been translated twice into English). Gabriel García Márquez called this novel the best Spanish novel written after the Civil War; the younger Catalan intelligentsia, however, praise *Mirall trencat* (Broken mirror), not yet translated into English, as her crowning glory. Rodoreda's cultivation of short fiction has been decisive, along perhaps with Pere Calders's, in making the *conte,* or very short narrative, a highly influential if not the most successful genre among the writers and readers of the younger generation.

"Summer" was first published as "Estiu" in *Vint-i-dos contes* (Barcelona: Editorial Selecta, 1958), and "That Wall, That Mimosa" as "Aquella paret, aquella mimosa" in *La meva Cristina i altres contes* (Barcelona: Edicions 62, 1967). Both stories also appear in Rodoreda's *Tots els contes* (1979) and *Obres completes* (2 vols., 1976 and 1978).

MERCÈ RODOREDA

Two Stories

SUMMER

She stopped to look at a shop window full of umbrellas, and her friend, who had stepped ahead, suddenly turned around: "Carme, I'm going to lose you!" Her name was Carme. He'd been following them from the Travessera, where he'd been working for the last eleven years, all the way to Carrer Pàdua.

Now, leaning on the railing of the rear balcony, he could still see that vaporous, pearl-gray dress, with a flower print of very pale pink, almost mauve. A cool and sweet dress. "Carme, Carme." She would stop at all the shops that displayed nice things and her friend would pull her by the arm and drag her away from all those hooks. On Pàdua, near Carrer Saragossa, they popped into a laundry. "Fine Pressing." The sun fell fully on the shop's window and one couldn't see inside. That's how he lost track of her. It was late, and a boy who had been playing ball stopped playing and eyed him with some curiosity and some suspicion. And now he could not get her off his mind. He could not get her dress, her legs, off his mind; she had smooth skin, brown, matte; her skirt's hem made waves at every step, at every step. With the slightest of movements.

Standing, with his hands in his pants' pockets, his shirt unbuttoned, he watched the sky as it turned dark and, little by little, was sprinkled with stars.

"Why don't you help me clear the table instead of acting the lord of the manor?"

A swallow came in with a shriek. There had been a nest on their balcony for three years now; every spring the bird brought back more mud for it.

"My work is never done, and you——Did you forget that the clothesline broke and that we have to change the mosquito net on the boy's bed? Of course you did. You never think of anything. We're taking in the scenery. His lordship is taking in the scenery: no one is to disturb him. Instead of stargazing you could go get your son. You'll soon complain he's a bum."

"He's old enough. He knows how to get home."

"When he's run over by a car we'll see what you say."

How the hell could he be struck by an automobile if their street didn't even have carts? It seemed she read his mind:

"The other day he went to Carrer Wagner all by himself; and he didn't ask for your permission, to my knowledge. If you don't act soon, any day he'll be killed by a truck on Plaça Bonanova."

"We can't keep him tied up with string, can we?" he shouted.

The scent of flowers rose from the gardens. He could see all the gardens from his balcony. The Codinas' palm tree opened its dusty fans in the thick air. The darkest of the trees was the medlar: tall, old, with smooth trunk, not a gnarl on it, and with stiff leaves as if they were made of cardboard. He felt his neck, his forehead; he was perspiring. A mosquito was raging around him. If by some magic he could find himself now suddenly in a forest . . . If he could spend the night in a forest . . . After all, life . . . The only good thing in life is this. Only this. Night. A girl. Only this. And it is terrible, as if you'd suffer, as if you'd die from it . . . For a girl like her one would give everything. "Carme, Carme." How is it that a pretty girl always has an ugly girl as her best friend? The friend had a parcel. Clothes for ironing, must have been. "Fine Pressing." The sign's letters were black, except for the capitals that were red. Carme . . . He would call her name softly and would make her his just by repeating her name.

"Will you empty the bucket? I don't have the strength."

"What?"

"Are you asleep? I'm asking you to empty the bucket on the sink; I'm not strong enough to lift it."

"Coming."

"What's the matter with you?"

"I'm hot, tired . . . it's nothing."

He drained the bucket. He spilled half the water on the floor. The whole kitchen filled with the smell of diluted bleach.

"I'd have been surprised if you'd done it right."

He lit a cigarette and went out to the balcony again. After a while, from the dining room, his wife's voice was saying:

"I can't go on, you hear me? If our son isn't back by ten, go get him, O.K.?"

"Will you stop pestering me?" He turned brusquely with his eyes full of anger.

"Go on, shout . . . After all, if the Puigs have asked our son for supper so much saved. We're not exactly living high off the hog."

"Will you go to bed once and for all? You're in some mood!"

His wife had never been as pretty as the girl he'd seen that afternoon. She never wore such a becoming dress. Where could she have found the fabric? He had been selling silk and wool, wool and silk, for eleven years, and he'd never held in his fingers a gray crepe with those pink flowers and branches so nicely printed. He had never felt such a sharp desire as he did that night. To take her away to a forest. A forest with the scent of pines; and where the pines would be full of moon. Perhaps the years had changed him, but not like other people. Perhaps his youth was arriving now, when he was nearing forty; or perhaps it lasted longer than people claimed. True youth, with this taste of fire and of earth coming from his heart.

Someone's foot was knocking on the apartment door with violent bangs. He went to open. His son rushed in like the swallow and went straight to the dining room.

"We've caught a cricket!" He was all sweaty, flushed, and had a lock of hair stuck to his forehead.

"How many times have I told you not to bang the door with your feet?"

"Get me a bigger box. It'll suffocate here."

"Get to bed right away. Your mother got tired of waiting for you and has been in bed for quite a while. And wash your face; you look like a gypsy. And your hands."

The boy obeyed. His eyes were gleaming with excitement. When he came out of the kitchen with a clean face he took the matchbox where he was keeping the cricket and went to his room.

When he and his wife were old, even dead, his son would also feel that way. When he was married and had children, one day, all of a sudden, in summertime, back from work, he'd be hankering for a silk skirt over naked legs.

He went out to the balcony once more. Night had fallen. He wiped his forehead and his neck with his hand. Thirty-eight in the shade. Thirty-eight degrees in the shade. His age. He felt a burning on the back of his hand. The mosquito had stung him while he was looking at the gardens. He realized his carnations were dying of thirst. The basil was all yellowed; it had always been a scraggly plant. But . . . He didn't feel like watering, or like doing anything.

"Son! Come here and water the carnations."

The boy came out of his room with his shirt pulled over his pants.

"Did you find me a box for the cricket?"

"No. Tomorrow is another day."

The boy went back to his room. He felt like grabbing him and spanking him until he watered the carnations. For he was sure his son had heard him. "Never mind!" He didn't feel like doing anything either. If it had been less hot he could have gone to a movie. Go out. Leave everything and get away.

The boy came back to the dining room and got closer.

"Good night, father."

They were both thinking about the carnations. He would also go to bed and, if the heat wouldn't let him sleep, he'd come out to the balcony and lie on the floor until dawn. He took off his shirt, his pants, all his clothes. He got into bed slowly so as not to wake his wife. He might see her again tomorrow. His wife turned. She was small, weak. She had been very ill three or four years ago and had changed a lot for the worse. She got tired over nothing and spent her winters coughing. The doctor said it was nothing to worry about. She sighed unexpectedly. A small sigh, just to give a sign of life. He felt a great sorrow. Yes, yes, a great sorrow. And he didn't know why.

THAT WALL, THAT MIMOSA

My girlfriends found it very funny when Miquel left me; he got the itch to see the world. He said he'd come back, and they still tell me he'll be back, but as they say it, they are thinking I'll never see him again.

I think so too. Because Miquel . . . He wanted us to sleep together right away, and I didn't feel much like it. I only wanted to go out. But as I am a good girl I couldn't say no to him, because he said if I didn't go along I would set him on the road to ruin. Maybe he'll come back, and if he does, I don't want anything to do with him. Not even if he comes wrapped in gold. What all my friends would like to know is why I'm happy when I have a cold. Let them squirm. They wonder why I sing when I'm coughing like a dog and my nose is running like a drain pipe. I've never told them I like soldiers and I melt when I see them. Whenever I see those guys with their boots and their pea-jackets I feel a kind of sorrow. They wear wool and have to exercise in the heat, wearing wool. But some of them, when they cock their caps over one eye . . . As they walk around, three by three, and stroll, and talk to the girls going by, because they miss them, they are like plants without soil. The ones from small towns are homesick a lot! They miss their mothers, the way they lived there, the way they ate. They miss the girls going down to the fountain and they miss everything. And with their woolen khakis, to make matters worse. The three of them were walking, and I was strolling in my bright pink dress and a scarf around my neck; it was the same pink as the dress because it was a leftover piece of the material. And a tortoise-shell barrette on a wave in my hair, with a marcasite bow. All three stopped in front of me, blocking my way, and one of them, who had a very round face, asked me if I had a streetcar ticket and would I give it to him. I told him I had no streetcar ticket, and the other soldier said: even if it's old. And he looked at the soldier next to him and they laughed, but the one that had remained a bit apart said nothing. He had a little freckle on his cheek and a smaller one on his neck, next to his ear; they were both the same color, like dark earth. The two who wanted a streetcar ticket asked me what my name was, and I told them my name right away; I wasn't going to hide it. I told them: Crisantema, and they said that I was a fall flower and that it seemed incredible such a young woman was a fall flower. The soldier that had not said anything yet told the others, let's go, that's enough, and they told him, wait a bit, now Crisantema will tell us what she does during the week, and finally, when I was getting used to them, they went away laughing, and the one that had said nothing, after a little while, came back, and started walking next to me; he had left his buddies and said he'd like to see me again because I reminded him of a girl in his village called Jacinta. He asked me, what day? And I told him Friday, late. It was the day the people I worked for went to Tarragona to see their grandchild and left me guarding the house and waiting for Se-nyora Carlota, who was to come from Valencia. I told him where I worked and asked him to write it down, but he didn't write it down because he said he had a very good memory, and on Friday he was waiting for me outside the door, and I can't explain the strange thing that ran through me I don't know where, maybe through my veins, maybe through my skin, I don't know, but it was something very strange, because I figured that if he wanted to see me it was because he missed his folks a lot. I took along two rolls split in two with some roast meat inside, and after we'd walked a bit I asked him if he was hungry; I unwrapped the rolls and gave him one, and to eat them we leaned against a garden wall where tree branches and rosebush branches were sticking out. I ate biting with my teeth and pulling; he didn't. He would pinch off a bit of bread and a bit of meat with his fingers, then put them in his mouth. Country folks can be very dainty. He ate slowly, and as I looked at him eating I no longer felt hungry. I couldn't finish my sandwich and gave him the rest of it, and he ate that too. His name was Angel, it's a name I've always liked. That day we said almost nothing to each other. But we got to know each other a lot. And on the way back a group of kids thumbed their noses at us and chanted: they're gonna marry, they're gonna marry! The smallest of them threw a handful of dirt at us, and Angel chased him, because when the boy saw that Angel was coming near him, he took off running; Angel caught him by the ear and pulled on it, just a little and gently, to give him a scare, and told him he'd throw him in the stockade and then he'd put him in the mess kitchen and would make him peel potatoes for two years in a row. On the first day that was all. On the second day we walked down that street and we stopped to chat by that wall where a part was crumbling away. In front of us, on the other side of the street, there was a row of cottages each with a gate and a window with a grill on each side of the gates. And the cottages were always locked because the people who lived there only used the back where they must have their terraces and gardens. One day, when we were at the foot of the wall and the sky was that night-blue that hasn't quite begun to blur things, they turned on the street lamps and I saw the tree over us was a mimosa. It was beginning to bloom, and for the whole time it bloomed it was very pretty; it was one of the good kind of mimosa, with few leaves the color of ash, and many little balls, and each branch looked like a yellow cloud. Because there are those with hard leaves and flowers as long as worms, and more leaves than flowers. Under the light of the street lamp the mimosa flowers seemed to burst out of the sky . . . We got used to eating before they turned on the lamps and I always brought two rolls with roast meat inside and, as he was eating slowly and with his fingers, I felt like kissing the freckle on his neck. One of those evenings I felt a chill because, to look good, I was wearing a pearl-colored silk blouse and, when I got home, my eyes were watery and my head felt about to split. The next day I went to the pharmacy; my mistress told me to go, for, she said, more than a cold I'd caught the flu. The clerk had very light eyes, almost gray. I've never seen the eyes of a snake, but I am sure the eyes of that pharmacist were like those of a snake. He told me I had a spring cold. I explained to him that I'd spent a couple of hours in a silk blouse under a mimosa. And he said: it's the pollen, don't ever stand under a mimosa again. One afternoon, while I was by the wall with Angel, at the nearest corner I saw a head. It's not that I was seeing visions or that it was a severed head, no. It was a young man's head. At night, thinking of the head at the corner that had been watching us until he realized I'd noticed him, I thought I recognized him and I could have almost sworn it was the head of one of those soldiers that showed up with Angel the first time I saw him and asked me for a streetcar ticket. I told Angel and he said it couldn't be, because they had completed their service, both of them, and had left for their hometowns. It was the last day I saw him; I've never seen him again. I went many times to the wall to wait for him and finally I stopped going, but some days I was anxious thinking he might be there . . . He hadn't even given me a kiss, ever. He would just take my hand, and hold it for a long time under the mimosa. One day, after eating, he looked at me so intensely that I asked him what he was looking at and he shrugged as if to say: if I only knew! I gave him a piece of my bread and he went on looking at me. My cold lasted like it was going to last my whole life; I thought it was over, and it broke out again: a tickling in my nose and sneezes, and coughing fits at night. And I was happy. Later, when I would go to the pharmacy, even if only to buy boric acid, the clerk, as expected: watch out for the mimosa . . . And now, whenever I have a cold, it's as if I had just caught it by the wall, as if he were still there . . . I had a good time with Miquel, of course, and I became his fiancee because a girl must marry sooner or later. But at times, when I was with Miquel, I closed my hand because I thought I was holding Angel's; and sometimes I opened it so that he could withdraw his if he wanted to, not to force him into anything. And when my friends think I live thinking only of Miquel, who's left to see the world, I think of Angel who vanished like smoke. But I'm not unhappy, no. While I think of him I have him. There is one thing that's a little sad: they have a new clerk at the pharmacy. And if I ask for some aspirin, the new clerk, who doesn't know me, says: here you are, two and a half pesetas.

And, clink-clink, the cash register. And if I ask for lemon verbena, the clerk doesn't even look at me and says: half a peseta. And clink-clink, the register. Then I go, mechanically, but before opening the door I wait a little while, without moving, I don't quite know why. As if I had forgotten something.

II.

Time

A Note on Porcel's
"A Succinct Explanation of Catalonia for Castilians"

 Baltasar Porcel i Pujol was born on the Catalan-speaking island of Majorca in 1937. The Civil War, started in 1936 when a military coup against the Republican government of Spain divided the country into "loyalists" to the Republic and "nationalists" supporting General Francisco Franco, was to last until 1939 and leave the country ravaged, poorer by about one million dead, and in the hands of Franco's dictatorship until his death in 1975. For Catalonia the Civil War signified an added conflict as Catalan conservatives were forced to choose between the far-left loyalists (an uneasy combination of anarchists, socialists, and communists) and the rabidly anti-Catalanist nationalists. For Catalan culture the war was the end of a period of normalization. The repressive regime that ensued forced all Catalan activities to either exile or an underground existence until the passage of time gradually softened the situation and Catalonia regained its cultural life.

Porcel's essay translated here was presented as a lecture in Madrid's Club Pueblo on February 12, 1970, and was published in Catalan three years later by Editorial Selecta of Barcelona as part of a collection under the title *Debat català*. Written toward the end of the Franco dictatorship, it discusses the contradictions which Catalan cultural life must overcome. The piece is valuable not only as an interpretation of the past but also as a look toward the new realities, in Spain and in Europe, which Catalans must face.

Porcel began his literary career as a dramatist but soon turned to the novel and to journalism. Among his several novels, *Difunts sota els ametllers en flor* was awarded the Josep Pla prize in 1969 and the Critics' prize in 1970, and *Cavalls cap a la fosca* the Prudenci Bertrana prize in 1975. As a journalist, writing both in Catalan and Spanish, he is best known for his interviews (collected in *Grans catalans d'ara*) and his travel accounts.

BALTASAR PORCEL

A *Succinct Explanation of Catalonia for Castilians*

I am, ladies and gentlemen, one of those strange Mediterranean creatures called Catalanists. I do not know if today this affiliation is, as it was a quarter of a century ago, unlawful. Nor do I know whether it is still considered a synonym for wilted anachronisms, as it was then. In any case, I can assure you I am a Catalanist out of neither rebelliousness nor nostalgia. I am such, simply, for natural and geographical reasons; and to be precise, because I come from Andratx, an old town of sailors, smugglers, and hotel keepers on the westernmost vertex of the island of Majorca. I was born in 1937. An uncle of mine was then mayor of the town; my grandfather, justice of the peace; my father went about with a shotgun, standing guard more or less voluntarily during the fragrant island nights; my four cousins were at the front. All together, at the front and in town, we were on the "nationalist" side, which was to win the war. Seven persons, then, who did not belong to any of the four Catalan "provinces" nor had intervened at all, before the conflict, in Catalanist politics. But also seven persons whose native language was Catalan and who manifested their personality and related to one another and to the world in Catalan, in the dialectal variety of Catalan spoken in Majorca. Seven persons, besides, who were never taught either Catalan grammar or Catalan history. Rather:

in school they only learned Castilian. A runty, stiff, and shaky Castilian they used only for document writing and spoke only when, in the café, they ran into the Civil Guard sergeant. I found myself, therefore, thrown into a childhood and adolescence within a crazed and disjointed cultural setup: the only language I had and spoke I could not write; I only understood it and was able to speak it passably, as I speak French today.

But French leaves me cold. I only use it as a vehicle for communication, just as I use my car, which is only good for moving me around. For a language is not simply a functional tool but a creation of the world. A child does not learn that a table is called table. Rather a child places the image and concept of table in its mental universe through the word *table*. It took me a while to understand, being a gradual observer of reality, that I lived submerged in an illiterate bastardy: all that was superstructural, important, and grandiloquent, from politics to science, including literature, came to me from outside, and in Castilian; all that was basic, daily, and domestic, my life and that of my people, was carried out in Catalan and enclosed within my island. On the other hand, I saw no books or journals in my language; few titles were allowed to be printed in Catalan during those forties. From there to fall into an extenuating outcast complex, to think myself a savage living inside a fossilized society and culture, on the margins of history and the future, there was only one step. I took it.

I decided, when I was fifteen, to learn a language, the only one I had access to: Castilian. First I learned it in books, and later, thanks to an Andalusian friend, the son of a marine officer and the only kid in town whose home language was Castilian, I was able to practice it orally. On hot summer afternoons the two of us would walk down dusty paths toward the sparkling sea. I, out of necessity, sputtered my Castilian; he, out of necessity, sputtered his Catalan. It was Babel, but in the long run it was to bear fruit: we both learned to express ourselves in both languages.

But as I was moving ahead into my life, speaking was not enough for me, as I also felt the need to write. And that language, so useful to converse with the marine commander or to read novels by Baroja or Valle-Inclán, was showing itself harsh to me whenever I tried to compose an article or a story: words got stuck, descriptions became long and unfocused. It was then that, quite casually, two books in Catalan with nineteenth-century realistic topics fell into my hands, two short novels filled with scenes of city and country life: Miquel dels Sants Oliver's *L'Hostal de la Bolla* and Salvador Galmés's *Flor de Card*. I can assure you, ladies and gentlemen, that I was astounded beyond belief: I devoured page after page, and with each new line I read it became more and more evident that

that was also the world I wanted to describe and also the way I wanted to write. Which came to mean that, in the twinkling of an eye, I found myself literally condemned to a fossilized wildness, to a marginality without an iota of importance. It was a disagreeable discovery. It seemed to me I was being forced to return to the caves. But I wanted to write, and with the same voracity with which I had taken to learning Castilian I undertook the learning of Catalan and the reading of books in this language. What followed was grotesque: between the ages of fifteen and twenty, a high school student, and the citizen of a civilized state, had to learn two languages in order to speak with my fellow beings and to write to them, since from childhood I had been deprived of a normal language.

And I wrote. I wrote a lot in Catalan from that moment and would only use Castilian for bare-bones newspaper copy. Until the day I experienced a strange phenomenon: I *discovered how to write* in Castilian. Precise wordings, sensual and correct adjectives and adverbs, phrases with the musical naturalness of the language came to my pen. The explanation, once I found it, had a radical simplicity and logic: since a language is at once a creation of the world and a means for communication, I was able, in the first place, to describe a world, my world, as soon as I could put together my experiences and my Catalan speech within their proper cultural context. But underneath, unconsciously, my brain was carrying out another job—muted, deep down, like an IBM computer. My brain looked for the Castilian equivalent to all that I was creating in Catalan and brought about in Castilian a second creation based on the world created in Catalan. Then I managed to write in Castilian with a certain expressive decency and without the rhetorical dryness that characterized my grandfather's judicial sentences. As a matter of fact, it happened that as I freely pursued the search for my own roots and personality, I was granted, unexpectedly, that which before had been denied me by the laws of a national education.

I am a Catalanist, as I said, for reasons of nature and geography, of history and culture. For the same reasons that make me who I am. Constitutionally.

You may believe this linguistic autobiography is excessive. It might be so, were it merely the reflection of the vicissitudes of one apprentice writer. But it is basically the biography of a good six million Catalan speakers, the inhabitants of the old Crown of the counts of Barcelona: the present inhabitants of Catalonia, the old kingdom of Valencia, the Balearic Islands, and the Roussillon. People whose ancestors have been speaking the same language for centuries, since, during the late Roman Empire, vulgar Latin broke down into Romanian, Dalmatian, Italian, Sardinian, Provençal, French, Galician-Portuguese, Castilian, and Catalan. A language, Catalan, that from the thirteenth century produces eminent literary figures, as their political and commercial empire expands along the Mediterranean to reach Greece. Sociopolitical circumstances, however, beginning in the fifteenth century, provoked a chain of changes that resulted, ultimately, in decadence. At Caspe, the crown went to Ferdinand of Antequera, a Castilian king of the Trastámara dynasty; the plague decimated the population; Mediterranean commerce weakened because of the new Atlantic routes; and so on. So, from the time of Ferdinand and Isabella, the inexorable prostration of the Catalans was sealed and the spirited Castilian expansion took off. Beginning in the fifteenth century, pluralistic Roman Hispania gave way to a Castile-dominated and unified Spain. A Catalan decadence that was to last until the end of the eighteenth century. A decadence that affected the country only partially: its superstructure, that is, its written culture, its politics, its initiative. Private papers, from legal briefs to correspondence, people's conversations, liturgical and folkloric events went on in Catalan. Even in some places, as in the island of Minorca, which for a good part of the eighteenth century was under British rule, Catalan remained the official language. And so it is, today as ever, in the Principality of Andorra.

An approximate idea of the great medieval writers should follow from naming the most notable ones: Ramon Llull, whom you call Raimundo Lulio, and whose fabulous lexical inventiveness made his literary, philosophical, and theological work one of the most illustrious in medieval Christianity; Ramon Muntaner, James the Conqueror, Bernat Desclot, and Peter the Ceremonious, authors of four extraordinary chronicles, lush testimonials of a nation; Joanot Martorell, the genial author of *Tirant lo Blanc*, the most realistic and ironical of all romances of chivalry; Ausias March, whose poetry has seldom been surpassed in dramatic intensity; Anselm Turmeda, the apostate friar and corrosive satirist; Bernat Metge, the profound humanist. The list could go on. Do not think I merely want to inflate our honor roll stupidly and lavish my praise on a few defunct mediocrities. Those are authors whose value is recognized worldwide as Catalan literature is studied along with all other Romance literatures in universities in Germany, England, the United States, Sweden, the Soviet Union. Only recently has it begun to be timidly studied at two universities in Spain.

But let us return to the eighteenth century, during which Cata-

lonia underwent an economic and demographic renaissance that awakened
its aspirations for cultural recovery. This materialized during the first half
of the nineteenth century, basically with the work of the poets Bonaven-
tura Carles Aribau and Joaquim Rubió i Ors, and in the collective revival of
the Jocs Florals poetic competitions in 1859 that were to restore Catalan to
its status as a language for culture and to herald the return to it of writers
mostly from Catalonia and the Balearics.

That renaissance was not, as has been said all too often, the
simple result of the rise of Romanticism and its medievalizing dreams
which provoked the limited awakening of some old European languages
such as Provençal. Catalonia underwent a formidable economic expansion,
gestated during the previous century, that gave birth to a multiplicity of
textile factories and became, in the Iberian Peninsula, the only solid version of the Industrial Revolution. The calico factory owned by Esteve
Canals of Barcelona in 1738 has been considered the first modern industrial factory in Spain. Soon thereafter, Canals mechanized completely his
textile factory, while the English-made Highs machine was transformed
into the Catalan "Berguedana." In 1790, Simó Pla patented what he
called "a double-injection fire pump" that was nothing other than Watt's
steam engine patented twenty-two years before. During the eighteenth
century Barcelona grew from 35,000 inhabitants to 111,000, ten thousand
of whom worked at its four thousand looms. This growth was so phenomenal that it left public functionaries as befuddled as they were over-
whelmed, unsure how to deal with those energetic men who called
themselves calico makers. Finally, the civil servants opted to inscribe those
workers as *vagos,* meaning people of unknown or imprecise occupation.
The Catalan nineteenth century is the cultural and economic expansion
brought about by those *vagos.*

Toward the end of the nineteenth century, Catalan literature
again had writers of a caliber comparable to our medieval classics and to
authors in Europe or America. The poets Miquel Costa i Llobera, Joan
Maragall, Josep Lluís Pons i Gallarza, and Jacint Verdaguer; the play-
wrights Angel Guimerà and Santiago Rusiñol; the novelists Narcís Oller
and Marià Vayreda; the thinkers Valentí Almirall and Josep Torras i Bages,
and so on, are exponents of the amazing reentry into existence of a culture
that fifty years before was justly seen as a mere reminiscence of things
past. Verdaguer, Oller, Maragall, Guimerà, Rusiñol, Costa i Llobera were
translated into Spanish, French, Italian, and other languages. Narcís Oller,
for example, was enthusiastically introduced in the Spanish versions of his
novels by José Maria de Pereda, and in the French by Emile Zola.

Guimerà's theater almost won him the Nobel prize the year it was awarded to the pompous and superficial José Echegaray.

In the meanwhile, conditions in nineteenth-century Spain underwent a change that was to prove decisive for the channeling of all that ferment. From the monarchy of Isabella II to the Restoration, including the time of the First Republic, all of Spain shook under confusing and piercing internal divisions that manifested themselves in a number of ways, from military uprisings to regime changes, with the added curse of the Carlist wars, all this while the old overseas empire was crumbling. The process culminated in 1898 with the loss of Cuba and the Philippines and the undertow of a voluminous national pessimism. Catalonia felt the '98 pessimism as well, for its industrialists were losing their best markets. But at the same time, Catalan society had no internal cleaving; rather, with its economic upsurge and the daily growth of its reborn culture, it enjoyed a feeling of solidity and safety it had not felt for centuries. As for the loss of markets, Catalan industry still held those within Spain with no competition. The Catalan pessimism of '98 was not a feeling born of frustration but one more consequence of the power of the Madrid-centered government and state, along with taxation and military drafts. *Modernisme,* which at the time was spreading in Catalonia like a huge, beautiful, and fantastic bonfire, may be seen as further proof of that euphoria. Buildings appeared everywhere, as did pieces of furniture, works of art, poems, choirs. Their capricious arabesques born of the latest Parisian fashion allied themselves with the indigenous towers and crowns of medieval origins. Antoni Gaudí, the genius of Park Güell and the Sagrada Família, is the formidable creator of Catalan modernisme, its highest mark. Gaudí shows a prodigious faith in an almost feudal religiosity, and at once astonishes by his use of popular and artisanal materials and motifs, all together in a great blend within the modernist style. Old Catalonia, popular Catalonia, and new Catalonia come together in the overflowing and daring forms, in the bursting stones of Antoni Gaudí. When Prime Minister Antonio Maura, accompanying the young Alfonso XIII, came for a visit, Gaudí refused to speak in Spanish to the prime minister, who, being a native of Majorca and therefore Catalan-speaking, ended up addressing the architect in Catalan and breaking the protocol in front of the king. There was, all told, an attitude of Catalan affirmation, spanning the range from petulance to the creation of regionalist and republicanist programs, which was to leave the central power stupefied and on edge. In 1906, Solidaritat Catalana, a euphoric movement for Catalan political vindication, inflamed the whole of Catalonia and managed to send to Congress in Madrid a good number of representatives. By then

Catalanism is already a political force—and I mean Catalanism in general, encompassing movements both from the Right and the Left—and it will be a decisive one in the peninsula until 1939. It will be decisive not by dint of electoral trickery nor for the role it would play in the closed pact of the Bourbon restoration, but rather because of its natural robustness, in spite of all its opposition to traditional Spanish politics. Catalonia is like a growing tree.

With the turn of the century, modernisme is replaced by *noucentisme*. All that historical, riotous, Romantic, rustic frondescence of the modernistes becomes European and urban civility in the noucentistes. Poets no longer sing the *almogàvers* or the mountain of Canigó, but rather appear ironic and delicate. Noucentisme is full of neoclassical reminiscences. Eugeni d'Ors is its pontifex, writing daily his short column in *La Veu de Catalunya* under the pen name Xènius. Ors rationalizes, consecrates, disdains. The cultural and bourgeois metropolis looks at itself in those daily mirrors by Xènius. Josep Carner promenades his verses in the salons and on Passeig de Gràcia, with his genial smile, his simple but steely satire always ready, grandly standing on his profound mastery of the language. Prat de la Riba creates the Mancomunitat de Catalunya, bringing together the four provincial diputacions, and from that vantage point undertakes an autochthonous and ambitious cultural politics culminating in the creation of the Institut d'Estudis Catalans, a body that will undertake many and great projects, from the setting up of lending libraries to the reformation and grammatical standardization of the language (the work of Pompeu Fabra). Prat also consolidated the conservative Catalanist party, the Lliga Regionalista, from which people such as Cambó, [Jaume] Carner, and Ventosa will become active in Catalonia and elsewhere in Spain.

The new literary armies have nothing to do with the almost miraculous emergence of a Verdaguer, a Maragall, and the writers of the previous generation. Essayists and historians such as Ors, Rovira i Virgili, Nicolau d'Olwer—who was to be a minister during the Second Republic—Joan Crexells, Joan Estelrich, Jordi Rubió; poets such as Joan Alcover, Joan Salvat-Papasseit, Jaume Bofill i Mates, Josep Carner, Gabriel Alomar; novelists such as Joaquim Ruyra, Víctor Català, Prudenci Bertrana, and Joan Puig i Ferreter, become popular and professional, and form a lucid, profound, and effective intellectual body. The frenzied will for Catalanization has functioned as if propelled by centuries of tradition. Let us not forget that a nation is defined, as Renan said, more by its willingness to be than by its culture, its race, or its history.

But there are quite a few mirages in modern Spain's history. I cannot say if these are comparable to those of the dialogical universe of the Greeks or to those of the hallucinating deserts of the Arabs. I cannot say if, here as in those places, there continues to be a strange and aberrant capacity to create merely verbal illusions, independent of the surrounding reality, fascinating mirages that will crumble at once. The lack of a modest and constant pragmatism brings about gigantic tragedies. Did it not seem that the Catalan society born of the industrial bourgeoisie would last a century? But the Catalan bourgeoisie made three formidable mistakes: first, believing that its light industry, the manufacture of socks and rags, could attain the importance of the French or English manufacturing networks; second, engaging in a political pact with the central power, a democratic fiction filled with archaic conceptions of government and even of state, in exchange for customs protectionism; and third, failing to see that its factories were packed with an increasingly strong and demanding working class. The First World War represented a period of bonanza as the countries in the struggle needed goods from neutral Spain. But the war ends, and a period of spectral scarcity begins. Easily conceived enterprises come to a stop, workers organize and strike, the monarchy wavers. General Miguel Primo de Rivera, Catalonia's captain general, boards a train in Barcelona to go to Madrid for his coup d'etat; the bourgeoisie sees him off, the Lliga Regionalista stands by his side. It is the end of a dream. Bourgeois Catalonia, if not downright reactionary, will be, at least to this day, mired in a liberal conservatism. The Lliga Regionalista will stand by the king, will declare itself against the Republic, and will side with Franco's nationalists during the Civil War. Cambó, now a leader, arrived in Madrid on April 4, 1931, to unite forces with Gabriel Maura and create the Centro Constitucional party. The Republic was then in power. Later, from 1936 to 1939, Cambó will finance, from Italy and France, an information service to work against the Republic. The bourgeoisie was left without any real power in Catalonia, without any say in the Spain of Primo de Rivera or in that state installed after 1939.

Other forces will be rising: Esquerra Catalana, which will unite intellectuals and the middle classes with the workers' parties—FAI, CNT, UGT. Catalan, immigrant workers, and ideologically alert intellectuals will all mix, grow together, and work in the Republic's Catalonia with the belief that their existence is to prove everlasting, that a new dawn has risen. Again the mirages, the incredible and persistent mirages which, this time, however, will not lead to a general boarding a train for Madrid but rather to the bitter and paltry and disastrous roads to exile. In exile, all thrown together, Catalan writers next to CNT militants, will gush forth onto the world or end their days in French or German concentration camps. From that original thrice-mistaken blindness of the bourgeoisie we fell into collapse and hecatomb. Catalonia, as an autonomous entity, remained doubly tied to the Republic during the Civil War. It was twice a loser: the workers' parties saw in the members of the autonomous government of the Generalitat a suspect shadow of the bourgeois past, while the new state was to consider Catalonia as separatist. The people and their culture were to pay for the damaged goods of both Right and Left. For in Catalonia, Catalanism, I insist, is a fact by itself, an essence to be later colored with many hues, but existing independently of all.

Culture will, of course, reflect those crises, beginning in the twenties, but its growth will remain unaffected. It is then that a whole array of writers begin to publish and make a name for themselves: Josep Pla, the formidable and sharp essayist; Carles Riba, the refined post-symbolist poet; Josep Maria de Sagarra, the author of populist and baroque dramas and songs; the journalists Carles Soldevila and Gaziel; the great historians Ferran Soldevila and Ramon d'Abadal. They will be joined by the generation beginning to work under the Republic: the novelists Mercè Rodoreda and Llorenç Villalonga, the poets Joan Oliver and Joan Teixidor, the philosopher Josep Ferrater Mora, the historian Jaume Vicens i Vives. Catalan culture during the Republic is a wave that has reached the most recondite corners of the Catalan world. Schools, libraries, newspapers, and books play in Catalonia a well-deserved role. And even in Majorca and Valencia one begins to see a reformulation of the autochthonous structures.

And now I shall return to what I mentioned a few minutes ago: the separatist issue. Catalonia has had and has separatists. Just as much as it has stamp collectors, spiritualists, and lottery vendors. And just as much as Madrid or Valladolid have their conspicuous anti-Catalan barons whose only obsession is to confine Catalans within as many linguistic and administrative prohibitions as possible—these are the other separatists. The problem, however, lies elsewhere. Speaking of separatism whenever one addresses the Catalan question is like speaking of the Masons whenever one poses general Spanish problems. The reality of Catalonia's society and culture is much vaster. In Catalonia the radical separatists, the bourgeois in league with the armed forces, the FAI militants dreaming of libertarian communism, the Moscow-led communists, the post–Vatican II Christian

Democrats are all Catalanists. Waving the separatist flag or claiming that the Masons lurk in the darkness to pounce on the Ministry of the Interior is like parading scarecrows, if not inventing them. Catalonia is a complex society, unrealized as yet, with many internal tensions. An encompassing and rejecting attitude toward separatism can only be provoked from the outside, from Castile, as happens with the systematic prohibition of all that is Catalan, separating it from the rest of Spain, which is understood as a uniform state under Castilian rule. Most Catalans become separatists whenever they are forced to be unionists. In any case, the problem will be seen properly only after a period of total freedom. We are at the threshold of Europe. Catalans feel European by their geography, their history, their economy; they aspire to join Europe. Catalonia's problem is not one of separation but of internationalization, union, dialogue, treaties, understanding, and expansion in Spain and in the world. To achieve such recognition Catalonia must first affirm itself, reconstruct itself, bring to fruition all the cultural and social possibilities it lacks today. I feel of course no resentment for Castilian or Spanish culture, no matter how much I define myself as a Catalan writer or how much I write also in Spanish. I cannot accept, however, any restrictions for or negations of Catalan culture. This is my modest intellectual position. Should you call me, seeing my attitude, a separatist and sinful ghost? I stand against nothing and am in favor of all.

A Note on Vicens's
"The Catalans and the Minotaur"

In the preface to his *Revolt of the Catalans,* the English historian J. H. Elliott wrote about Jaume Vicens i Vives: "His death in 1960 at the age of only fifty was a calamity for modern historical scholarship. Single-handed he set in train a complete reappraisal of the traditional dogmas of Spanish and Catalan history, and his stature, already great in his lifetime, will continue to grow." Indeed, Vicens revolutionized Catalan historiography. Catalan historians before him had followed a Romantic tradition and had articulated a communal, almost epic history of national affirmation against a despotic Castile. Breaking up with his predecessors, Vicens created a new school, analogous to the French Annales, devoted to the consideration of a larger body of documentation in which economic data loomed at least as large as biographical facts. In addition to an impressive production of specialized works, his own or his team's, Vicens wrote two book-length essays in which he reflected respectively on the history of Spain and of Catalonia. From the latter volume, *Notícia de Catalunya* (A panorama of Catalonia), comes the essay translated here; the earlier volume on Spain, *Aproximación a la historia de España,* has been translated into English by Joan Ullman as *Approaches to the History of Spain.*

Vicens's view of Catalonia takes issue with his predecessors' notion that Catalans are endowed with a guiding and predominating virtue, *seny.* The word, pronounced /señ/, is related to *sense* but has no clear equivalent in Castilian or English and is popularly considered as untranslatable, as befits a quality that is supposedly the essence of the Catalan soul. Vicens sees *seny* as bespeaking short-sighted conservatism as much as judiciousness, and as only one of two poles of communal behavior. In his view Catalans have oscillated between *seny* and *rauxa,* or frenzied political abandon; Catalan *rauxa* (the word is etymologically related to the German *Rausch,* "fury," and to the English *rush,* as in a drug-induced "rush") has shown itself in the many revolutions that have bloodied the country's history (and which in a later chapter of *Notícia de Catalunya* are tallied as more frequent than those of Castile, France, or England). Indeed, the country's *rauxa* and not its *seny* would explain the spread of anarchism in twentieth-century Catalonia.

For Vicens, Catalonia's history must be seen in the light of the region's underdog position, of its alienation from the centers of political power, which he here calls the Minotaur. The main feature of that history may well be, Vicens argues, the continued tug-of-war between the ruling classes in Catalonia and the people in power. This conflict began in the Middle Ages and is implicit in another key word in this essay, *pactisme.* I have coined the word *pactism* to translate this term here, as *pactisme* derives from *pacte,* "pact," meaning the covenant or agreement between the monarch and his subjects with which the king swears to defend certain of their freedoms; *pacte* in turn derives from the Latin word for peace, *pax,* a term dear to the feudal contract (as it is surely to the Mafia). While pactism had been considered the pride and joy of the Catalans' democratic nature, Vicens posits that the series of pacts between the Catalan upper classes and an increasingly distant monarchy during the Middle Ages ultimately reconciled the Catalans to their alienation from true political power. Pactism thus opened the door to the shifting of that power from the Catalans first to a Castilian family, the Trastámaras, later to the Madrid-based Habsburgs, and finally to the centralist Bourbons. *Pactisme,* or alienating compromise, *seny,* or conservative judiciousness, and *rauxa,* or extremist rashness, form, according to Vicens, the vertices of the Catalan triangle. The history of modern Catalonia is the history of the efforts to find a point of balance among the forces that constitute that triangle.

Notícia de Catalunya was first published in Barcelona by Edicions Destino in 1954. The selection here is taken from the revised 1960 edition, one of the last projects completed by Vicens.

JAUME VICENS I VIVES

The Catalans and
the Minotaur

T*he Failed Experiment.* The Minotaur plays a key role in history and in the news. He is Power. At times disguised, he adopts benevolent and peaceful shapes; from his palace, he pretends to invite people to handle the mechanisms which control the affairs of this world: he awards a medal to a scientist or approves bonus pay for a worker. But such sharing of power is an exception. The Minotaur is normally aloof and commands respect, more so with every day that passes. Power is peace and war, revolution and reform, justice and injustice, the common good, and evil. Abstract in theory, it is a daily reality one needs to know how to handle. Some countries are familiar with it; others do not seem to get the hang of it. The latter is the case in Catalonia.

The Minotaur had been yawning throughout the Middle Ages. He barely remembered his happiest times, during the decline of the Roman Empire, when there was a single man—the Universal Boss—controlling all the levers in the machinery of the state. Feudalism had gotten that out of step: a dust cloud of miserable feudal lords had come to eclipse the sun of royalty! But, little by little, things got straightened out. Great wars and calamities came, they had to be overcome and the world reordered; population grew and became wealthier, people's comforts had to be ensured; social classes clashed over issues of property and distribution of monies, intervention was necessary. Toward the middle of the fifteenth century, the Minotaur was back on his feet; a century later, in Western Europe, he was revered; and a century beyond, the Universal Boss made his comeback in the brilliant courts of Europe. Since then, each revolution attempting to reform some defect of society has only added its grain of sand—or a whole quarry—to the imposing edifice of the State.

Catalonia's downfall began precisely when the Minotaur was pressing upward in the shape of national or plurinational authoritarian monarchies. We Catalans had a long experience of Power in its waning form; whenever it revived, we succeeded in restraining it through the imposition of pactism. That was enough for us. We did not proceed beyond that crossroads. We did not play dirty with the Minotaur. And from here stems, I believe, a sensational historic disappointment: that of a people without the will to Power, without the desire to occupy its palace or pull any of the levers.

The Political Process of Pactism. Pactism was the great formula used to achieve practical and concrete relations between Power and the Catalan people. As a system of political equilibrium it lasted more than three centuries, and left good memories. Its very persistence, however, sets us on the tracks of a particular flaw in the political behavior of Catalonia.

For the Catalans, royalty was something unsurmountable. It lacked the magical sheen of the French throne, but not by much. The adoration of the monarchy, which represented the unity of the nation, arose from the old feudal nobility of the mountains and from the new patriciate of the cities. Both these social classes saw the throne as the justification of their privileges. Monarchy, nobility, and bourgeoisie had grown together, and the glory of the first was also that of the other estates—in the Iberian Peninsula as well as throughout the Mediterranean. True, the king could have bad advisers, rash connivers who might entrap the nation in private profiteering and neglect of the land. But pactism had been invented to avoid such clawing. The monarchy stood above all contingencies, even though at times some writer would echo the theories of tyrannicide so abundant in Scholastic political treatises. Such expressions, however, didn't even amount to a baring of the teeth.

When the fifteenth-century revolution broke out, pactists won the first skirmish. They had two options then: to declare themselves independent from John II and transform Catalonia into an aristocratic republic in the style of Venice—which would have installed them fully on the

Minotaur's ship—or to press for a contract with the king, which would also have been a system of shared Power. Pactists found neither of these solutions good; the first was too revolutionary, the second excessively conservative. And so the compromise they arrived at unleashed a civil war. The monarchy of John II was erased from Catalonia, but not the monarchy as the mystical lightning rod for the nation. In their eagerness, revolutionary Catalans sought the help of Castile, Portugal, and France, and they proclaimed as their king, successively, Henry IV of Castile, Peter of Portugal, and René of Anjou. The radical solution—Barcelona and Catalonia as an Italian-style *Signoria*—was never considered. To do so would have polarized things, and then the end of the war would have made it clear either that the Principality really held Power or that it really yielded to Power. Neither happened. The solution of 1472—the Pedralbes Capitulation—consisted in declaring the inviolability of both monarchy and pactism.

It was at that very moment that the political mummification of the country began. Romantic historians, fond of mysterious turnabouts and secret confabulations, accused Ferdinand II of having burdened Catalonia with the introduction of absolutism, the abolition of the freedoms of the Diputació del General and of the Barcelona municipality. Poor Ferdinand II! His great historical responsibility lies in having tied for good the preservation of pactism to his politics. Catalonia wants that form of government; let us allow it then. The Constitution of the Observance of 1481 laid the foundation for Catalan pactism of the sixteenth and seventeenth centuries. These constitutions and property rights were to be defended tooth and claw. Ferdinand also created the two definitive administrative organisms of pactism: the viceroy and the Council of Aragon. Catalans were thankful to him. They felt certain that they lived in the best of worlds.

Accustomed to the absenteeism of monarchs since Alfonso the Magnanimous, Catalans were unsurprised by the establishment of the new Habsburg kings' court in Castile. Let us say there was a transition period before Madrid became consolidated as the bastion of the Spanish Chancellory and the capital of the monarchy. Still, that caused few headaches. The Catalans had their own little court in Barcelona, with the viceroy or captain general, the lawmakers of the Royal Audience, and the notables of the two great corporations of the land. They did not realize until much later that the viceroy and the Council of Aragon were not organs of the country by which to communicate with the Minotaur but rather screens blocking access to him. Therefore, while the Castilians became familiar with the Minotaur by dint of receiving his blows—defeat of the *Comunidades*, exploiation of municipal treasuries, complete separation between the Cortes and public life—the Catalans basked in the most absolute ignorance of the State and of the mechanisms of Power. It was then that Castile took command, and the symbiosis between the Hispanic monarchy and the Castilian state was achieved.

No one in Catalonia raised a voice against pactism, because from the early seventeenth century it had become, after being the tie between king and people, a series of oppositions *against* the Minotaur. We suspect that many were irked by those formulas which no longer satisfied the spirit of the times. But no one proposed their modification. On the contrary, at the high point of the seventeenth-century revolution, when Catalonia separated itself from the sovereignty of the Spanish king in order to fall, exhausted, into that of the French king, it did not even have the brawn to propose a more agile solution to the political and administrative crisis of the country. In the agreement made at Perona, on September 19, 1641, between Louis XIII and the representatives of Catalonia, the new monarch not only accepted the pactist theory—"the pact and convention made between His Majesty and the Province"—but also all the institutions of government in Catalonia, including, alas, the viceregal institution that had provided so many bitter proofs of incompetence and inefficacy.

An almost absolute lack of imagination presided over the Catalan political scene during the pactist period. Unable to develop a new mental scheme, afraid of the distant State, but satisfied with the crumbs that were their great institutions, the Catalans hesitated between tradition and innovation until they finally fell on the well-known bed of contractual pacts. From the fifteenth century onward pactist theory had lost its greatness; what was constitutionalism of a certain ambition in Eiximenis and in the Corts of Alfonso the Magnanimous became mere bargaining for later jurists.

So, during the sixteenth and seventeenth centuries, viceregal Catalonia gradually lost contact with the realities of Power. The success of the uprising against Philip IV and the last Habsburg's adoption of the formula of administrative immobility were elements added to the fatality of the game of history. For history forgives no instant of belatedness and, as soon as one forgets, it comes back with full force. In Catalonia the next move in the game took the form of the State of Philip V and the Nova Planta.

The Unattainable State. The Minotaur made himself felt in Catalonia under his least comfortable guise. Catalan constitutionalism had grown old, but some of its important pieces could have been used with some judiciousness by the French, Castilians, and Catalans who discovered and applied the new regime. Such possibilities went down the drain in 1714. And so the Catalans came to know the modern state under the least favorable of circumstances: imposed by conquest, organized so as to maintain that conquest, without any kind of contact with the local traditions or with the reality of the moment. As Joan Mercader has accurately pointed out, the idealist administration Patiño imagined for the restoration of peace in Catalonia gave way to an upwardly mobile carcass of bureaucrats, courtiers, and military men. Only the passage of years could achieve a certain congruity between the Principality and the Bourbon administration.

But the essential fact is that the State thus became something definitively distant and unattainable. We do not mean to say that Catalans failed to be part of the routine within the Bourbon administrative machinery during the eighteenth century. During those times some Catalans could not avoid jumping onto the wagon of the State apparatus. Some profited notably from it, and even acquired titles of nobility, such as Joan Canals, a famous technician and manufacturer of textile dyes, whom Charles III made Baron of Vall Roja; others tried their hand at espionage and sabotaged as many Catalan initiatives as they could. But in general the congruence between the interests of the State and the Catalan bourgeoisie allowed things to go on without much hindrance. As far as the administration went, therefore, the worries were few; but as for the State itself, the rule was total incomprehension and distance. How much more astronomical could the distance between Madrid and Barcelona have been when, during the eighteenth century, and in spite of the influx of personalities from the Peninsular periphery into cabinet posts, not a single Catalan served in the courts of Ferdinand VI, Charles III, or Charles IV?

Catalonia's absence from the government of Bourbon Spain may be justified, as we see it, by two reasons: one is the slowness in the exchange of ideas, the hard transition from a pactist spirit to that of subordination to a centralist state; the other is the oppressive character of the administration in Catalonia, based on the principle that no coin could circulate without finding its way into the coffers of the Royal Treasury. We must also consider that municipal offices, the only ones available to the locals allowing even limited intervention in public life, were given to the petty nobility, a provincial class with limited horizons that saw things with the same eyes as the *corregidor,* the subtreasurer of the government, and of course the captain general.

The situation improved toward the end of the eighteenth century. The Chamber of Commerce, created in 1758, allowed a select nucleus of Catalans—landowners, merchants, bankers, industrialists—to reestablish the tradition of government, practically lost since 1714. Soon after, in 1766, as a consequence of the disturbances that the scarcity of bread provoked throughout Spain, a new disposition created two deputies of the commonwealth and ombudsmen in the town governments, with some input from the guilds. That did not amount to much, either, but through this minute opportunity a small group began to acquire administrative experience. Let us say, however, that the new political mentality of the country was formed either in the back shops of Barcelona, where the journals that came from revolutionary France were read and commented on, or in the classrooms of the University at Cervera, where the Jesuits had created a school that, by way of Suárez, grafted itself onto the scholastic doctrine of the people's rights and, consequently, onto Catalan pactism. Within this atmosphere we can understand the hostility awakened by the government of Godoy, even though his friends, people such as Cabarrús, engaged in activities that were very favorable to the textile industry. But Godoy, the Prince of Peace, was accused of cabinet despotism, of severing all ties between the Crown and the old statutes of the monarchy, and of conducting a foreign policy contrary to the interests of the nation (which was only partly true). Toward 1800 Barcelona society had changed its skin and had become an articulation of wholesale merchants, industrialists, and capitalists, a group anxious for a new political regime in which to intervene, even if it were just to protest and plead.

The fall of the old regime in 1808 forced the Catalans to hasten to create some sort of regional state, the Junta Superior del Principat de Catalunya. Because the reformist ferment remained in French-occupied Barcelona, the leaders of the Junta did not have great horizons. Most of them were graduates from Cervera and very judicious conservatives; in a provincialist mode, they only advanced some timid political reforms and accepted the unifying theses issued by the Cortes at Cádiz. But they were good administrators. At the center of an uninterrupted struggle—Catalonia was a true victim of the war against the French—in between military campaigns and counter campaigns, skirmishes for prestige, offensives and retreats, the Junta managed to levy armies and supply them, organize elections and carry them out, maintain cohesion with the Central Spanish Junta and the Regency of Cádiz and with the other neighboring juntas, and impose its criteria on the corregimental juntas, which were often under the control of demagogues or split by infinite rivalries. In spite of criticism from the military, who thought its efforts insufficient, the reams of paper left by the Junta suggest a positive reentry of the Catalans into the art of governing. The Junta even took the time to think of the Catalan language and used it as an instrument for political propaganda and military education.

But that spontaneous blooming of an activity that had been dormant for so long was not to have a future. Once again, with the restoration of Ferdinand VII and with the moderate dictatorship of Narváez, that is, from 1815 to 1833 and from 1843 to 1854, the Minotaur left Catalonia. The surge of political enthusiasm in the Catalonia of the Romantic era was stopped by a state that feared having to share with the Catalans a part of their economic and social vitality. Time and again, the impulse toward the state, begun in 1833 when the Barcelona bourgeoisie entered the city government and revived in 1835 with the creation of the Junta d'Armament de Catalunya, was frustrated. The manufacturers organized themselves politically with their Industrial Institute of Barcelona and, with General Prim, carried off one of the most cohesive campaigns to break the barrier imposed by the Madrid government, but they ended up tiring of their own persevering opposition. The artisanal class, eager for progress and a thoroughly liberal state, suffered the whippings of Baron de Meer and the bombs of Espartero. And the workers saw the State shut the doors to them as they postulated their right to form associations just as the manufacturers had done.

So, toward 1855, Catalonia, having made a true political incursion into Castile, fell back deeply disillusioned. The moment was decisive. Catalans began to reflect and rejected that incomprehensible, abstract, corrupt, and inefficient State. The choices made by manufacturers and intellectuals are very clearly manifested in people such as Mañé, Sol, Illas, Cortada, and so many others who formulated the program for the new Catalanism. Of what the workers said or thought we know almost nothing, gagged as they were by General Zapatero.

Catalans reacted by either combating or denying the inimical and unattainable State. The constitutionalism of Isabella II was never popular in Catalonia. The Carlists endeavored to maintain the country's statute laws, and the conservative elements sought a solution in direct democracy, either corporate or municipal; democrats dreamed of revolutions that would put the people in the forefront of political life, and the workers abominated an administration that made them familiar only with prison and bondage. That collective disappointment had to give birth to the antistate attitude of Catalans during the second half of the nineteenth century and also, mostly based on the theory of the inherent evil of the State, to the anarchistic uneasiness of the working class.

Between Pragmatism and Mysticism. From the middle of the last century on, Catalonia lived an unreal experience: that of a people refusing to intervene in political life and to control the power of the State. Let us leave aside for now the revolutionary movement between 1868 and 1874, which brought to power so many Catalan personalities, starting with Prim and Figuerola and ending with Figueres, Pi i Margall, and more than thirty civil governors. That experience was not so absolutely negative as to make us want to hide it under a pious veil. The problem is very different. The Catalans in command in Spain during the September revolution made the mistake of believing that Castile and Andalusia were as evolved as their own region, and so they unleashed gigantic forces that they were unable to control or tame: internationalism, cantonalism, anticlericalism, and so on. In the hands of those at once generous and naive politicians, the apparatus of the State became the scaffolding for revolutionary constructions.

Let us insist that, between 1856 and 1901, Catalans accepted the State as the greater evil, and bossism—the State's local manifestation—as the lesser. Good folks stayed clear of public organisms, even though, under the table, they were forced to deal with those monopolizing the carcass. The intellectuals obviously were in solid disagreement with that stark regime, which was incapable of any material progress and, worse yet, given to the unpleasant habit of exercising tyranny against the most delicate feelings of the country. Finally the workers, forced to risk their bread or their skins at the slightest economic crisis, leaned more and more toward the Proudhonian doctrines that Pi i Margall had spread before 1868 and that were now traveling from mouth to mouth and were, therefore, deformed. Petty bourgeois individualism, transformed at first into proletarianism, became the Bakuninists' antiauthoritarian libertarianism, then emerged as the strong vein of anarchistic mysticism that was to affect all of Catalonia during the final decades of the last century.

Balancing in between these two extremes—the pragmatic optimism that accepted reality and the millenarism of the redeeming catastrophe—Catalonia walked a tightrope toward recovery of a sense of state and administration. Here lies the true and unexceptionable merit of the generation of 1901 and, singularly, of Enric Prat de la Riba: enabling a team of Catalans to manifest their high competence as governors and administrators of the public good. Their success soon crossed the Ebro and reached Castile as a possibility for political and social reform without subversive worries. But Madrid had other fish to fry, and the great primates of the parliamentary or bossist regime did not want to hear a word. They had other methods. And with their charming tentacles they brought the Catalan politicians to the Minotaur's levers only when they no longer had the will to pull them—in the direction that would effect the Hispanic reform Catalonia was promoting. It was an experience from which no one recovered very soon.

Among the workers and the petty bourgeoisie whose individualism became extreme during the catacomblike years of the dictatorship of Primo de Rivera, mistrust of the State developed into a revolutionary mystique. Reading the papers of the time, I have been shocked more than once by the gratuitous apocalypticism in the union leaders' or even a humble town government's revulsion against any form of the Minotaur. The denial of all government, of any formula for legal relationship, of any instrument for general association, was frequent in the literature written even by the clearest heads. Imagine what effects that attitude had on the minds of the workers who felt unjustly treated and poorly paid—conditions for which they blamed the State, the arm of the bourgeoisie—and on the minds of the immigrants who had just left Murcia for Catalonia and to whose poverty the State had offered no other solution than the sacrifice of their native homes and a life-or-death thrust into an industrial city that seemed unwelcoming and greedy. This antistate mystique expanded in the 1920s and 1930s; the surge was so intense that, through capillary action, it impregnated quite a few intellectuals and the key members of the petty bourgeoisie. This phenomenon, the degradation of a sense of responsibility toward political power, was most remarkable during the period beginning in 1931.

And here we may bring to a close our analysis of the relationship between the people and the Minotaur in Catalonia. To summarize: the high administrative capabilities of Catalans were strangled by their false conception of the State, which they considered an alien phenomenon; that brought about in some circles the acceptance of a narrow-minded pragmatism and in others the development of the mystique of direct action. This dualism is one of the leitmotifs in the mechanics of political and social subversion in Catalonia.

A Note on Fuster's
"Maragall and Unamuno, Face to Face"

On April 23, 1898, the United States declared war on Spain; on July 26 Spain asked for peace terms; on December 10, by a peace treaty signed in Paris, Spain renounced its sovereignty over Cuba, Puerto Rico, the Philippines, and Guam. The short Spanish-American War, known in Spain as the Cuban War, made it obvious that Spain was no longer a colonial power but a rather backward and impoverished country on the margins of Europe.

The loss of the last overseas colonies influenced modern Spanish culture deeply. The disaster of 1898 was seen very differently by intellectuals in Madrid and Barcelona. In and around Madrid a brilliant group of writers, which soon came to be known as the Generation of '98, acknowledged Spain's defeat by singing the values of a new era—a new era, however, grounded in Castile's past glories and its stark, deforested landscape. They saw the crumbling medieval towns, such as Soria, and the stern pride of the bankrupt *hidalgo* as icons of an aesthetics and ethics that set Spain radically apart from the pragmatism of Europe and the United States. From Barcelona the colonial defeat was seen as the final demonstration of the failure of Castile's political hegemony and as an urgent prompting to turn a new leaf. An industrialized and relatively prosperous

"European" Catalonia demanded to play a role in the governing of the country and in its own self-determination. For Catalan intellectuals, Spain emerged from the 1898 crisis as a colorful and tragicomic mosaic of failed conquistadors, feisty bullfighters, dreamy mystics, despotic landowners, hungry children, ornate churches, and flamenco dancers. The Castilians (as Catalans call those from non-Catalan-speaking areas of Spain) replied with their portrayal of cold, avaricious, humorless, spineless, mistrustful, and generally dull Catalans. The polarized clichés of modern Spain— austere but despotic Castile vs. superficial and money-minded Catalonia— had been established.

Generalizations do not become clichés without an uncanny vitality or without some attraction for the intelligent minds of the times; only today, with the forty years of Franco's dictatorship well behind and with an altered economic situation, is the bipolar fiction of that Spain beginning to fade. In this essay, Joan Fuster examines how two of the most representative talents of early twentieth-century Spain reacted to and helped shape that fiction.

A Castilianized Basque, Miguel de Unamuno (1864–1936) was a prolific essayist, novelist, poet, and dramatist and an influential social and religious philosopher. At the height of his academic career he was named rector of the University of Salamanca, Spain's oldest. Unamuno viewed "the problem of Spain" (as the question of national identity was called) from the barren high plateau of Castile: Catalonia was to contribute to Spain, even to "Catalanize" Spain, but lose its language in the process. As a philosopher, Unamuno searched for the meaning of life in the "tragic sense" that a nonmaterialist tradition inspires. He made a virtue of postcolonial Spain's poverty and even of its backwardness; "let them invent!" he aphoristically derided the more scientifically advanced countries of Europe and urged his compatriots to "Hispanize" Europe rather than to undertake the Europeanization of Spain.

In Catalonia the bourgeois Joan Maragall (1860–1911) groped for hope in what he saw as the purity of the collective spirit and language of his people. He opposed the image of an open, vital, forward-looking Catalonia to Unamuno's Spain. Maragall was essentially a poet, and one of the last to win during his lifetime both the admiration of the intelligentsia and wide popular support; he was a poet of almost epic dimensions, and is still today held to be one of the capital figures in Catalan literature. As a theorist Maragall is known for his romantic view that the best poetry is the unstudied expression of pure emotion, a view he propounded in his famous

essay "La paraula viva" (The living word). He was also an active colum-
nist, both in Catalan—the language of his poetry—and in Spanish; most of
his essays and letters are written in Spanish.

The positions of these writers were too neatly antagonistic not
to have much in common, and indeed the two men engaged in a lengthy
correspondence. They were two symbols ultimately unable to convince
one another. They express, however, the intellectual mood that characterizes Spain during most of the twentieth century. If not opinions, they
shared the agitation of their times, and in particular the events that range
from "the great week in October" to the "Tragic Week." The first phrase
was coined by Maragall to refer to the week of October 14 to 21, 1906,
when an exultant popular demonstration was organized in support of Catalanist politics while the first International Congress for the Catalan Language opened and proceeded to become a flag-waving and massive political
rally for Catalanism. The "Tragic Week" (July 26–August 1, 1909) was
marked by violent anarchist demonstrations and subsequent brutal repres-
sions. Unamuno was in Barcelona for the first one but not for the second, a
fact that may have prompted his dismissal of Catalanism as mere spirit of
festivity; he derides Catalonia as "a suburb of Tarascon," the southern
French town made famous by Alphonse Daudet's Tartarin de Tarascon, a
bourgeois and comic Quixote figure. Maragall reacted with enthusiasm to
the first set of events and with judicious compassion to the second—although his views were mostly ignored by contemporary authorities.

Their correspondence is discussed in the following pages by
Joan Fuster. Unamuno's self-promoted independence of mind is ques-
tioned by Fuster as it would be by most Catalans, since Unamuno, like
most non-Catalans of his time, failed to understand the importance that
the vindication of their own language had for Catalans. Unamuno wanted
the Catalans not to be a problem, a rather facile attitude in a man of his
intellectual stature. At the same time, Fuster sees Maragall with a certain
rosiness, not so much to defend him against Unamuno as because Maragall, after his death, fell from favor among the intellectual elite of Barcelona: Maragall's romanticism and his "living word" theories were soon
derided by the emerging noucentistes, whom Fuster here implicitly de-
nounces.

Born in 1922, Joan Fuster i Ortells is a poet, essayist, and
literary scholar. The Gran Enciclopèdia Catalana calls Fuster "without a
doubt the most considerable writer of the post–Civil War generations."
Fuster's historical studies are attempts at drawing the personality of his
native Valencia and of the Catalan area in general; in his essays he presents

a learned, witty, often aphoristic philosophical commentary on the world. His critical stance has influenced his style: his sentences are often broken by asides, parentheses, and footnotes; interrupted by sudden periods; and clarified by constant adversatives—a style that is itself a confirmation of his notion of the fallacy of linear thinking.

The following essay, written in 1952, appeared as part of the book *Les originalitats* in Barcelona (Barcino, 1956) and is translated here from volume 4 of Fuster's *Obres completes* (Barcelona: Edicions 62, 1975), 197–222.

JOAN FUSTER

Maragall and Unamuno,
Face to Face

The *Epistolario entre Miguel de Unamuno y Juan Maragall*[1]
presents a few but nevertheless highly interesting documents by—and
about—two of the greatest figures of contemporary Iberian literatures.
Everyone knows how uncommon the publication of letters is in the cultural milieus of the peninsula. The simple fact that this collection has
come to light, with notes and other texts appended to it, lends it an exceptional interest. Readers will find here testimonials of singular importance
that will help them penetrate the intimate world of the correspondents and
clarify some contrasts found in their works or biographical anecdotes. In
the case of Maragall and Unamuno we barely have the characteristic reserve of a literary correspondence, that which makes us think the letters
were written "for posterity." Better yet: in Maragall and Unamuno the
epistolary mode shows no more—and no less—affectation than the rest of
their writing; and it is well known that when those men were producing
their literature they were, by principle and by temperament, little given to
"literature." This book holds no surprises. From their essays and poems to
their letters, in both Maragall and Unamuno we see no brusque transition,
no change in tone or tension. The correspondence shows, yes, the "broth-
erly friendship" that united the Salamanca poet with his Barcelona col-

league;[2] such friendship allows, at times, digressions filled with warm familiarity. In particular we witness the fecund contact of their ideas and temperaments. Here lies the enthralling strength of these pages. If they add nothing new—nothing substantially new—to the writers' thinking as we know it from their works, these letters help us delineate the play of affinities and differences underlying the authors' relationship. At first sight there appear numerous concordances between Unamuno and Maragall: so many that they deserve a detailed analysis and explanation.[3] But beneath these concordances, and above them, something, something unique and uncompromising, renders their attitudes irreducible. Perhaps we ought to begin by sketching those attitudes, before we can fully understand the agreements. This is my goal in the present paper. As far as possible I shall center on their human attitudes: those of the man Unamuno and those of the man Maragall, as the first would have said. There is room of course to consider another subject at least as intriguing as this central theme: is the essential disparity between the two men merely symbolic or is it a response to their respective national situations? This new theme raises questions on two key points of contemporary Iberian history: the Generation of '98 and theoretical Catalanism. But I shall merely allude in passing to these issues in so far as they are inevitable. What matters is that two men of the stature of Unamuno and Maragall be compared and contrasted and that we see their live encounter. They appear imposingly as the protagonists of a sharp drama, even a noble tragedy. Yes, a tragedy. Whatever attitude the reader takes toward its plot, and toward their plots, I believe that its *performance*—and their performances—call upon us to meditate on the spectacle and make it ours. Nothing could have pleased Unamuno and Maragall more.

Since most of the letters the Catalan poet wrote his friends were published some time ago,[4] the strict novelty of the *Epistolario* belongs to Unamuno. The rector of the University of Salamanca was afflicted, as he confesses, with letter-writing mania.[5] But, to my knowledge, only a small part of his correspondence is available to the public. This small part, as could be expected, has not rectified the "public" image of Unamuno, "of the Unamuno of our legend, yours and mine," as he himself said.[6] I am referring now to Unamuno as a monologue writer. A correspondence is, by definition, a dialogue; Unamuno violates that definition, with more or less conscious pleasure. Unamuno was unfit for dialogue. I trust that this judgment will not be contradicted by his still unpublished writings. At most he *monodialogued*—a word that carries his brand: he spoke with himself. Dialogue requires speaking to others and a willingness to meet them on a level of truth. And such willingness asks for availability and enthusiasm. Unamuno prefers—or says he prefers—combat and believes that "one of the most intimate" of possible solidarities is that among antagonists.[7] Deep down, his incapacity for dialogue follows from a secret lack of interest: "I am not, in effect," he wrote, "in favor of polemics; I like to speak my piece and then go on my way, without a glance backward, as I let all others speak theirs."[8] Jean Cassou called him "a man of civil war,"[9] and Unamuno spoke of *monodialogues*. Both terms fall within the orbit of his personalism, that personalism recurrent in Castilian proverbs; his invitations to others were pure formulas. He fought with himself. He sought in his inner being the solidarity of foes, which is a solidarity simply in the desire for the fight. And in fight he saw his reason for being. From this to a sporting sense of dialectics there is but one step; Unamuno took it, often unawares. If it did not operate on the innermost realm of the human, Unamuno's agonism would appear as nothing more than a tiring sophism, even an egotistic one in spite of all of his fits against "filthy logic." He is also saved by passion: his own passion, lyrical sometimes, or histrionic. Unamuno assumed, just like the other writers of his generation, the role of gadfly, a necessary agitator in a Spain that, either stupidly calm or ostentatiously complicated, was clearly inert.[10] He wanted to inject Spain with his intimate civil war, even though the country was to have its own. In any case, those were civil wars without a solution, without even the "*abrazos de Vergara*"—which are never more than mere cease-fires. Without a solution: this impasse is implicit in Unamunian expectations for both his philosophy and his country. In an old article (1915) published in the Buenos Aires *La Nación* and now issued as an appendix to the *Epistolario*,[11] he made the reproach that "Maragall refused to understand that one writes to make others doubt, think, become uneasy." True: Maragall did not write to make others doubt or to make them gratuitously uneasy, but to make them think and even exult and burn; to take them along.[12] This was the bull's-eye Maragall proposed for the writer's effort, quite a different goal from Unamuno's. Here lies Maragall's greatness, a quality that made itself flesh in his time and in his land. Here too lies his weakness for today's readers, who would not go along with Maragall in many of his faiths. Tomorrow will speak for itself.

Our poet was also an instigator, but not for the sheer sake of instigation. For him, instigating meant awakening, stimulating, suggesting. As a man, Maragall wanted to and knew how to understand; these abilities were an uphill road for the Castilian. Maragall did not follow his way without turning his head after speaking his piece; he rather stopped to hear

the word of others. He could "enter someone else's skin"[13] without remaining therein as Unamuno would. Maragall was the man-man, partaking
of whatever humanity he found in those near him. And partaking of it not
in order to assimilate it into himself but to rejoice in the pure fact of its
existence, in the pure manifestation of life implied in it. The theory of the
"living word" and the theory expressed in his *Elogi de la poesia* are but one
aspect, the literary aspect, of Maragall's way of being.[14] "Maragall believed
with those who believed," wrote Josep Pijoan.[15] One of the poet's texts—
an almost exact equivalent to some of Unamuno's sayings—tells us of
Maragall's faith in faith, in any faith, granting it be sincere. Maragall—as
partly, too, Unamuno—elevates sincerity to the maximum place in his
scale of values. If the rector of Salamanca, obsessed solely by his personal
and exclusive sincerity, follows his way and lets others be in turn as sincere
as he is but alone, isolated, itinerant, Maragall, on the contrary, sees in
sincerity an opportunity for living together and moving one another. Such
moving was already a sacred gift—and so he speaks of "that shivering
which is my only criterion in poetry and in art."[16] Whenever he ran into a
person radically different from himself—Unamuno, for example—the very
force of his sincerity helped him find a point of communion in feelings or
thoughts opposed to his. They were the occasion to vibrate with an energy
that was above all a human energy with fruitful consequences. Discussing a
book by Salvador Albert, a book that had wounded him "as if they had hit
my head with a rock," Maragall says it gave him "the strange sensation
that the rock that had wounded him had the virtue of curing the very hurt
it brought, and of turning it into good."[17] I do not know if this shows
Nietzsche's influence or if it obeys a kind spiritualist pragmatism, but
Maragall seems animated by the idea that the good and therefore the
beautiful—the beautiful being the good for this very reason—is whatever
contributes to evincing and fostering the superior vital powers of humanity
or, at least, contributes to transforming all powers into superior ones.
"Whatever diminishes the faith in the ultimate goodness of life is im-
moral," he wrote.[18] For this reason he could not consider writing to provoke doubt, doubt for its own sake. Effectiveness in his view was already a
measure of value. And to be sincere is always to be effective—of course,
every sincerity in its own sphere and considered only as a force. Because
the essence of sincerity is its "turning itself into good," its giving forth
fruit, its being "creative," that is, "poetic."

Maragall therefore had to accept whatever was positive in
Unamuno. Speaking to Unamuno about his poem "En el desierto," he
writes: "If your idea of God is different every time, your feeling for God

seems to be always the same, but this saddens me as it is a depressive feeling. For those who are not depressive, such feeling could be, at best, a frightful exaltation. But how strange!—excuse me, no, it is not strange—your exaltation, in becoming poetic, does not hurt, and your dismay does not depress. That is why I do not complain about your poetry but regret the feelings that have preceded it; later, by his own virtue, the poet appears redeemed to me. That is also why I think your poetry will reach the world at the right time, as this kind of poetry is always timely; but if you said the same in prose, coldly, systematically, I think it would always come at the wrong time."[19] It seems to me that this paragraph suffices to reveal Maragall, and no matter how little you know Unamuno you will understand the distance that separates their orbits in this significant aspect. But Unamuno, to his greater glory and validity, never wrote the systematic and cold prose feared by Maragall. In a letter to Carles Rahola, our poet comments on the visit the Salamancan paid Barcelona, by the time of the Aplec de la Protesta and the International Congress on the Catalan Language: "Even though everyone here finds him a *poseur*, he appears to me as a man of great sincerity; at worst, he is deceiving himself."[20] According to Maragall, Unamuno, locked inside his own metaphysical obsession, could barely perceive the possibilities of reality surrounding him—the living reality—and even reality itself.[21] In spite of his comparison of Maragall's *Cant espiritual* to his own poetry on the theme of death, Unamuno felt obliged to confess: "but my heart, a clepsydra running with blood, does not allow me to enjoy beauty in peace."[22] And not only beauty. To what his generation called the problem of Spain Unamuno gave—he could not do otherwise—a response with an arid ethical resonance. It was the response that the exuberant Keyserling, with the exaltation of a tourist, praised in his wide-ranging analysis of Europe. For Unamuno, man is always simply and solely man, a tower of flesh and bones; he can only be infected with the anguish for his own immortality, and he will see everything as a function, to a greater or lesser degree, of that anguish. He cannot conceive, and in general neither can the other writers of the Spanish Generation of '98 conceive, what we may call "related man." They were rabid individualists, clichéd Spanish individualists, and recalcitrant Jeremiahs immersed in a politics they disdained. They maintained their humanity or "personality" as an axis, as a singular and living nucleus, and never believed one can open up to other people and undertake a common task. Neither Unamuno nor Baroja nor Azorín nor Maeztu could have guessed or shared the deep and popular sense of the *sardana*, as Maragall did in a famous poem;[23] nor possibly could they have defined the collective as the sum of innumerable

individual and shared "moments of grace," as did our poet.[24] In all this
Unamuno would see, exclusively and contemptuously, "aesthetics," the   115
playfulness of the Mediterranean people—"You will always be children,
Levantines!"[25]—who do not feel they are a dream of God nor hunger for
abstract eternities.[26]

I find it difficult to admit that such extreme opposition between
Maragall and Unamuno is due only to what we vaguely call temperament
or psychology, to what those in the know reduce to hormones or to even
more arcane and ungraspable explanations. Nor do I admit as decisive the
variance in their intellectual upbringing, always an important factor, but a
relative one.[27] To their temperament and education we must add the eth-
nic factor or, to be more precise, their respective national situations.[28] It is
impossible to imagine a Maragall in Castile and an Unamuno in Catalonia,
particularly in the Catalonia and Castile of the early century. If Unamuno
was that way, it is because Castile (*his* Castile) was that way; if Maragall
was that way, it is because Catalonia (*his* Catalonia) was that way. But with
this I do not mean to establish a cause and effect relation between land and
time, on one hand, and these men, on the other. I would rather resort to a
more intelligent explanation, in the manner of Eugeni d'Ors: their relationship is *functional.*[29] Maragall for example was at once cause and effect
of his Catalonia. Let us not forget that in his conception, the country is
"mother" and "daughter" of its people; it is what we receive and what
molds us, and that which we mold as we make it: at once a legacy and an
undertaking. Maragall always speaks as a Catalan and from Catalonia, from
that Catalonia undergoing a material and spiritual rebirth; from that flour-
ishing Catalonia that had accomplished its double rebirth and become the
motive and the stage for a revolution. He would call it "ardent."[30] A country and a time in ferment, in which "life" was opening, splendidly, with all
its potential and all its dangers. Maragall felt and nursed the enormous
gravity of Catalonia. He held a magisterial job in it, with tender responsibility. He knew that his voice, if not followed, was heard. To be a poet
there amid parliamentarians and anarchists, amid bourgeois and petty
bourgeois, had, after all, a far-reaching influence. When he addressed his
people or the bourgeoisie, of which he—a vitalist rebel—was a part, or the
complex image of his city, Maragall mixed diatribe with praises, love and
pain. His first reaction—in his youth of 1890—was that, a mere reaction:
"Oh, Barcelona, Barcelona, a bourgeois, humid, crushing city. Oh, bourgeoisie, oh your fences and blankets, soft fabric of poor consistency! Oh
you who are average in wealth, in position, in everything, oh symbol of all
mediocrity, you, Barcelona, have really screwed me! And I must still thank

God, and I resign myself to being a Barcelonese in all the power and extension of the word. . . . How Phoenician we are!"[31] He resigned himself to it, and as a bonus got to discover something more than the mediocrity erected before his impatient romanticism. He resigned himself to it and kept the leaven of dissatisfaction. His *Oda a Barcelona*, the articles he wrote after the Tragic Week ("La iglésia cremada" and "La ciutat del perdó," so timely) and about the works in the Sagrada Família show us a Maragall just as far from what Unamuno would call "*desahogo*," or ease, as from any jovial patriotism. Our poet never fell for naive and ponderous rhetoric when he spoke about Catalonia: gone was his period of nostalgia. He appreciated justly all the effervescence of his people, both positive and negative; because it signified so many bids for life, and life itself, it was for him valuable and encouraging. Maragall was as drawn by the concrete as he was annoyed by the abstract. And the concrete was Catalonia, that pregnant reality. Whenever he wrote, he wrote thinking of it. He needed this Catalonia to "speak in the raw." Read, for example, two of his most characteristic articles: "El ismo" and "Evocación";[32] they exude the same disinterest, an identical fear of abstraction. Abstraction for him was emptiness, lifelessness, something very different from death; something that could bring about no "greater birth," transcendent or otherwise.

Next to an agitated Catalonia, with its bombs and its prosperity, its new parties and new ambitions, the Generation of '98 described, on its own, Castilian Spain.[33] Or rather two Spains. One, the real, anti-European Spain with its political thugs and bullfighters and lukewarm religiosity: "the inferior Spain" berated later by Antonio Machado.[34] And the other, the ideal Spain they, the men of '98, sought in Castile, in the revival of Castilian myths and stories: the Spain some of them would call, for better or worse, eternal Spain.[35] Both Spains are sad and desolate, variants of the same topical "black" Spain.[36] The repertory of solutions proposed by the Generation of '98 stems from this primary consideration. Their intellectual *arbitrismo* followed a tradition of patches, recipes, and panaceas that began in the time of the Habsburgs. Unamuno's *arbitrismo* is a religious one.[37] He flaunts his agonistic Christianity like a war wound, and sometimes like a *banderilla*. His quixotism leans more to the mad than to the knightly; just like all other quixotisms—madness striving towards the knightly—[38] it ends up as a renunciation of what constitutes Maragall's ultimate purpose: efficiency. Unamuno complains of the futility of his efforts. "It cannot be, my dear Maragall, it cannot be, it cannot be," he wrote in 1907.[39] "I feel embittered by what I see and hear."[40] He does not realize that this consequence—what "cannot be"—is implicit in his ideas.

Maragall subscribes, from another angle, to the same pessimistic vision of Spain. Castile's mission in Spain, he says, has ended.[41] Unamuno is its surviving representative: "Those of us who have been born facing the Mediterranean, or the moist children of Portugal, will never be able to rally under your flag"—Unamuno's—"but we all feel the duty to put down our arms for a moment and bend our heads in a salute to the last Castilian hero."[42] "It always seems to me that you are the last Spaniard alive," he wrote to him on another occasion.[43] Because Maragall believes that "a country is only alive when it beats to its own spirit and its consequent mission,"[44] and in all of Spain he only finds Unamuno conscious of the spirit and of the mission proper to Spaniards.[45] And certainly, Unamuno embodies that spirit, the Castilian spirit, as Maragall understands the spirit of a collectivity, an untransferable essence, a fidelity to the land, authenticity. Unamuno embodies that spirit, but not the mission—he embodies no mission. Unamuno was too much himself to assume any other mission than being Unamuno, if that was a mission. His pen gives forth the swan song of venerable Castile. What has happened after him is something else.

As for contemporary Spain, Unamuno and Maragall are united in their dismay and in what they blamed. Steering clear of politics, they both felt compromised by politics, or rather against politics.[46] Unamuno, even in his most boisterous moments (the ones he recollected in his *Dos artículos y dos conferencias*[47]), was fundamentally antipolitical. Yet few intellectuals of those times show for the politics of the peninsula so attentive an interest, an interest so inflexible in its judgments, so compassionate in its lucidity, as our two poets. For the politics undertaken and for the politics that should have been undertaken. "In Spain," wrote Joan Maragall, "political passion is but the disguise for other more primitive passions that seek in politics a hidden satisfaction; for this reason we see a violence disproportionate to its objectives: because those objectives are other."[48] And he adds: "Therefore, Spaniard, my brother, let go of all political fiction and go into your soul." Maragall condemns the farce, the absurdity and artificiality of government "deals," the mystification, be it blamed on Romero Robledo or on anyone else. His "go into your soul" is his nostalgia for truly living energies, fully popular energies that have been denied, distorted, or blurred by bad politics.[49] Unamuno's little faith and Maragall's big faith in politics[50]—the patriotic order of "renaissance" or "regenerationism"—center in social vitality. They always thought of people as their living and free material, without interferences from routine or hypocrisy. Politics, the politicians' politics, found a good ally in the collective deadness, in the fatigue following—and preceding—the colonial losses; but it clashed with the first symptoms of a partial perking in a Catalonia set in motion. Maragall found a hold on the smooth wall of that deadness: hope. "You do not believe in the barbarians surrounding you," he wrote Unamuno, "nor in your brothers nor in us; and you spew out the truth to all of us, but only the bitter truths, the only ones you feel. I do not rebut your reasons, and yet feel no sadness because I have hope. This is my secret. This is also the secret of Catalonia's present strength: we are a people who hope. We have all the defects and all the excesses you claim, and many more; but we hope; and this is our strength."[51] These words were written in 1907, during the eclosion of Solidaritat. Unamuno felt doubts—it was his calling, almost his trade—about what was then happening in Catalonia: "A moment of beauty . . . All right! But, its fruit?"[52] The fruit could not be what Unamuno asked for, nor what Maragall dreamt. But there was a fruit, and a little in the sense of our poet: "How far will it go? To what end?" Maragall continues, speaking of Catalonia.[53] "I do not know it, and I can almost tell you I do not care, because what is substantial, what is essential, the piece of eternal life, is the one [our country] now lives as it advances and hopes. This sentimental actuality of ours is worth more than the whole of the Roman Empire. This fire of ours is what we would like to imbue into all Spanish peoples, not to this end or that, but for our living fire's own sake, and this fire would go where it should go, because being a path of living enthusiasm, it will always turn out for the best." Once again we find here Maragall's supreme conviction, his supreme confidence: before politics and before all. Creative life.[54] "Our programs do not need to be too concrete," he wrote to Pere Coromines.[55] What matters is the living enthusiasm, living fire, hope. Automatically these will take us to "a good end." "We have, here, something living ruled by something dead, but the dead is weightier than the living and drags it to the tomb in its fall," he said in "La patria nueva."[56] The issue is to make the "something living" overcome the "something dead."At that moment, according to our poet, Catalanism—a part of the "something living"— managed to become "a national palingenesis."[57] It was the moment when Catalanism became interventionist, at least among the theoreticians of the then preponderant sector—Prat de la Riba and his idea of "Big Spain." But the Generation of '98 never noticed: they were not looking at their fellow citizens. The politicians did; but they were interested in no palingenesis. And if Unamuno affirms—some years before, in 1905, although the political and spiritual circumstances were identical—that "Catalonia's duty toward Spain was to try to Catalanize it,"[58] his intentions were radically opposed to those of the Catalans.

No one has thought of a better word to define Maragall's thought than the rector of Salamanca himself. He qualified it as "panpoeticism."[59] Rising from the etymological definition of poetry, a simple synonym for creation, and enlarging it beyond the literary realm, Maragall's philosophy—"if one may speak of a Maragallian philosophy"—is an exultant panpoeticism.[60] An admirer of Novalis, Goethe, and Nietzsche, Maragall was a romantic, as was Unamuno.[61] He believed in the spirit—in the fecund and avenging spirit—and in life.[62] His sense of the transcendent, therefore, had to be a modality of that Mediterranean Christianity we could call Franciscanism. Perhaps with a slight bent toward pantheism. He was a poet with the full conscience of being one; his personal vocation was confused with a redeeming vision for his people. He wrote to Unamuno: "To Catalonia we have given this strength, this hope—we can say it with no false humility and no false pride—or rather we have awakened it, we, the poets, each according to his possibilities."[63] Poetry, then, is the revelation of the soul of a community, the concrete soul that abstract patriotism drowns.[64] Unity may be realized in this revelation, and then "poetry," he assures us, "would be the best politics."[65] Not a literary politics, nor a mere *entente* of minorities, because "true sublimity in poetry lies in its power to become popular,"[66] and if the poet manages to communicate his conviction "in words vibrating with poetry, his people will believe what he feels, what we feel," and will begin to feel it too.[67] Spirit and mission will be identified, and the people will *live*. Maragall preached this politics to Unamuno around the theme of Iberian nationalisms. Poetry will reveal *the Iberian soul,* the subjacent common ground. "We must search inward for this Iberian soul only a few of us can feel; the Castilians inside their Castile; the Portuguese inside their Portugal; the Catalans inside our Catalonia, until we reach the common root. Inside each modality, until we find the one cause for modalities."[68] But it was in vain. Unamuno confessed his impotence to understand Catalonia, and he saw unity not in the "common root" but in real fusion. For him, as for the few Castilian writers that have approached Catalonia, this country could only contribute to Spain its work and its enthusiasm, and had to renounce its soul and its language.[69] It was useless to ask of the Salamanca Basque that "first recognition of diversity, irreducible to a simple unity but not to a compound," of which Maragall spoke: "In this compound, yet unrealized, lies the secret of Spain's greatness."[70] Unamuno did not believe in compounds but in impositions: Spanish unity was for him the result or the advantage of a victory. He was really a man of civil war, not a man of dialogue. Maragall, on the contrary, was a man of civil peace, of concord: "a hopeful worker." This discrepancy undermines all the affinities both men had and sought. When, in 1911, Maragall's death put an end to the *Epistolario*, people and deeds would prolong, in other terrains, the themes that occupied and preoccupied both writers. But our recent history and what has not yet turned into history have been, from one side or the other, more Unamunian than Maragallian.

NOTES

1. Barcelona: Edimar, 1951.

2. See Unamuno's foreword to Joan Maragall's *Problemas del día* (vol. 17 in Maragall's complete works); reprinted in *Epistolario*, 171–179.

3. I know of few studies of Maragall and Unamuno. José María Valverde is the author of a brief and intelligent note in his essay "Cuatro apuntes sobre la poesía de Juan Maragall" (in *El Español* of Madrid, 1946, no. 165). Among other interesting notions, Valverde points out a certain "Pirandellism" *avant la lettre* in the dialogue between the Poet and Adelaisa in Maragall's *Comte Arnau*.

4. I shall quote from the latest edition of Maragall's *Obres completes* (Barcelona: Selecta, 1947). His letters occupy pages 1625 to 1881. I know that some other letters from Maragall to Unamuno have been published; they do not appear either in the *Obres completes* or in the *Epistolario*.

5. *Epistolario*, 11.

6. Unamuno, *Ensayos*, vol. 2 (Madrid: Aguilar, 1942), 961 (foreword to *Contra esto y aquello*).

7. *Epistolario*, 46.

8. *Ensayos*, vol. 2,627 ("A la señora Mab" in his *Soliloquios y conversaciones*).

9. The idea and expression *civil war* are a constant leitmotif in Unamuno's writings (in his last years it took the name of "Cainism"). In general, combat or struggle plays a decisive role in his philosophical thought: strife, the equivalent of contradiction. Unamuno unearthed the etymological sense of the word *agony* and made it the axis of his meditations. Maragall, on the contrary, wrote: "Strife is repugnant to my nature, which searches for a core of harmony and serenity in all things" (letter to Pere Coromines, January 22, 1902; *Obres completes*, 1961). If at some point Maragall dares speak of strife and of "civil strife," it is in a radically different sense: "You speak of necessary strife," he told Pijoan in a letter of June 18, 1906, "but I consider that the noble, the civil battle can be, ought to be, indirect: what Henry IV told the universities when they asked him to remove the Jesuits: 'Faites mieux qu'eux.' " (*Obres completes*, 1763).

10. See the curious words of J. Ferrater Mora in *Unamuno: Bosquejo de la filosofía* (Buenos Aires: Losada, 1944), 182: "Unamuno, unlike Ortega, is no spectator, nor, unlike Eugeni d'Ors, is he a preceptor, but as Ernst Robert Curtius has suggested, he is an exciter: *excitator*, and not *praeceptor* or *spectator Hispaniae*."

11. *Epistolario*, 164.

12. Maragall, in an article on Campoamor (*Obres completes*, 915) says that to make people think is a defect in a poet and in the artist in general. The philosophizing yearnings of poets induce them to "sacrifice all poetic emotion to an a priori concept of life and to a logical mechanism that deforms and freezes it." Great poets, he says, limit themselves to "intensifying life" by expressing it. He also says

that the virtue of the great pure poets is to enthuse, to inflame. (O. Saltor, in his article "De Unamuno a Maragall" published in the *Diario de Mallorca* of June 23, 1953, formulates exactly our poet's attitude: "Maragall, in the most priestly sense of the concept, preaches, proselitizes.") (1953 note.)

13. Letter of January 3, 1907 (*Epistolario*, 44).

14. See *Obres completes*, 561ff.

15. Josep Pijoan, *El meu don Joan Maragall* (Barcelona: Catalònia, n.d.), 71.

16. Letter of December 19, 1906 (*Epistolario*, 40).

17. Letter to Salvador Albert, April 22, 1908 (*Obres completes*, 1630).

18. In his article "Campoamor" mentioned above (*Obres completes*, 916). Through his affinities with Nietzsche, Maragall joins the new vitalist philosophy, which was then erupting in Europe. Its connections and spread would make a good topic for study.

19. Letter of November 26, 1906 (*Epistolario*, 29). The poem mentioned is reproduced on p. 118 of the book.

20. Letter of February 5, 1907 (*Obres completes*, 1791f).

21. Maragall referred to Unamuno's attitude during the aforesaid visit to Barcelona in his article "La gran setmana d'octubre" (*Obres completes*, 648). Unamuno "had not come because of the Congress but in order to see what all the noise was about. And all of a sudden he found here the fiery inaugural session of the Congress, the feverish movement of the fight against the Commerce treaties, and the strident scenario of the great 'Aplec de la Protesta' of Solidaritat Catalana against the militarist laws." But the rector of Salamanca—"the representative of today's Spain whom we could call the hero, in Carlyle's sense, of the extreme Castilian decadence"—was a "man fascinated by his own inner abyss, absorbed by personal contemplation." He was "a brain of fearful activity, turning around the mystery of life and death, the idea of God and individual conscience"; but he barely realized what was happening around him.

> His tall, straight, noble figure of a Basque weaned in Castile walked, unmoved and disdainful, through this "vast suburb of Tarascon" (as I know he told someone) without deigning to cast more than a glance at the surface, and, disgusted, turning his gaze immediately to his inner self where he would find the peace of the noble steppe immensely restful and empty, in order to take up again in silence his terrible battle with the invisible God of his insomniac nights.

Unamuno wrote up his impressions of that trip in a note entitled "Barcelona" (November 1906), which he published first in a Buenos Aires newspaper and gathered later in *Por tierras de Portugal y España* (Buenos Aires: Espasa Calpe Argentina, 1944), 97–102. "In Barcelona one feels one is in a vast suburb of Tarascon," he says, "and one thinks one hears in Catalan, a language so close to Provençal, the battle cry of the good Tarasconians: *fem du brut*, that is, let us make noise." Unamuno accused Catalans of being "petulantly vain" and "greedily avaricious"; they have the vices that "emerge from a quality"—let us remark that the word quality sneaks in—"which is sensuality," a quality shared by all Mediterranean peoples. He foresees that "should these lines be read by a Barcelonese" he will be accused—and Maragall did raise this objection—of not having understood what he saw. Such objection, he proceeds, will be dictated by "the boastfulness of collective selfishness." The Catalans are the people "whom I have seen less given to self-censure." "They are always on the defensive, even when they appear to attack," and this reveals ultimately "a very vacillating, very dim, very insecure faith in themselves." This is not the moment to try to elucidate the rightness of those observations. But I will point out that, in so far as they are exact, Unamuno showed his bad faith in hiding their causes from us. If the Catalans are as he says we are, it is not out of the blue, and Unamuno knew it or should have known. Josep Ferrater i Mora, in different terms, has discussed this psychological and social trait of today's Catalans in his "Prefaci per a catalans" of his *Les formes de la vida catalana* (Santiago de Chile: Edicions de l'Agrupació Patriòtica Catalana, 1944), 9–18. Ferrater also ignores the question of the causes, historical or otherwise, of the phenomenon. Unamuno (loc. cit., 99) wants to give the alleged Catalan boastfulness a retroactive reach and considers it a constant in our collective temperament. To prove it he quotes line 960 of the twelfth-century Castilian poem *Cantar de Mío Cid*, which, speaking of the count of Barcelona, says: "the count is cocky and has spoken vainly." Let us say that this is not a valid historical argument, nor should one extend it from the count to the whole nation. On the other hand, texts such as this are frequent from all ages and places among neighboring countries. We have—to give but one example—a perfect response to the *Mío Cid* text. When Saint Vincent Ferrer tried to justify the verdict of Caspe before the people, he attempted to deny the Castilianness of the chosen king, Fernando of Antequera, and said: "Castilians are very wordy, to wit: 'Ferrán Ferrández de los Arcos de los Mayores'; but our king speaks sparingly, and takes care of business," like a good Catalan. Roc Chabàs, "Estudio de los sermones valencianos de San Vicente Ferrer," in *Revista de Archivos, Bibliotecas y Museos* 8 (Madrid, 1903), 121–122.

22. Letter to Romà Jori dated February 21, 1911, and inserted in *Epistolario*, 142.

23. First of all because a dance could only put them in a bad mood. At least during those times.

24. See *Elogi de la poesia* (*Obres completes*, 566ff).

25. From Unamuno's poem "L'Aplec de la Protesta" (see his *Antología poética* [Buenos Aires: Espasa Calpe, 1946], 32).

26. José María Valverde, loc. cit., points out that both poets share the dream of preserving things beyond death. He adds, however, that this is barely visible in Unamuno, while it constitutes the backbone of Maragall's poetry. I am convinced that Unamuno and Maragall do not refer exactly to the same *things*. Valverde quotes Unamuno's "Elegía a la muerte de un perro":

> . . . World of the spirits!
> But there, won't we have
> around our soul
> the souls of things which feed
> the soul of the fields . . . ?
>
> The other world is one of pure spirit!
> Of pure spirit!
> Oh terrible purity,
> inanity, vacuum . . . !"

We see, then, that Unamuno speaks of "the soul of things," and in a questioning sense. Maragall—primarily in his "Cant espiritual"—speaks, in contrast, of things in a sense we could term wishful:

> With what other senses will You make me see
> this blue sky above the mountains,
> and the immense sea, and the sun that shines throughout?
> Give me in these senses eternal peace. . . .

> . . . This world, whatever it is,
> so diverse, so vast, so temporal,
> this land, with all that grows on it,
> is my country, Lord, and why should it not be
> also my heavenly abode?

Maragall, in love with the sensual world, would like to remain in it. Unamuno, on the contrary, conceives of personal immortality exclusively as the atemporal immortality of consciousness. In a word: their difference lies in the fact that Maragall, as a believer—in his own way—in the immortality of the soul, would like this immortality to be accompanied by the things of this earth he loves, while Unamuno, since he does not believe yet in his own immortality—or understands it the way he does—does not bother to imagine its conditions. Besides, Unamuno never felt great enthusiasm for things.

27. The *Epistolario* shows them united by their admiration for Goethe—somewhat unsuspected in Unamuno—for some German Romantics, and for Spinoza, and also by their shared revulsion for French writers. Unamuno, however, utilizes a larger repertory of authors, particularly philosophers. Some of the more constantly admired in his writing do not appear, or do so only in passing, in Maragall's: for example, Pascal, Augustine, Kierkegaard. These are after all highly significant names.

28. "The sweet Maragall, in this jubilant Catalonia, is the fraternal replica of an Unamuno tormented in his learned and severe Salamanca," Joan Estelrich wrote in his preface to the French translation of José Ortega y Gasset's *Ideas y creencias* (Paris, 1945). Cf. J. M. Corredor, *Un esprit méditerranéen: Joan Maragall* (Toulouse, 1951), 163.

29. "The cause does not always precede the effect," wrote Ors. "The cause that follows the effect is called finality; that which accompanies it, function." See his *Gnómica* (Madrid: Euro, 1941), 108, and his *Teoría de los estilos y espejo de la Arquitectura* (Madrid: Aguilar, n. d.), 60ff. Poets and their people are, as mathematicians say, in mutual function. Leaving aside Taine's theories, of course.

30. "Dulce ley" (*Obres completes*, 994).

31. Letter to Antoni Roura of May 16, 1890 (*Obres completes*, 1813).

32. *Obres completes*, 934, 999. This is from "Evocación":

> The poet is the only one who can speak alone without going mad. But the orator, from a platform or a newspaper, needs an audience, and to see that audience—with any kind of eyes—and hear its heartbeat—with any kind of perception—and also to share that beat and return it to the audience intensified. The orator needs, in a word, communication. If I am not in your heart, I will be unable to speak to your heart. And if I do not speak to your heart, what does it matter if mine displays before your understanding a theory of far-away ideas like a procession of corpses? . . . For this reason I loath sitting down to write, in the oratorical genre, for a distant audience.

Maragall needed "to speak in the raw," to have a concrete, familiar audience before him; "otherwise I feel I am speaking to the clouds outside my window, I feel I am writing a letter and do not know to whom. And, what do I have to say to the clouds about my general ideas? What can I answer to those who have asked me no question?"

33. The bibliography on the Spanish Generation of '98 is as abundant as it is well known. César Barja's *Libros y autores contemporáneos* (Madrid, 1935), 467ff., provides a bibliographical appendix of publications to 1933.

34. "El mañana efímero" in his *Poesías completas*, 5th ed. (Buenos Aires: Es-

pasa Calpe, 1949), 171. We must point out, however incidentally, the latent seed of violence in the members of the Generation of '98, who all somewhat resemble the "civil war man" that Unamuno was. "The dawning Spain" to which Machado refers at the end of this poem comes "with an ax in its avenging hand" and is the "Spain of rage."

35. See Pedro Laín Entralgo's *La Generación del Noventa y ocho* (Buenos Aires: Espasa Calpe, 1947).

36. I do not know if those who have studied the Generation of '98 have remarked on the ninety-eightish character of Darío de Regoyo's little book *La España negra de Verhaeren* (Madrid: Cuadernos Literarios, 1924); we need only recall one of its ending paragraphs: "If this artist," Verhaeren, "would come today to Spain, he would find us all deader than during his last visit. His remarks seem written during this sad year of 1898." Of course, when recalling in my text the label "black Spain," I refer to the viewpoint we could call European, somewhat superficial but not totally inexact, which was held by the Belgian poet.

37. José Luis L. Aranguren (*Cuadernos Hispanoamericanos,* no. 38 [Madrid, February 1953], 139) discusses Unamuno's attitude before the problem of Spain:

> For Francisco Ayala, modern Spain's spiritual history is based on the fact that against "the peaceful and trivial bunch of traditionalists, stuck to the static bottom of our being and seeing problems nowhere" again and again rise the "dissenters," forever in the service of "Europeanizing intelligence." Until Unamuno arrived to put an end to this wretched historical antithesis: "His personality cannot be fit in either of the two opposing attitudes; but it does not oscillate between them either, it rather encloses both of them." That is to say, since Unamuno, Spaniards, while conserving a certain margin of dissidence vis-à-vis their history, are able to express with full consciousness their opposition to the unilateral orientation of "modern civilization" and their proud fidelity to "our radical positions in life." This and no other has been, according to Ayala, Unamuno's great undertaking.

Aranguren extracts the quotations from Francisco Ayala's *Razón del mundo: Un examen de conciencia intelectual* (Buenos Aires: Losada, 1944), 114ff, and 146. (Note from 1953.)

38. I am not quite convinced of Catalonia's quixotism as proposed by Josep Ferrater Mora in *El llibre del sentit* (Santiago de Chile: El Pi de les tras branques, 1948), 46. Saint George—to whom this writer refers—is not Don Quixote; what we may call Saintgeorgism is no "essential quixotism" because Saint George killed the dragon while Don Quixote never triumphed over men, or over beasts, or over windmills. Eugeni d'Ors used to oppose Ulysses to Don Quixote and Tristram: the first was the efficient hero, the other two the heroes of failure. Ulysses, wilier than chivalric, ultimately bourgeois, represents the Catalans better than any other mythical character, the Catalans as well as any other Mediterranean people. Now: if we must find a symbolic archetype for ourselves, and if we are not pleased with Ulysses—because of his wiles and his presumed and anachronistic bourgeois character—let us retain Saint George, simply, without quixotizing him.

39. *Epistolario,* 69.

40. This letter, of May 15, 1907, became an open letter, published in *España Nueva* (Madrid, May 1907) under the title "Contra los bárbaros" (see *Epistolario,* 129ff). Both the private and the open letters have some of the most violent paragraphs Unamuno ever wrote:

> For barbarians abound. . . . When they go to hear someone, they are not going to hear what is said, but what they imagine will be said to them. . . .

The barbarians have their mental schemes made up, and if one talks to them they do not hear. It is impossible, my dear Maragall, impossible. One can make a sculpture in granite, but not in sand. And this country is pulverized. It is a matter of their mental structure. You know where the barbarians' energetic will comes from; you know that when refusing to do something they say: "My c[*ojones*] don't want to do it." In their "heads, inside the cranium, instead of brains, they have prairie oysters. Their brains are c[*ojones*]' brains! And let the barbarians laugh, believing that blood spurts from irony or humor, and let the imbeciles, whose number is infinite, speak again of paradoxes. . . . And here, my good friend, here in this poor and forlorn Castile, the spirit suffers and sighs under the barbarian's dominion. Near Fontiveros, in the middle of the dusty steppe, I asked myself: How could this have been the birthplace of Saint John of the Cross? And I concluded, to console myself, that the spirit is not dead but sleeping. From time to time it moans in its dreams.

41. *Obres completes*, 1372.

42. Letter of December 19, 1906 (*Epistolario*, 39).

43. Letter of March 7, 1907 (*Epistolario*, 61).

44. Ibid.

45. "You understand," Maragall adds (loc. cit.), "that if there is anything here in Catalonia, it represents, at least for now, a disintegration."

46. It is worth transcribing some sentences of Josep Ferrater Mora (in his *Unamuno: Bosquejo de una filosofía*, 30) that clarify and complement what I try to say in my text:

Spain is precisely the country where nobody, and less than anybody those who call themselves intellectuals, can ignore politics, if by politics we understand something more than electoral propaganda or the pursuit of public office. Politics in this sense is working for the moral regeneration of the country, and that is why one can play politics even if locked up in the ivory tower, even writing the most intimate lyric poetry or the sternest philosophy. But poetry and philosophy are not listened to by those who ought to listen and, for this reason, the poet and the philosopher must say in plain words that which they ought to translate to politicians.

47. Madrid: Historia Nueva, 1930. This book shows an extraordinarily rash force. Here Unamuno outdoes even Baroja. See my note "Los energúmenos" in *Verbo* (Alacant), no. 17 (October 1949), 11ff.

48. "La espaciosa y triste España" (*Obres completes*, 1493).

49. On this positive aspect of Maragall's political thought, see Josep Maria Corredor's chapter "Un cri de renaissance parmi les dangers" in his *Un esprit méditerranéen: Joan Maragall*.

50. It seems that toward the end of his life, Maragall felt the diminution of his optimism: "For—I confess to you—even I have been losing my faith in our people for anything that is a collective and disinterested task." Letter to Carme Karr de Lasarte, n.d., but written after October 18, 1911 (*Obres completes*, 1705).

51. Letter of May 23, 1907 (*Epistolario*, 72).

52. *Antología poética*, loc. cit.

53. Letter of May 23, 1907 (*Epistolario*, 73).

54. Needless to say, life is also a value for Unamuno. "Truth is what makes one live, not what makes one think," he wrote in his *Vida de don Quijote y Sancho*. This may make us believe in another essential point of convergence between both writers. Yet we would have to analyze in detail what each understands as "life." For

one thing, Unamuno takes off from his "tragic feeling" of life; this sets him radically apart from Maragall.

55. Letter of October 29, 1909 (*Obres completes*, 1662).

56. *Obres completes*, 1394. In this article, as in other writings by Maragall, we notice a clear *progressive* tone, very nineteenth century, which may have displeased Unamuno and which to today's reader—even if we accept the enormous political transcendence the Catalan poet's progressive arguments had, and have—must seem something out of archaeology.

57. *Obres completes*, 1372.

58. *Ensayos*, vol. 1, 743.

59. "Leyendo a Maragall," an article published in *La Nación* of Buenos Aires on March 7, 1915 (*Epistolario*, 154). Arturo Farinelli, in his *Poesía del Montserrat y otros ensayos* (Barcelona: Bosch, 1940), 58–105, draws an explanation of Maragall's thought that would have pleased Unamuno.

60. Ibid. See Ferrater Mora's admirable essay "El 'Cant Espiritual': Sentit d'un poema" in his *El llibre del sentit*, 51ff.

61. See the essay "Juan Maragall" in Eugeni d'Ors's *Estilos del pensar* (Madrid: Espasa, 1945), 55ff. Leaving his evaluation aside, Ors acutely and exactly places our poet in that baroque coordinate of his invention. His assessment of course follows the rationalist principles—or predominantly rationalist—of Ors's ideology.

62. "The spirit takes revenge! The spirit takes revenge!" ("Esta es my fe," *Obres completes*, 1480).

63. Letter of May 23, 1907 (*Epistolario*, 72).

64. Maragall spoke at times (*Obres completes*, 1279) of that weighing and depersonalizing "administrative verbosity" that feeds the official rhetoric and ideology in the great modern states.

65. Letter of April 10, 1908 (*Epistolario*, 85).

66. Letter of January 3, 1907 (*Epistolario*, 43). Maragall's statement is as romantic as it is optimistic.

67. Letter of May 23, 1907 (*Epistolario*, 73).

68. Letter of March 5, 1911 (*Epistolario*, 97).

69. Maragall's position vis-à-vis Unamuno's idea to "Catalanize Spain" "in Castilian" was defined in his article "Catalunya i avant!" of October 5, 1911 (*Obres completes*, 1495ff).

70. Letter of January 3, 1907 (*Epistolario*, 44).

A Note on Roig's
"Catalans in Nazi Death Camps"

 Montserrat Roig i Fransitorra (her first surname is pro-
nounced something like *Rotch*) was born in Barcelona in
1946. Her first book of stories, *Molta roba i poc sabó*, was
published in 1971 and awarded the Víctor Català prize.
Since then she has devoted her professional life to fiction, feminism, and
journalism. Among Roig's narratives, her 1977 novel *El temps de les cireres*
won the Sant Jordi prize, and a significant fragment of another novel,
L'òpera quotidiana (1982), has been translated into English. Roig has published two collections of essays on women, in Castilian: *¿Tiempo de mujer?*
(1980) and *Mujeres hacia un nuevo humanismo* (1982). As a journalist she
has written countless interviews and hosted the popular television talk
show "Personatges." As an extension of her journalistic work she has issued a biography of a Catalan politician, *Rafael Vidiella. l'aventura de la
revolució* (1976), and the impressive reportage *Els catalans als camps nazis*
(1977), which was awarded the *Serra d'Or* Critics' Prize; its first chapter is
the selection that follows.

The Spanish Civil War, surely the most consequential event of
twentieth-century Spain, has naturally provoked a great deal of writing. In
English, George Orwell's *Homage to Catalonia* described the struggle for
power in Barcelona among the main factions of the Left—anarchists, Trotskyites, and communists—culminating in the bloody events of May 1937.

Roig takes a different approach to describing the conflict. Shortly after Franco's death, she traced and interviewed Spanish Republican survivors of the Nazi extermination camps and told the story of those idealist leftists who, vanquished, found themselves exiled in a Europe dominated by Hitler. Hair-raising as their adventures in the Nazi camps were, I have selected the opening chapter of the book, which discusses the origins of the deported and the ideas that, in their own recollections, influenced their destinies. In Roig's narrative we see an aspect of the sufferings caused by the bloody Civil War; we are also introduced to a significant segment of the Catalan population that followed its youthful ideals in the hope of changing history.

MONTSERRAT ROIG

Catalans in Nazi Death Camps

T he war was coming to an end. On January 15, 1939, General Franco's troops had captured Tarragona; on January 26 they entered Barcelona; on February 4 they occupied Girona. For thousands of Catalans who, three years before, had risen in opposition to the insurrection against the Republic, the exodus began. Some of them were to feel on their own skins the disasters of another, more terrible war. Our deported men and women were to die or survive in despair in the death camps at Mathausen, Dachau, Buchenwald, Ravensbrück. Our people, along with republicans from all over Iberia, had fought against what Wilhelm Reich called the resurrection of the Middle Ages. They had also fought for a living Catalonia, for a freer Catalan zone.

On February 27, 1939, the "democratic" governments of France and England recognized the Burgos government. This body, presided over by General Franco, had decreed in 1938: *"The character of each region will be respected, whenever it does not threaten national unity, which we want absolute, with only one language, Castilian, and only one personality, Spanish."* Our deportees were excluded from that definition. They had the grave defects of speaking another language, Catalan, and of seeking from their left-wing ideologies clarification of the concept of "only one personality, Spanish."

Our deportees could not have been very pleasing to General Franco. They were aware of it, and so, brokenhearted, they crossed the border early that February. Our deportees knew they were fully implicated in the law of political responsibilities of February 13, 1939:

> We declare the political responsibility of all persons, be they legal or physical bodies, who from October 1, 1934, until July 18, 1936, contributed to create or aggravate the many forms of subversion that victimized Spain, and also of those persons who, from the second of the above-mentioned dates on, have opposed the national Movimiento by either deed or grave passivity.

Later, according to the newspaper *El Heraldo de Aragón* of February 29, 1939, those political responsibilities were extended:

> We also include those who held office with the "Popular Front" in the central administration.
> Those who made public declarations of support for the Popular Front, or members of the above-mentioned parties, or those who contributed to them with their economic support, in a free and voluntary manner, even if they never held office or membership.
> Those who opposed the Movimiento.

The only exclusions from these responsibilities were those under fourteen, those who had served the Movimiento, and those who had received in its defense the Laureada or the Military Medal. Also the seriously wounded who had enlisted voluntarily in the armed forces from the beginning of the war or six months before their draft date; those holding the title of Mutilated Knights. Those who had publicly recanted before July 18, 1936, and then adhered to and collaborated with the Movimiento would benefit from either exemptions or attenuations according to the judgment of the tribunals.

Our deportees were fully affected by this law. They could not return. They had opposed the Movimiento with their participation in political life here. They were men and women affiliated with the CNT, PSUC, Esquerra Republicana de Catalunya, Estat Català; they were union people, socialists, anarchists, communists, Catalanists, and some simply loyal republicans; men and women from the working class who never repented having chosen the republican side. With the naiveté of all idealists, one deported man who spent five years in Gusen, a branch of Mauthausen, told me:

I have suffered a lot defending democracy and social justice. From an early age I followed the ideas my father also had: "do good, and don't care for whom." I joined the party with the greatest enthusiasm of my life. It was my first love, with no egoism or treachery. After a lot of hard work I was dragged into the Spanish Civil War, and we lost. Because the whole world, or the greater part, was against us, because we were people full of good faith.

What kind of people are these deportees? During my interviews I have found that they come mainly from the working class, a few from the middle class, some were farmers. Those who ended up in Mauthausen were mostly rounded up by the Germans from the retreating work companies during the *drôle de guerre*. The ones who went to the other extermination camps, and some who also went to Mauthausen, were captured by the Nazis because of their participation in the resistance. If we consider the birthplace of all we see that most are Catalans from little towns and not the big city, and that on the 19th of July many were employed as house painters, carpenters, waiters, masons, specialized laborers who left their tools to enlist voluntarily in defense of the Republic in danger. Those who went to Nazi camps crossed the border at the Pyrenees; we therefore find in their number many Catalans and children of migrants established in Catalonia, mostly from the industrial belts. A case in point is the Cortès family; some of the children were born in Pechina, in the province of Almeria, but the younger children were born in Prat de Llobregat. Almost all the Catalans who were victims of Nazi fascism in the German camps came from the working class. They were the most destitute, and had been unable to find help so they could leave the French concentration camps. Intellectuals, white-collar workers, those with relatives in France, and the main cadres of the parties got away; those who could not find a crack to flee through remained. They had no one.

Joan N. was twenty-eight in 1936. He fought at the Aragon front, in Vedado de Zuera, Tardiente, Robles. He was in the quartermaster's corps; they were in charge of getting bread and water to the trenches. Joan once saw a soldier shot because he had drained the whole water supply during a raid; Joan did not know if the soldier had been a spy or simply very scared. Joan withstood the whole Aragon front and then the retreat toward Prats de Molló. On the way, he stopped in his town, Campdevànol. He was made lieutenant when crossing the border: "You are now a lieutenant in the Engineering Corps," he was told. But he did not care about rank and wanted to leave under the same conditions as all the others. It was February 13, and he was still carrying the typewriters from headquarters. Joan N. was a member of CNT because, he says, everybody in Campdevànol was a member of CNT.

"Deportation has really injured our feelings," says Francesc.[1] Francesc is now over seventy. His eyes grow moist as he tries to remember. Memories are painful, but Francesc holds on to them, afraid they will vanish. His story, like that of all the deportees who have talked to me, does not consist of flat, harmonious events tied to each other in a logical and natural manner. His story zigzags in his memory. Events come to him loosely, brokenly. Francesc has a hard time giving them a coherent shape. Francesc was thirty-two when the war broke out; he was a reservist and joined the militia. He had done his military service as a topographer, at headquarters in Ceuta and Tetuán. It was toward 1929, and there he met Franco, Moscardó, and Millán Astray. He was invited to remain in the army, but he said no, it was too much of a sacrifice. He did not dare confess that he was an antimilitarist. He was discharged as a reserve sergeant. But when he joined the militia to fight against those military men whom he had known seven years before, he was made lieutenant. He went to the Aragon front, to the Massaluca mountains; there they were surrounded by the fascists for nine weeks.

"Even though our ideologies were different—socialists, communists, or anarchists—we all fought under the same flag, the Republic's."

Francesc rejects rank. At Robles he was asked to make a Communist Youth flag with the motto "Spain will never be fascist."

"We were convinced that fascism couldn't last."

He dislikes the phrase "civil war." He says that *that* was really an independence war, and he firmly believed it because La Pasionaria had said so.

> Borders were closed to us; but they were getting weapons from Portugal, and they had lots of Germans and Italians. If it had been a civil war it would have been over in three months. At the front, I was tired of hearing "Don't shoot, brothers, I'm coming over!" I dare say that about 80 percent were on the republican side. A civil war is fought among brothers from the same country, and not against foreigners as I saw. Many of the prisoners we took were German or Italian. So it was a war of independence and not a civil war.

Roc Llop, from the CNT, was born in Miravet. He was a grade-school inspector and during the war he put his pedagogical ideas into practice. Salvador Figueres was a war correspondent for *La Publicitat*. Josep Ambròs was a schoolteacher; his widow tells me:

> My husband felt his calling deeply. He wanted to elevate the people; he only thought of people. After we married he was assigned to Portella and

began to teach school according to his ideas. Parents looked at him with suspicion, mostly a few who said their children were very bad, young thieves, out of control. My husband paid no attention to them and began to treat those kids like people. In no more than a month those kids had changed. Not only were they not stealing, but my husband trusted them to sell school supplies to the others. Then, in the evening, after classes, he took them to the riverside to continue the lessons. He made fishing rods and took them all. The town mayor, seeing he was such an excellent teacher, wanted him to tutor his children exclusively, but my husband refused. The mayor got mad at him and then, after the war, when "his side" came into Portella, he took his revenge: he didn't let my children enjoy the free tuition they were entitled to as a teacher's children. My husband was a member of Esquerra, even though during the war he leaned toward socialism, providing that it was a Catalan socialism. On July 18th I saw my life end.

Josep Ambròs was to die aboard one of the death trains en route to Dachau. His widow is right: for her, July 18th meant the end of a great love. She goes on:

We'd been attracted to each other since we were seven or eight. He came from a very rich family in town, and I from one of the poorest. When Josep turned fourteen he went to Lleida, to study education, and I cried and cried. I tried to go to Lleida; I convinced my mother to put me in a religious school, and since we were penniless, I had to go as a ward. But we never saw each other, we just ran into each other once, on the Passeig, and he bought me an ice cream. I kept the little wooden spoon for I don't know how many years. The nuns wanted me to enter the convent, and as I could never see him, I didn't know what to do. Some time later I ran into him again and he told me to forget about becoming a nun. "Don't you see you have to marry me?" he said.

During the war, Josep was in Lleida, in the quartermaster's corps, and he was always in trouble because he took care not only of the soldiers but of everybody. When the "nationals" were at the gates of Lleida, we tried to leave together, the two of us and our two children, but all the roads were flooded by the fleeing crowds and there was no room. . . . Josep was unable to find us a car and told me, "I can stay no longer; the fascists are here," and he left. It was the last time I saw him.

Josep Ayxendri is from Tarragona; he fled from home when he was seventeen to go to the war. Joan de Diego, who is one of the few republicans to survive the camp among those who arrived there on the first day, is from the Fort Pius neighborhood, by the Marina bridge in Barcelona, a neighborhood with a strong labor tradition. Joan de Diego feels great nostalgia for Catalonia, Barcelona, and his neighborhood; he tells me what it was like, draws me a plan so I can follow the street battles of the gangs of friends. But Joan de Diego has never returned, from the day he crossed the border as a defeated man, because he says "he is still angry." And he adds that he would not recognize anything now, that years erase everything. He knows that today's Catalonia is not the same as it was, just like when he saw his mother after many years apart and did not recognize her.

Joan de Diego remembers many things from his early days, including names he heard often at home, such as Francesc Layret and Lenin.

My father used to read the newspaper out loud every day at home; he had clear diction and was a learned man. The neighbors came to our home and sat around the table to listen to the news of the first World War. . . . I remember the time of the thugs. They killed a union man, near a cloth-sizing workshop. Two men, dressed in the smocks workers used at the time, went up to him and shot him in front of us, in front of the kids playing in the neighborhood. Then they shed their smocks and left. My father used to take me to union meetings, and I was scared hearing everybody's shouts. I am still terrified of crowds. My father worked for the railroad; he was from Segovia and my mother from Avila. I am Castilian in origin but Catalan in feeling. My mother was an active participant in the 1917 strike. Today she is over ninety and still roots for the Barcelona soccer club. My father lost his job because of that strike and wasn't readmitted until 1931, with the Republic. My mother was in the strike's women's committee; they looted groceries and went to the demonstrations with their offspring, their youngest in their arms. They breast-fed them in front of the Civil Guard, who didn't dare touch them. The women's captain was a certain Senyora Antolina, a colonel's widow. She must have been fed up with militarism for she was very brave and stood in front of everybody with her hands on her hips waiting for the guards to charge. The women went in groups to steal coal from North Railway station and dragged the guards from their horses by grabbing their legs. They also forced the "ladies" walking by with their maids behind to join them. When they marched to the Civil Government's office, they forced the Marquis of Pilares to flee through the sewers as they climbed the building's stairs. Someone loosened the banister and many women fell off and were badly hurt.

So Joan de Diego does not want to return, because he is still angry. Likewise Josep Arnal, the friend of the writer Joaquim Amat-Piniella and of Pere Vives. Vives wrote a letter to Agustí Bartra from the French concentration camp: "Arnal is another magnificent guy. Quiet, sullen, but when the pressure inside him mounts he says things that knock you out. There is a silent relationship between us, built on things we need not say and on things we'll never say, but there is affection, and a good deal of it."[2] I also saw him quiet and sullen when I interviewed him.

Incredibly solid, and a man of an almost heroic clear-headedness when he recalled the happy days of his youth, when he was a draftsman full of promise and dreams, when he could still think of a harmonious future. Remembering the time that distance has made idyllic, the nights at Bataclan and Madame Petit's house, the nights in a Barcelona that has nothing to do with the graveyard it is today. "At the time I was a playboy," Arnal winks at me, a Catalan draftsman who ended up in one of the worse *Kommandos* in Mauthausen, Steyr's. Josep Arnal, born in Barcelona in 1909 the son of Aragonese parents, sold his comic strips to *TBO, Pocholo, KKO.* "We were a bunch of young draftsmen, the first to adopt the American style of having our characters speak with their words inside a little cloud. We also wrote up the sounds: *paf!, pum!, xop!, glu-glu,* and so on." Arnal created the famous dog Pif, who, from the pages of *L'Humanité,* has spread to the whole socialist world. There is a puppet theater in Leningrad where they constantly show the story of Pif and its family. Arnal worked for *Papitu* and *L'Esquella de la Torratxa,* which published his first sketch of Cametes, "Little legs."

Josep Ester is one of the founders of the Libertarian Youths of Berga. He studied with the Christian Brothers, a private school, and he still marvels at the number of left-wing people in Berga who came from Catholic schools. One of his best friends was Father Armengol, who founded a very different group in Berga, the Marian Congregations. Some years ago there was a mass to celebrate the reunion of the Christian Brothers' alumni. Father Armengol, who died in 1976, spoke from the pulpit, regretting that historical circumstances had prevented the presence of his old friend Ester. Talking about his libertarian origins, Ester smiles wistfully. A faithful CNT member, Josep Ester ended up in Mauthausen because of his participation in the resistance; he was an NN (*Nacht und Nebel,* "Night and Fog"), which meant he could be executed at any moment. One of the few deportees from a well-to-do family, he has preserved the dignified and aristocratic air of an uplands farmer. He has been one of the most even-handed witnesses; he always has a word for his old friends, such as Montero, a communist who died a strange death in Asturias in 1946.

The Nazi camps also held office workers such as Casimir Climent i Sarrion, the son of a Valencian father and an Asturian mother. When Climent was six his father would take him to see executed anarchists. His father forced him to go and told him, "Look at them well and fix this in your memory so that you don't end up like them." He fixed it in his memory, but to a different effect from that which his father had wanted. Other office workers were Bailina and Joan de Diego. The work these three Catalans carried out within the bureaucratic apparatus of the camp was invaluable. They preserved the lists of those dead in the crematoria; Climent i Sarrion, for example, kept track of all republicans coming into the camp and made a second list. Thanks to him we know the exact number of dead in Mauthausen and its *Kommandos*. A clear head, a work method learned before the war, meticulousness, order, and a good memory were the virtues of those three Catalans that made their work indispensable for the clandestine struggle.

Dídac Sabater, who died at Coswig camp, was a member of the Estat Català Council in Barcelona; his father had been a high official in the Badalona Town Hall. Francesc Boix, from Girona, finished medical school in Madrid and joined Izquierda Republicana. Many of the Catalans who were arrested for their participation in the resistance had liberal professions, while the great mass of those who went to Mauthausen, captured in France after the defeat, came from the humblest strata of Catalan society. Bernat Garcia, captured as a resistance fighter in Bordeaux and deported to Sachsenhausen, had a business degree and a job in the commercial department of the publishing house Proa in Badalona. These publishers moved to Barcelona's Carrer Pelayo; their offices were set afire when Franco's troops entered the city. Bernat Garcia remembers affectionately the writers Andreu Nin and Puig i Ferreter; of the latter he told me he was "nervous" but also "a great sentimental." Antoni Blanco i Blanch, of the CNT and an aide to the union leader Joan Peiró, considered himself a Catalan from Badalona, even though he had been born in a village in the province of Huesca. During the war Antoni Blanco became the manager of the collectivized factory, Casa Gros. He died in Gusen on September 11, 1941. Some boxing champions also died in Gusen: Joan Tosca i Blanch, Greco-Roman style champion; Dídac Lorenzo i Ribera; and Llorenç Vitrià i Barrera, a professional champion whom friends called "the wonder of the ring." Also Salvador Galobardes i Fuertes, a member of Estat Català; he had participated in the events of Prats de Molló with Francesc Macià. Catalans of all political tendencies died in Gusen, the outer *Kommando* of Mauthausen: Francesc Aymerich, of Esquerra Republicana de Catalunya and mayor of Palafrugell; Josep Sedó, of Acció Catalana; Josep Pons i Carceller, a schoolmaster in Tarragona who had paid for his studies delivering milk every morning; Jaume Castells, a mason from Hostalets de Balenyà; Antoni Sayós, a carpenter from the same town; Josep Iglesias, born in Sierradefuentes, province of Cáceres, and a worker in a cork factory in Palafrugell. Iglesias was a member of PSUC. A streetcar driver from Barcelona called Alegria, a member of CNT, died in Dachau.

Joan Pagès has a ruddy face, thick and protruding eyebrows; his lips, pursed whenever he is listening, open from time to time in a contemplative smile. Joan Pagès has always been a man of action, and in Mauthausen he decided to resist and help the resistance. He is from Palamós, a calm man who speaks slowly, mindful of detail. Joan Pagès did not stop fighting when he left Mauthausen; he was jailed by the Franco regime in 1951 with Gregori López Raimundo, the PSUC secretary general. Now he travels all over Catalonia introducing the film *Nuit et brouillard* as he tries to explain to those of us who did not live it what it meant to be in a Nazi extermination camp. At times someone in the audience, steeped in the historical ignorance of so many years of silence, asks a childish question; Pagès answers with a smile that is both ironic and sad. Joan Pagès is very tired; he has a bad heart and a stomach condition and, during his crises, can eat only mush, like a baby. But he does not tire of introducing the Resnais film, that tireless reminder of the evils of Nazism. He joined the Partit Comunista Català when he was seventeen in 1934. They told him that to be a good militant he had to pass a test: to argue politics with the anarchists in a public debate and, after the debate, face the horses and swords of the Guardia de Asalto.

> At the front I was the political commissar of my company. I can say I became a volunteer from day one. I was not yet twenty-two. I defended Catalonia's right to express its own personality as a free nation. Perhaps a simple autonomy was not enough for me; I wanted to go further, even though I understood, as I think I understand today, that if circumstances remain the same we shall be unable to detach ourselves from the rest of the Spanish state, or from the rest of the world for that matter. But we ought to have the same decision power as any other nationality.

Nineteen people from Manresa went to Mauthausen; thirteen died there. They all had voted Esquerra before July 18. Later some became members of PSUC, CNT, or Estat Català. Two men from Manresa were shop attendants: Jacint Carrió and Bernat Toran. Carrió became vice-president of CADCI in Manresa when he was twenty; in France he was departmental secretary of Esquerra Republicana de Catalunya for the Dordogne, where, among other things, he organized an homage to President Companys. Bernat Toran, who worked at Jorba's department store, died of exhaustion in Gusen in 1941. Joaquim Amat-Piniella, also from Manresa, died in 1974, but he had been carrying his death inside since he was freed in 1945. Manresa still owes him an homage and an apology for having expelled him until the late 1950s, when he went there to sign copies of his novel *K. L. Reich*.

Josep Escoda was born in Loà, in the Priorat. When he was eighteen he went to live in Tarragona. His mother was a widow, and so as not to abandon her, he enlisted as a volunteer in 1935. The *alzamiento* caught him when he was serving. His regiment was sent to the front immediately and liberated Alcanyís. His whole regiment went into exile except for General Garcia Rebull, who participated in the infamous Burgos trials of December 1970, and the Landa brothers, who with some others hid and deserted to the other side. Escoda was wounded in Belchite. When the Popular Army's mixed brigades were formed, he joined Brigade 142 of the 32d Division under Colonel Manuel Gansedo. He was a militant of no party but a convinced republican and very progressive. As a boy he had lived in Terrassa and grew up among Casa del Poble people and in the spirit of Esquerra Republicana de Catalunya. Once, when he was fourteen, Francesc Macià shook his hand, and he remembers he did not wash it for a whole week.

Joan Sarroca's parents were farmers from Benissanet. His father, when he saw Joan's progress in his studies, sent him to the high school in Mora d'Ebre. He was sixteen when the war broke out; he was one of the organizers of the JSUC at his school and soon left as a volunteer for the front. He belonged to the 5th Corps of the Republican army whose commissariat he joined as a Joventuts instructor. The army had many illiterates, and Sarroca worked as a teacher. Later he moved on to the Servei Especial d'Informació Perifèric, a corps that tried to infiltrate the enemy camp.

> I was sector head, with the rank of lieutenant, until the end of the war. My parents crossed the border as refugees. There they separated and my father was sent to the concentration camp in Sant Cebrià. He ended up in Mauthausen, like me, but we never saw each other. He died in Gusen and I didn't know about it until a year later.

Eventually Sarroca learned that his father had died there, as had the fathers of the Cortès brothers, Alcubierre, Nos Fibla, Valsells, and Avinyó. These were the younger of the deportees, called *Poschacher*, most of whom were deportees from the Angouleme group. It was important to save them. It was important they not be "touched" in either body or spirit; this was one of the goals of the "older." Among the *Poschacher* some were thirteen, such as Quesada and the younger Cortès, both from Prat de Llobregat.

Ramon Milà was also very young; he had just turned fifteen when the war broke out.

I wanted to be a pilot and would build model airplanes, but couldn't enlist because they said I was too young. I worked as a kitchen helper in a restaurant in Aigua Fresca. My father was a good pantry man and had worked at the Orient, the Ritz, and other hotels. He was the treasurer of FOSIG, the hostelry division of UGT. He was captured in Figueres and could not escape. He spent a few years in prison; he was a fighter. He first belonged to Esquerra and later became a communist. The Franco regime condemned him to death, but he got spared because he was a great cook; the prison officers wanted him to cook for them. Toward 1950 he was arrested again and when he was released, was forced to report weekly until he was almost eighty. His age brought him no respect. I was not allowed to see him, and he was denied the papers to go to France. I finally saw him shortly before he died. He was eighty-four.

Ramon Milà had worked as a waiter in a German beer house on Passeig de Gràcia. It was frequented by the bigwigs, and he recalls people such as Líster, Trueba, Comorera. He wanted to go to the front, but they would not let him and he sat listening to the adventures of his customers. He wanted to participate in some way and joined Red Aid, and for a long time helped remove bodies from bombed buildings. When the Franco troops entered Barcelona his whole family had to flee because they had been active in the fight against fascism. Only one of his grandmothers remained; she saw the Franco people confiscate all she had in her home. Ramon Milà's mother went to the women's camp in Sant Cebrià; Milà recalls the last time he saw her:

I went over from my camp with a soldier behind me pushing me with the tip of his bayonet. I would see her no more. She went back to Barcelona and lived thinking that at any moment her husband would be shot and she'd never know what happened to me. In 1943 she suffered pleurisy and I think she let herself die. She looked for me like a crazed one. . . .

Another very young deportee was Miquel Serra, one of the witnesses who knows written Catalan well since he belongs to the "Republic generation" and learned it at school in Roda de Ter. Miquel Serra was the son of a basketmaker and, like Ramon Milà, was just fifteen when the war started. "My father belonged to CNT and I joined the JSU de Catalunya. But I might have become a *balilla* if I had been born on the other side. Only when I crossed the border did I realize the republicans were right in doing what they did."

Francisco Cortès fled Almeria and hunger with his wife and seven children. They found their way to Prat del Llobregat. There his children all learned Catalan and became assimilated. In Prat, the Cortès family would see one of their sons die at nineteen and two more children born. The father was a shoemaker and the eldest son, Pepe, soon found a job in the paper mill. Jacint Cortès was thirteen at the outset of the war; his brother Manolo was eleven. They wanted to join JSU de Catalunya but were not admitted as they were too young. They resigned themselves to joining Peoners de Catalunya, the Scouts. Their gang of friends would walk all the way to Gavà and look for iron in the rubble, wherever they could find any, and thus contributed to a war they felt was their own. They listened to their elders talk about the battles, read the letters from their brother Pepe who was at the Ebro front, and thought it all a great, extraordinary adventure. Pepe had left for the front full of enthusiasm and conviction; he was the family's idol and a master in political issues in the eyes of Jacint and Manolo. After the bombing of the Soviet ship Konsomol, these brothers sold stamps to collect money. Little Manolo was the champion collector in all of Prat. Jacint Cortès turned sixteen the day he crossed the Pyrenees into France. From that day he has never set foot in Catalonia again.

Jaume Arnaud was born in Montlluís in Roussillon and was barely twenty when the Nazis invaded France. He went to war against Germany in 1939, was made prisoner, and after fleeing the prisoners-of-war camp, joined the resistance. When I met him in the Amical de Mauthausen in Paris and he learned I was from Barcelona, talked to me in Catalan.

All the Catalan women who were deported had fought in the French resistance. Most of them also came from the working classes or from the peasantry. Two of them, Sabina and her mother, had immigrated to the Pyrenees area; Coloma Serós was a Lleida schoolteacher; Neus Català came from a farming family; three were textile workers; some were active militants in different political parties, such as Roser Fluvià and Mònica Gené of Estat Català; others belonged to CNT, PSUC, or, like Carme Boatell,[3] were union women:

> My parents had an offal meat shop on Plaça Sant Antoni in the Sants area of Barcelona. I worked in the Oller i Planells textile factory. During the war I belonged to the factory committee. A Red Aid group was also created there, and we named it Lina Odena after our fellow worker who committed suicide near Guadix in order not to be captured by the Franco people at the outset of the military uprising. During the retreat I was wounded in my legs by shrapnel. I had gone to Figueres as a volunteer, to the hospital, to help evacuate the wounded; the fascists half destroyed it. Franco's troops were entering Figueres; all who could fled, but I couldn't walk, my legs were damaged. Two anarchists came by and, in a jiffy, mounted me on one of their horses. An evacuation hospital was being set up in Port de la Selva for

a PSUC regiment, but only admitted men. They wouldn't take me because I was a woman. I thought: "I better give them my sob story, or else I won't get anywhere; I don't feel like crying, but more like slapping them." They took me in. Later I crossed the border with the hospital people. I was still wounded when I got to Perpinyà.

("I was the only 'red' in the family," Dolors Gener explains.)

I remember a day on the Barcelona Rambla—during the war—I ran into an uncle of mine, from the village. When he saw me, he came fast, all angry, his eyes on fire, but he controlled himself before he'd slap me. Even my first cousin was killed by our side.

In 1936 I belonged to the Lleida chapter of Joventuts Socialistes Unificades de Catalunya. I was a greenhorn and thought communists were janitors who cleaned *comunes* [communal toilets]. First I joined the group in my town, Alcoletge, on the road to Balaguer; later I was sent to the JSUC congress in Barcelona as a member of the Lleida province delegation. I slowly got involved. I was sent to a youth school in Lleida, and there met Avellina Pijoan, Aurèlia, Pere Ardiaca, a German comrade, and others who taught me many things. Years later in Ravensbrück's death camp, I saw three fellow women hanged, one of them, Mimi, a republican, and I remembered the Lleida school where I had learned so many things. That memory helped me stand the spectacle, gave me inner strength, and I did not lose my morale seeing those three girls die. I was also sent to the Huesca front, to Del Barrio's column, with the medics. They were all communists there, from the stretcher carriers to the doctors, and I really got the bug then—I mean, my eyes opened, for I used to be a devout Catholic at the time.

At the front I met my husband. We married in 1938 in Molins de Rei. When I crossed the border I wasn't twenty yet.

Joan Mestres still lives in exile. This is how he left his homeland:

I was born in Mola south of Tarragona, some fifteen kilometers from Mora d'Ebre. My parents were farmers and goatherders. My father got tuberculosis and had to sell his lands and goats. He then went to work in the lead mines of the Priorat, between Bellmunt i Mola, but he was no longer good for anything: the mines finished off his lungs. My mother would buy material from the dime store and sell it in the nearby villages. She earned the whole family's keep. When I was fourteen they sent me to the mine to work as a mechanic's apprentice. I worked my twelve-hour shift and then went to learn to be a barber. I was also in charge of the theater of the Societat Obrera Republicana; we performed plays by Guimerà and Iglésies. Theater was my passion, and it has helped me in my meetings and rallies. The Societat gathered people of many tendencies which helped me against sectarianism; there were anarchists—the dominant group at the time—republicans, radicals, and some of us who were the left wing of the republican youth. Macià was our hero.

In 1928 I went to Barcelona to work with a barber. "If you really want to live, go to France," he'd tell me. "No, I can't leave here; this is my country," I replied.

Was I wrong! I did my military service in Girona in 1932; I became the officers' barber and I soon saw that the republic ended in the mess hall. A group of us were convinced republicans, all friends. Some anarchists from Sabadell and some from the Bloc Obrer i Camperol were also friends. We had a rabid anti-Catalanist sergeant who called the roll, and we always answered "Present!" in Catalan. He punished us all, and a friend, Riera, was thrown in the lockup; he was to die at the beginning of the war. We refused to pledge allegiance if they didn't free Riera and went to see a congressman from Girona who was a republican. He told us Congress wouldn't touch the military. We replied that the military were not on the side of the Republic. Most of the officers in that fort had fought with Franco in Africa.

At the beginning of the war the most dynamic of us left at once for the front. I used to belong to Joventuts Republicanes, but as soon as it was founded I joined the PSUC. I was on the front in Aragon, in the Pàndols mountains, until the end, and I took part in the battle of the Ebro in Tagüeña's brigade. A week later, out of three thousand, only three hundred were alive. The fascists killed almost everyone. Bombings, explosions everywhere. I have never seen so many dead. Only in the German camps. But, dying or not, we were all fighting. We managed to swim across the Ebro; it was bodily combat. They said our brigade, the 140th, was the one that had fought the hardest. We stayed near the Segre until we returned to Barcelona. When we arrived, crossing Diagonal Avenue, we Catalans could not contain our tears because we had thought we'd never make it back. We saw the fascists coming down from Montjuïc, the empty streets, the women looting the flour warehouses. This is my last vision of Barcelona. And we retreated and retreated until we crossed over into France the night of February 10."

A taxi drops me off in a workingclass area on the outskirts of the French city of B____. The building walls are crumbling, their color is a dirty pink. House numbers have been changed and I cannot find T____'s house. He is an old fighter, one of those who organized the resistance at Mauthausen. I hear voices in Castilian, and I inquire about T____'s address. "Many Spaniards live here, you know. I think the person you want is a retired gentleman three houses down."

I go down three houses. The staircase is cold, humid, sticky. B____ is a foggy, quiet city. An old man opens the door. He is not very tall and I can barely see his face. He is wearing a beret, a scarf that girds his neck and mouth, a heavy sweater, and wool slippers. "Come in," he says. "I was just going to the balcony to feed the birds."

His apartment is dark, as dark as his neighborhood and city. It is difficult to picture a man like T___ in this atmosphere, so far from his past, from his memories. It is as if I had gone to meet a man who had nothing to do with his image: the shadow of a powerful past now seeping out among the mists of a provincial French city, his balcony birds, his retirement. He sits in a wide armchair, leans on a cane, and starts to speak. He tires easily; his breathing becomes heavy. Then he closes his eyes and rests for a few moments before he speaks again. The journey back into his memories is slow, almost painful.

"Exile lets you know a man," he says. "I don't recall who said that, perhaps Marx, or Lenin."

T___ explains to me that his nightmares did not subside completely until less than a year ago. He shows me the letter of a French deported woman who ended up in Mauthausen after Ravensbrück was evacuated. They met in the camp's laundry after he had been expelled from the officers' kitchen because there was a radio there and they did not want him to learn the news about the war. "My memories of the republicans I met in Mauthausen," the letter reads, "of your organized solidarity in favor of women, will never leave me. And I shall also remember you, my friend, who being my age, twenty-one, explained to me like a true comrade how to solve many problems in a most valuable manner."

T___ is the child of farmers. His parents fled hunger from their village of Vilosell near Lleida and came down to Tarragona. T___ became a bellhop in the Hotel Europa. He was nine. With the tips he got, he was earning more than his father, who worked other people's land. He had always liked his books, but had to miss the review sessions because evening was the busiest time at the hotel. His learning, he says, is quite anarchic. Later his father took a job as bricklayer, and he went to Madrid; it was 1930. There he joined the Juventudes Libertarias. But he came back to Catalonia with a thirst for learning about politics. He took a job as a waiter at the Bar Nin, in Tarragona. He felt hunger again because, for food, he only received a bun and sardines.

One day Valdés went to Bar Nin. T___ was reading a Trotskyite magazine edited in Vendrell. "What are you reading?" Valdés asked him. T___ showed him the magazine and Valdés explained to him that it was trash. "I'll bring you something better," he said. The next day he gave him a copy of Lenin's *State and Revolution*. T___ read it in one gulp and immediately requested admission into the Partit Comunista Català. He organized its Youths in Tarragona and later the waiters' union.

Then he met Lina Odena and her tailor friend. "One day in 1934 I was marching down the Tarragona Rambla with my raised fist,"

T____ tells me. "My friend Ayxendri was with me and we ran into his father. Right there and then his father slapped him. And he gave me a nasty look, Ayxendri's father, thinking that I was leading his son astray."

On the Aragon front, T____ served in the 31st Division commissariat. In 1937 his sector started the retreat toward France and crossed the border at Benasc. In Banyeres de Luixon the soldiers were sorted out: those who wanted to go with Franco from those who wanted to go with the Republic. The latter were locked up in the Casino. The police prohibited the people of Perpinyà from bringing them food. When he returned to Catalonia all the stations were crowded with people and red flags. The International Red Aid was there and gave them food, tobacco, and medicine for the sick. T____ rejoined the 31st Division, now reorganized and under Trueba's command, and was sent to the Tremp sector. Soon after, he was given home leave and saw his wife. He did not know then that it would take them nine years to see each other again.

"They were the worse years of my life," T____'s wife tells me.

> My father-in-law was in jail. To ward off starvation, I took a job at a factory in a village near Tarragona. My mother-in-law lived next door to a convent school which had been converted into a women's prison. Whenever I went to visit I would hear from the rear balcony the screaming and howling of the women who were being dragged off to their executions. Still some women would sing the *International*. I couldn't stand all that. And no news from my husband.

From Tragó de Noguera, Benissanet, Mola, Badalona, Manresa, Alcoletge, Palamós. Teachers, draftsmen, farmers, barbers, waiters, young scouts, adolescents, immigrants from poorer areas of Spain, volunteers to the Spanish war. These are our deportees, our "reds," the "criminals" who crossed the border early in 1939. These are the ones who were locked up like cattle, treated like subhumans in the Nazi extermination camps. From provincial towns, rural areas, the city; from the working or the middle class; farmers, fugitive Catalans, defeated, twice the victims of the irrationality of fascism.

They could not return home. Franco had stated so very clearly in his Law of Political Responsibilities of February 13, 1939. That law was against them; at home they would be welcomed by overcrowded prisons, the fear of execution at any dawn. Their crime had been defined by the Franco legislation: they had opposed the Movimiento, fought against the military uprising from day one, declared publicly in favor of the Republic and of the Generalitat de Catalunya, done so freely, and had certainly not recanted before July 18, 1936.

Their long exodus was beginning. Our deportees had experienced the most sinister aspect of that exodus that was to engulf thousands of Catalans. The lucky ones managed to flee to America; others remained in France and survived the Nazi occupation; but the deportees experienced the most turbulent aspects of German fascism. Many died during that exodus, some survived it and became another kind of person, one that had little to do with those who had enlisted to fight the Franco troops; they had become someone else.

NOTES

1. His name was Francesc Teix. I interviewed him in October 1974. He died in June 1975. He asked me not to publish his name; I hope I am not betraying his will by revealing his name now. He died in exile.

2. *Cartes des dels camps de concentració* (Barcelona: Edicions 62, 1972).

3. Carme Boatell died May 31, 1976, in Perpinyà.

A Note on Espriu's
"Two Parables"

Born in Santa Coloma de Farners but a resident of Barcelona, where he practiced law, Salvador Espriu i Castelló (1913–1985) nevertheless identified in his writings with his summer residence, the fishing town of Arenys de Mar, a few miles north of Barcelona. Espriu situated most of his writings in the mythical town of Sinera (for Synera, acronym of Arenys). He also assimilated into his fiction a number of Sinera characters, such as Ecolampadi Miravitlles, Pulcre Trompelli, and Efrem Pedagog, and gave them mythical as well as local dimensions. Sinera was Espriu's archetypal town, and he imagined stories from biblical narratives and Greek myths reincarnated there. His most famous plays, *Ronda de mort a Sinera* and *Primera Història d'Esther,* are productions in which ancient heroes mingle with the popular figures of Sinera: a schoolteacher, a concierge, a beggar, and so on.

This mythical bent and his interest in the Old Testament set Espriu apart from other writers of his generation. The ancient imagery shaped his allegorical and satirical modes. The two short stories or parables given here are clear examples of this. In his work Espriu idealized all of Spain under the name of Sepharad, the ancient Hebrew name for the Iberian Peninsula, and also under the phrase "the bull hide" (from the popular observation that a map of Spain looks like a bull hide hanging in a

tannery). "The bull hide," *La pell de brau,* is the title of Espriu's most
politically ambitious book of verse. Within Sepharad, in a number of Es-   147
priu's postmodern mythologies, Catalonia became the hapless Konilòsia
with its busy capital city Lavínia, all dominated by a profit-first spirit.

The two parables translated here evince Espriu's lashing wit.
One lambasts blind optimism in the figure of Doctor Mestres (who appears
almost as a New Age guru); the other chastises the proverbial greed of
Catalans and their lack of feeling for their own country.

Two details from the second parable require explanation. The
reference to Africa is of course an example of European ethnocentrism and
prejudice; it also refers to a well-known French dictum, "Africa begins at
the Pyrenees," a phrase meant to mark the backwardness of nineteenth-
century Spain. Catalans have often felt that the phrase ought to be modi-
fied into "Africa begins at the Ebro"; one of Espriu's best-known poems,
"Assaig de càntic en el temple," portrays the poet's desire to flee "up
north," where people are reputedly clean, wise, smart, and happy. The
reference to Aina Cohen is explained by Espriu himself in a note to the
original edition: "I have christened my character thus because I did not
think it proper to call her by any other name: Aina Cohen, the exemplary
creation in *Mort de Dama,* the admirable novel by 'Dhey,' Doctor Llorenç
Villalonga, the great writer from Majorca." A vapid and apolitical rhyme-
ster, the fictional Aina Cohen represents everything a poet should not be.

Even though Espriu was also a short-story writer and played a
pivotal role in the renewal of the Catalan stage during the Franco dictatorship, his reputation rests predominantly on his poetry. His works, whether
lyrical or satirical, prod his readers to a higher commitment to their country. One of his poems commands:

> Ara digueu:
> Ens mantindrem fidels per sempre més
> al servei d'aquest poble.

> Say after me:
> We shall remain faithful forever
> in the service of our people.

Catalonia's existence as a nation without a state invites writers
to assume the heroic mode more readily than their colleagues from nations
that have no problems of self-identity. Catalonia tends to have "national"
writers. For this reason Espriu is comparable to Joan Maragall; each represents for his respective generation the voice of conscience of the country.

But Espriu, whose literature came of age during the Spanish Civil War and the harsh dictatorial regime that followed it, could not share Maragall's romantic optimism. Espriu's portrayal of the corrupt upper classes in "Crisant's Theory," for example, would be unthinkable in Maragall. For Espriu, the poet is a seer like the Greek Tiresias, who dares speak uncomfortable truths; his portrayal of Catalonia within modern Spain is a harsh reproof to a people who have not risen to the challenges of their destiny.

These two parables were originally published in 1935 in the collection *Ariadna al laberint grotesc*. Espriu revised them for later publication, as he often did with his work; my translation follows the last revised edition, published in Barcelona by Edicions 62 in 1974.

SALVADOR ESPRIU

Two Parables

CRISANT'S THEORY

Crisant Baptista Mestres, an eloquent man with a medical degree and a taste for belles lettres and philosophical vagaries, which are, they say, most entertaining hobbies, had never felt the need to work for a living until he suddenly lost all of his rich patrimony. "Crisant, dear, there isn't a whole lot of food at home," his loving wife reminded him. "Let me orient myself, Laudelina," Crisant requested. "I've got it!" he exclaimed at last. "We'll soar, I'm telling you." "Don't forget we need bread," Laudelina started again. "Think with purity. That's it! My theory," declared Crisant, satisfied. "OK, but what'll we do to eat?" insisted his wife. "Nothing more than thinking with purity," Crisant cut in. "An infallible system for prospering, my girl. Oh, what a brain, mine, what a man I am, one of the best! You'll see what results! And in no time!" Crisant promised, full of optimism. "Purity Thinking: a method for conserving a healthy body, combatting all ills, and lengthening one's life. Office: Dr. Crisant B. Mestres. 15 Carrer Galatea." He broadcast this notice throughout the country. "Think with purity. How intelligent you are, my young friend!" he told his first client. "Think with purity and you'll get well." "What'd he tell you, what'd he prescribe?" people asked the first one to try the new system. "He didn't mention any prescriptions, but told me very profitable things instead." "I get it, he's a psychiatrist," people guessed. "Or perhaps a psychoanalyst," they hesitated. And in order to find out they rushed to Number 15 Carrer Galatea. "Come in, ladies and gentlemen, come in," invited Crisant. "I will straighten you all out very soon. What a noble cranium you have! Think with purity," he told one of them. "You are rich and, besides, you know how to be rich, I can tell. You deserve your wealth, and whoever would vilify it would commit a monstrous wrong; think with purity," he advised another. "How bold you are! No, no: *bold,* not old, didn't I speak clearly? Think with purity," he waxed before a third one. "What a charismatic man, and he has cured me completely; he is a thaumaturge," the lucky ones exclaimed. "Oh, Master Mestres!" they intoned. "You're the best," Crisant granted them. "What, do we have enough food now?" he asked his wife. "We won't be able to eat it all, dear," Laudelina replied enthusiastically. "You really *are* the best." "Think with purity," Crisant reminded her. "I do, I do," agreed a very happy Laudelina. And the sick filled the office at Number 15 Galatea at all hours, and they all strove to think with great purity and were sustained by their simple conviction of being the best. "I am the best, am I not, doctor?" asked old Tobies Comes, rotten with earthly possessions. "I am the best, am I not, Crisant?" inquired Count Trinitat Castellfollit, who at the time was the first purse of the country. "You are the best," Crisant confirmed separately to Tobies and the count. "All you need now is to think with purity." "Hooray!" exulted both principled gentlemen and the legion that followed them. "Long live Crisant the Psychopathologist!" And they all enjoyed in private the sweetness of the news, of Crisant's gospel. "I am the best, I am the best," decrepit Tobies chanted as he pruned himself in front of a mirror. And, snap, he fell to the floor as if hit by lightning and debuted as a corpse. "Crisant, my old relative Tobies was seized all of a sudden, and he's now stiffer and colder than an Englishman, and he had the same condition I do," Crisant was informed by Count Castellfollit, who, rigid with fear, nevertheless boasted a sense of humor. "Do not take it that way, my dear count. Quite different cases, yours and Tobies's. Frankly, I never managed to make our defunct friend think with purity. He was not one of the best, that Tobies Comes. But you, my dear Castellfollit, you *are* one, for sure," Crisant pacified him. "Thank you, thank you," cried a euphoric count. "Charge me what you will." "I want nothing but to do good deeds; I am a modest man," said Crisant. "I understand. You're a soul that would earn beatitude before its time, God forbid, if your friends didn't take care of you. No, I insist, not before you sit among immortals, for example, in the Academy of the Language," the all-powerful Trinitat told him. "No, no, please," Crisant sputtered most adroitly. "No way. Relax. Make this sacrifice for me," the count begged him. And Crisant was made Academician (one of the unconfessed dreams of his life), appointed to the Board of the

National Bank, elected as a deputy to the Parliament, chosen as president of the Fellowship of Discalced Indians, and endowed as professor of Characteriologic Graphology at the University, where he was immediately surrounded by many disciples, and among them his favorite: Amaranta, Pupú Alosa, Ludovicus Baronet, Maria Victòria Prou, Mimí Pitosporos, and two or three silent supernumeraries; they formed a closed, hermetic circle, that of Crisant's orthodox doctrine. "How they love him!" people said as they saw that distinguished coterie. "You are the best," Crisant graded them in his intimacy. And he spread the praises of his apostles. "What beautiful hands you have, Amaranta! And you, Alosa, how well you move them! And you, Baronet, what beautiful silence! Silence is the best of qualities, because it allows us to think with purity," he indoctrinated them. "And you, Victòria, what fineness of spirit! And you, Mimí, what a voice, how talkative! The art of talking is the best quality, because it allows you to express your thoughts with purity. And you," he told the two or three remaining supernumeraries, "you are also the best, because you admire me, and you admire so purely your fellow students." "Glory to Crisant!" the whole country cheered. And he was offered, as an homage, a dinner for five thousand guests. "Thank you, ladies and gentlemen," Crisant started at speech time, "thank you for your showers of one and many flowers." "A poet, man, a poet! A thaumaturge, a financier, an academician, a patron, and now a poet," people ejaculated. "And above all, a teacher. How he loves his disciples, how he stimulates them, how he helps them, how he knows them, what a great school of clinicians he has created! What about Baronet's silence, Amaranta's hands, Alosa's gestures, Mimí's conversation, or Victòria's delicacy of spirit?" "You can be sure about it, they are great clinicians," the audience acknowledged. "I have heard, my dear professor, about yesterday's honors," Princess Bijou Fontrodona told him the day after the gala. "N'est-ce pas, maman?" "Oui, ma fille, une journée tout à fait historique," the moth-eaten duchess Stephana Martin agreed, eating up a yawn. "I am sure I was missed there, as I am the only princess in the country," Bijou added. "And the best," the great man interposed gallantly. "You are adorable," said the princess, pleased as Punch. "But I was unable to attend, as you can imagine, because of the prince, my husband." "Yes, of course, the prince," said Crisant. Then the three of them sighed. "And what do you plan to do now, what are your projects?" Bijou was interested. "Just a book," the great man revealed confidentially to her. "A book in which no doubt you will expound your curative doctrine; how terrific," the kind princess reflected. "Yes, and also a kind of confession, an autobiography. For I am to disclose to you, my dear ladies, my hidden tragedy. In reality I am not a clinician, nor a financier, nor a patron of discalced Indians, or a characterologist, or an academician, or a poet. I am a philosopher. As a young man I followed the teachings of Efrem Pedagog, a sublime genius, and Efrem considered me the best of his disciples. I owe him all of my doctrine. Then life and circumstances took over, and no one has been able to perceive the philosopher in me. But I am nothing else—or I am a failure: this is what I want to tell in my book." "Really, a philosopher?" commented Bijou with a certain dryness in her voice. But she soon reacted. "How naughty you are, Crisant! A philosopher, a failure. Your ambition has no limits, my dear friend." They all laughed; Crisant's ears turned red because of his psychological blunder. "This reminds me," the duchess said when they all calmed down. "I wanted to ask you to do me a favor, Crisant: nothing much, an obligation I have contracted. It's about Melània, an old student of yours." "Melània, Melània," Crisant tried to remember. "Ah, yes, Melània attended my classes for three years in a row. Duchess, not another word, I beg you, she is an unbearable girl. She never accepted my theory, she slanted it, she thought on her own, and I do not like such independence. Melània does not belong, so to speak, in the elite of the best," Crisant explained. "Ask me, instead, whatever you will for Mimí, or for Baronet, or as a favor to Amaranta, Alosa, or Victòria."

THE DYING COUNTRY

The country that had lost its soul sat empty-handed near the port and was sadly eyeing the dead waters when I arrived. "I shall soon be like them. It's obvious; I express nothing, nothing authentically mine. I shall soon be like these waters, an indifferent mirror," it exclaimed. "Not at all!" I replied. "You're a great, a formidable country." "How do you know?" shouted the poor old country, reviving a little because there is nothing more prone to ephemeral revivals than poor old countries. "How do you know?" it said, falling again into despair. "I am a shadow, a carcass. You see, this was the hub and the way of my glory," it said, pointing to the port. "From here the ships sailed toward their conquests, from here came the wise laws of the seas, my proud banner. Now, however, it is old and dying like myself. And its senility is disguised, like my own, under a makeup of theatrical adjectives. Lost are the cadences of my imperial language. It is now shouted, clauses are left hanging, emphasis is conveyed by blasphemies and paleolithic gestures. It has become a Volapük with neither intimacy nor delicacy, without hues, clotted with sibylline, cold, pedantic, unbearable words. Nobody reads in it, and the little literature they cultivate in it, measly, amorphous, gray, without personality or enthusiasm, has no other purpose than to serve electoral ends. My children take no interest in their own minds and have lost all tradition of culture and finesse. Materialists that they are, they imitate alien techniques. I am, you can see, a country without a soul. And precisely now, dying and tired, I am forced to live a grotesque masquerade, the dream of an ambitious mind, a mean grimace. I am but an anachronistic medieval silhouette." "No, you are a great country, a country with a future, damn it!" I interrupted. "A medieval silhouette? So what! Do you know how important that is? Haven't you read Spengler, Berdyaev, the papers, people who have seen God face to face, the university-trained descendants of the prophets? Your time is come, the time for your sea, for your language, for your empire, for your glory, for your mind." "The best in the world," shouted a distant and patriotic choir. "You're rich, you're learned," I went on. "What do you say about your dance?" "The most beautiful in the world," the choir intoned. "And about your popular song?" "There's none other, tra-la-la," sang the choir. "And about your prosperous hospitals, your public peacefulness, your urban neatness, the goodness of the people of your countryside? You can no longer spit, no longer mobilize more beggars, no longer ignore more than you ignore. Everything has a limit, you have reached it, you cannot demand anything else from your effort. Dying? Many would like to be as healthy as you are, as stalwart! You want proof? What other proof do you need but your great city, a model of anarchy, pretentious, nouveau riche, without comforts?" "The best of all," exulted the choir. "Of course, we cannot deny that none other has its Palau de la Música, its Gran Metro," the country concurred. "And you may add the critical sense of its inhabitants, listen to them," I told it. "One cannot live in this hovel," said the voice of Efrem Pedagog. "What will Adler and the Hungarians think of us?" "Hélas, hélas, la bêtise humaine!" recited the harmonious throat of Pulcre Trompelli. "We belong to a fifth- or perhaps sixth-class country," Ecolampadi Miravitlles stated with clear satisfaction. "Not long ago the Germans organized a colossal competition. The theme to develop was: 'African origins of cretinism among peoples and countries.' We won it." "We won? This is the pleasant, the only good news!" an excited Aina Cohen, the illustrious poetess, said. "Can't you hear the nightingale's song in celebration of victory? There, in the old folk's manor, while the old man—

"He listens to the birdling's song so sweet
and weighs his figs in the realm of sleep.
His venerable head feels the congestion
under the simmering rhythm of a pot of rice."

"Don't forget, brothers and sisters, that we are the favorite of our lord,"
the smooth rhapsode added, after unleashing and accepting enthusiastic
applause. "Didn't you hear Aina, didn't you hear her? Are you convinced,
now?" I asked the country. "Yes," it said, moved. "But I am so ancient! It
is cold, my head spins, I'm dying!" it screamed suddenly. The stroke was
fatal, and I had no time to help. Its body fell with a splash into the calm
waters, at a solitary spot, and I was the only witness. "Must I get wet for its
sake?" I pondered. "We'll find another one, a better one. I am going to
cable in the news, it's more important than attempting to save it. What a
scoop!" I reflected as I left the spot. "What's this idiot saying?" my fellow
citizens demanded the next morning when they read my telegram.
"What's it say?: 'Old country drowned yesterday port waters. Body uniden-
tified.' Well, the country died. Great! We even have a country that dies.
Let's see, we want details." That day the city desks at the newspapers
worked feverishly and compensated for the usual editorial penury: at least
fifty newspapers in our language were sold, in that language which with
such delicate adoration some call our vernacular.

III.

People

A Note on Pla's
"Antoni Gaudí (1852–1926)"

Josep Pla i Casadevall was born in Palafrugell on March 8, 1897, and died in nearby Llofriu on April 23, 1981. Both towns are in the area called Empordà, an area that, in great part due to Pla's writings, has acquired a reputation for natural beauty (the famed Costa Brava is in its littoral) and for the indomitable spirit of its people. The *empordanès* Pla, however, earned his living mostly as a journalist and in particular as a foreign correspondent, and thus traveled far and frequently.

During his lifetime Pla became the most popular—meaning he had a most substantial sales volume—of all Catalan authors. He was also prolific, the author of a vast body of work consisting mainly of his observations of contemporary reality. His writings may be considered, as he himself implied, as a large autobiography or rather an ongoing essay on everything he saw. An early literary model of his was Michel de Montaigne, whose conception of the world as *ondoyant,* "wavy," Pla echoed. Pla's mature prose is steeped in the kind of detached irony practiced by Montaigne.

In spite of his popularity, Pla received little critical acclaim until late in his career. He was the bête noire of the Catalan literary establishment after the Civil War, considered by many a traitor to the Catalan cause. This reputation stems mainly, it seems, from the fact that during the Civil War Pla fled to Rome. How he managed to earn his keep there is unclear (the writer himself never threw any light on this subject), but he came to be suspected of spying for the Franco side while working for the exiled conservative politician Francesc Cambó, who did aid the Franquistas. This skeleton in Pla's closet kept him from ever receiving the much-coveted Premi d'Honor de les Lletres Catalanes, for which he was proposed but always turned down, in favor at times of much lesser writers.

Pla's literary ambition was to write as keen a portrait of Catalonia as he would have time to do. Indeed, many of his pages are devoted to *el país,* "the country," Catalonia. He also excelled at travel literature, writing many informative and amusing pages on most of the countries in Europe. One of his projects was the series called *Homenots.* The word *homenot,* an augmentative of *home,* "man," signifies something in between "great guy" and "big man" but in any case is a rather irreverent term that caused a few raised eyebrows among his more pious readers. The piece on Gaudí translated here is one of the essays from that collection. The intention of the *Homenots* was to provide, in some forty or fifty pages, a portrait of a man (all the characters in his series are men) in a way that would be informative, precise, readable, and true to the human aspects of his subject. In this homenot Pla concentrates on Gaudí's most ambitious work, the Sagrada Família, a building planned by the ecclesiastical authorities as an expiatory temple and popularly considered a cathedral (which it is not, canonically speaking) because of its grandiose proportions. Pla's essay seeks to illuminate why such a monumental project was undertaken at a time when cathedral building could only be seen as anachronistic, and how such a fundamentalist group as the one that promoted the temple came to accept the innovator Gaudí for its chief architect.

Pla's stylistic ambition (for readability more than simplicity) caused him to part ways with the *noucentista* school prevalent at the time of his literary debut. His view of Gaudí should be contrasted with the passing references to the architect's work we saw in the selection by Carles Soldevila, "The Art of Showing Barcelona." Not only does Pla defend Gaudí, but he shows his contempt for the snobbish intellectual world that rejected him. If the present state of affairs in matters of taste is any indication, Pla has proved farsighted in his appreciation; Gaudí is nowadays considered one of the great names in the history of architecture (see, for example, the passing praise lavished on Gaudí by Baltasar Porcel in another essay in this anthology). Yet the polemic about his great unfinished work has not died down; the more fashionable intellectuals in Barcelona still oppose quite vehemently the continuation of the work. Today the

polemic spares Gaudí and centers on Josep Maria Subirachs, who accepted
the commission to carve all the sculptures for the temple.

Pla compares Gaudí to the great medieval philosopher and
mystic Ramon Llull (known also by the Latin adaptation of his name,
Raymundus Lullus, and in English as Raymond Lull, or Lully), who con-
structed in words an architectural system of thought, called the "Art,"
which spread his influence throughout Europe. These were two great Catalans of passion. Pla, a hyperrational verging on the cynical, manages however to present an evenhanded portrait of the impassioned architect and
homenot, warts and all.

The version of Pla's essay followed here is that of his *Obra
completa* (vol. 11, 187–236), published in Barcelona in 1969 by Edicions
Destino. The homenot was first published by Editorial Selecta in 1958.
The biography of Llull referred to is E. Allison Peers's *Fool of Love.*

JOSEP PLA

Antoni Gaudí
(1852–1926)

Antoni Gaudí i Cornet was born on June 25, 1852, and died on June 10, 1926. He was just a few days short of his seventy-fourth birthday.

It is highly likely that Gaudí was born at the Mas de la Caldereta, the usual residence of his father, who by family tradition was a caldron maker, and that he was baptized at the parish Church of Sant Pere in Reus. He was baptized at the Reus parish because the Mas de la Caldereta was closer to Reus than to Riudoms. This circumstance has given birth to the picturesque confusion over whether Gaudí was born in the township of Riudoms or Reus.

Endless papers have been written on Gaudí. New ones are published every day, all over, even in the most distant countries of the earth. Gaudí's glory is on the rise. Gaudí is the Catalan of his time who, having been most intimately tied first to Catalonia and then to the Mediterranean, has the vastest universal dimension, the widest span of all.

We still lack the complete book we would need on Gaudí—on his life and work—the global biography that the Anglo-Saxon world devotes to its great personalities. In Catalan we have three excellent books on Gaudí: one by the architect Ràfols, one by the architect Martinell, and one by the architect Bergós. All three are excellent—primarily Bergós's, which does not mean the other two are less than notable. We still lack, however, the great, complete—to the point where human things may be complete—authentic, hiding-nothing, truthful book. Truth cannot hurt Gaudí in any way, from any viewpoint. In the lives of people there are some things that are important, others less so. But often these last things explain the others, the decisive ones. Everything is always more complex than it appears at first sight.

While Gaudí was being formed at the School of Architecture and in the life of Barcelona, Ferdinand Brunetière was one of the more important and listened-to social and literary pontifexs in Parisian intellectual circles. A brilliant professor of the Ecole Normale, he was also editor of the *Revue des Deux Mondes,* which at the time had a decisive influence on European society, Russia included. His Barcelona contemporaries read a lot of French publications, and the wealthy snobs were fascinated by Parisian life. At a given moment, Monsieur Brunetière published the following judgment: "The Gothic cathedral is exactly the same from one end of Europe to the other; it is an architectural form revealing no distinct personalities." By saying this, he continued a French tradition but with a different slant. Just as the people from the French eighteenth century had said that the Gothic style was a savagery from the Dark Ages, now Brunetière found that Gothic did not have enough personality, that it did not reach that degree of savagery demanded by his taste.

We bring up his opinion here, not because of its intrinsic interest, but because its very singularity makes it a slogan, one of those propelling pronouncements that are found at the base of all "isms"—in this case at the base of modernism. All the avant-garde movements begin with scandalous credos based on disdain. In any case it would be interesting to know if Gaudí knew Brunetière's opinion, directly or indirectly. Given the relationship he had with the intellectuals of his time who were most sensitive to the ferment beyond our borders—Yxart, Toda, and others—it is quite likely. Brunetière's judgment lends itself to deductions that, aided by such a formidable vitality as Gaudí's, are bound to have great consequences. From many points of view, in any case, Gaudí is inseparable from the modernist movement. Gaudí, however, was a modernist with such an enormous personality that he can be considered a much more important branch of modernism than the trunk itself.

I also think it correct to view Gaudí in his time, and consider the tributes he had to pay to his times. Given his overall development, this is an incidental and quite unimportant issue, after all, but an issue we cannot neglect because it explains the passion characterizing, in one sense or another, the great architect's mind. Cold people tend to be immutable. Gaudí was never cold, either when he held a specific opinion about religion or when he held its opposite.

In the critic Feliu Elies's biography of the painter Simó Gómez, an award-winning book published by the Junta d'Exposicions de Barcelona, you will find, on page 109, the following news:

> The cenacle of the Cafè Pelayo had an interesting appendix. It was a small coterie . . . of the irreligionists who, as was said, used to gather exclusively to share their profanities in a nightly ritual. The coterie consisted of the architect Gaudí, another architect called Oliveres, and a certain Senyor Fargas. Gaudí, who was then a novice in architecture, was full of talent and of good initiatives; he was collaborating in the building of the Ciutadella Park, designing the elegant lamps for Plaça Reial, and so on. He was so passionately anti-Catholic that he never held back from the most loud-mouthed demonstrations of anticlericalism, to the point that he would stop in front of the gates of churches and then curse the faithful (on their way in or out) calling them "woollies," an eloquent way to refer to the faithful's obfuscated eyes.
>
> Once the blaspheming ceremony ended, the club adjourned with the satisfaction of a job well done, except for Gaudí, who remained alone for a few minutes and then joined the coterie of Guimerà, Yxart, and Vilanova.

This information intrigued me, and one day when I met Feliu Elies—an excellent friend—in the library of the Barcelona Ateneu, I dared make a reference to it. "What you have written about the coterie in the Cafè Pelayo and Gaudí is surprising."

"Right you are!" he answered. "The information is crude, but unfortunately true. I have it from one who was present, I mean one of the most assiduous and notable members of Guimerà's group, the architect Domènech i Montaner. When it comes to personal things, Domènech is a bilious, pitiless, and gruff man, but he knows many things, and when he speaks of his time he is bottomless, a living archive of firsthand, live, authentic evidence. Whenever I have checked on some piece of information coming from him it has turned out to be accurate, fully confirmed."

Forty years after that conversation, I spoke about Gaudí to Josep Pijoan in Lausanne. "I have not read Elies's book on the painter Simó Gómez," Pijoan said, "but what he says of Gaudí, as you report, does not surprise me in the least. Gaudí was a man loaded with contradictions to an indescribable degree. Particularly during his youth he must have gone through moments of great passion. His religious crisis lasted many years. His life is full of shadowy zones on which perhaps no one will see fit to

throw light. Our country shows an excessive interest in keeping fictions
alive, even though from time to time we set fire to a bunch of churches.
Gaudí was a Catalan with a tragic depth, like Maragall himself."

And after a brief pause: "You know that I am convinced that
emigration is good for Catalans, mostly if they are intelligent. This is true
for the whole peninsula. Once abroad, they feel nostalgia, certainly, but
living amid a more authentic society, one more open to positive merits,
they can produce great things. In general, the Catalans' output at home is
quite weak, excepting some rare cases, mostly those of erudites; work at
home is by and large disconnected from the tenor of the times. You may
object that Senyor Prat de la Riba, Gaudí, or Maragall needed no exile to
produce something really positive. This is debatable. About Maragall, certainly, it is hard to prophesy, very hard. About Gaudí, let me tell you he
would have been the person—the only person in the world—capable of
building the cathedral for New York had that city decided to build a cathedral in proportion to its volume and its spirit. Gaudí is the last spiritual,
religious architect in the history of architecture. There have been, after
him, exceptional architects, extraordinary builders, but all devoted exclusively to making practical things, works in the service of material comfort
for endless masses looking for an easy life. And I am not speaking as
someone with an architect's degree or out of personal experiences with
architects. No. What I am telling you can be seen by a babe in arms. Gaudí
was a great man of passion, and for this reason I have defended him and
will always defend him. Maragall was one too, but in a different way.
Gaudí's passion came from his religious concentration, from his internal
flame. Maragall's passion was more complex, was manifested more cautiously, using euphemisms, although for me Maragall is eminently clear,
literal, and explicit."

While Pijoan talked to me in this tone, people in Barcelona
were arguing, in the pages of a magazine, which was Gaudí's exact birthplace. They all thought he had been born in Reus, but it turns out that
Riudoms also has many possibilities. I thought of the old ditty:

> From Reus to Riudoms
> the trip takes an hour,
> and from Riudoms to Reus
> the exact same time.

That is a senseless discussion. The confusion may be explained
by what we said earlier, which is not a personal opinion, but one coming
from the people who keep the flame of Gaudí's spirit in the strictest sense.

But the fact is curious because it proves that when the government is in the hands of one group their truth is personal, and when in the hands of another, truth is different, it is theirs. Since Riudoms, as opposed to liberal Reus, is a village marked by its conservatism, agrarian economy, and religiosity, someone was interested in having Gaudí born there—although he was born in the Mas mentioned above, within its municipality, and was christened in Reus. The problem is grotesque. From Riudoms to Reus the trip takes an hour—on foot!

All references to Gaudí have a great interest. In my modest opinion, this interest is independent of the reasons one may have for expressing one's admiration or contempt for his work, for saying that one likes or dislikes it—more or less. Gaudí is one of the top names of our times. His celebrity grows every day, within and without our borders—it probably grows more abroad. The creator of the Sagrada Família is becoming one of the greatest architects of his time. Any contribution to the knowledge of this figure—no matter how small—is a positive step. Those who knew him in person are fewer every day. Time goes by, people grow old and pass inexorably away, quietly, without leaving the slightest trace we can use—in written form—tiptoeing, as people have always done. For this reason any direct testimonial is appreciable as a contribution to the biography that some day will be written of Gaudí.

When I arrived in Barcelona during the second decade of the century, Gaudí had great fame, but his work stood at the center of a great polemic. Many sectors of Barcelona's intellectual life aimed constant criticisms at it. In general the libertines, the so-called "strong spirits," mostly artists, almost all of them in love with Parisian life, the fashionable slanderers, opposed Gaudí's work. Most of that cabal felt repulsed by the architect's religious feeling. Carner came up with his usual jokes. The *noucentistes*—principally Ors and Riba—were testily contrary to Gaudí's architectural conceptions. Being classicists, they found him burdensome. At times they clenched their teeth in rage.

On the side of the architect, at least on the surface, were Bishop Torras i Bages, the Academy of Sant Lluc, Prat de la Riba, Father Casanovas, S.J., Senyor Maragall, Cambó, Josep Pijoan, some, not many, architects . . . and that was about it. Cautious types said nothing, kept their mouths shut, waited, as usual, for things to settle. Those I mentioned first dominated the salons and the newspapers; they were the brilliant froth of the Barcelona of their day. Meanwhile the Sagrada Família was going up—with the slow rhythm of cathedrals, but it was going up.

The decision to found the Asociación Espiritual de Devotos de
San José was made in Montserrat in 1866. Senyor Josep Maria Bocabella i
Verdaguer, a bookseller with a shop on Carrer Princesa, brought the idea
to action. The year is significant. It was a time of political unrest. Those
elements we may call progressive had placed all their hopes in the person
who, the most in Catalonia, seemed to embody liberalism: General Prim.
Traditionalists were having a rough time. As a consequence of the process
of Italian unity, the Vatican was in trouble, and the creation of Italy, with
its capital in Rome, obliterated the temporal powers of the popes. In our
peninsula the September revolution had sent Isabella II into exile and put
Don Amadeo on the Spanish throne until, a few months later, he left
holding his head in his hands. Then the Cortes voted in the First Republic,
a second civil war—really the fourth—ensued, and Cánovas, helped by the
Foment del Treball Nacional, Duran i Bas, and Mañé i Flaquer (owner of
the *Diario de Barcelona*), restored the Bourbons to the throne. For active
Catholics, the moment was crucial. The Asociación Espiritual de Devotos
de San José was called, in short, the Asociación Josefina, and its goal was
"to get from God, through the intercession of Saint Joseph, the granting of
the full triumph of the Church during the difficult and hazardous circumstances of the world in general, and our Catholic Spain in particular." One
of its first activities was the publication of *El Propagador de la Devoción a
San José*, inspired by the journal a Marist brother, Josep Huguet, was
publishing in Saint Foy, Burgundy, under the title *Propagateur de la Dévo-
tion à Saint Joseph.*

The historical notes in the catalog for the Graphic Exhibition of
the Expiatory Temple of the Sacred Family, held in Barcelona in 1940,
give ample information on the promoters of the temple and the turbulence
of the times. Bocabella was a traditionalist, but, living in Barcelona (a
liberal city for the most part), he had no choice but to enlist in the National Militia where, following his pacifist temperament, he got into the
music band by pretending he could play the flute. Bocabella—his contemporary Francesc Arenas has written—"felt a horror for things of a mixed
nature and a foreign origin; he mistrusted all banks, and bought no French
products as they reminded him of the French occupation of Barcelona, and
even refused to eat any supposedly imported foods."

The Asociación Josefina decided to build an expiatory temple
devoted to the Sacred Family, and as they advertised their project, they
collected, almost in secret, in just seven years, 150,000 pesetas, which
paid for the temple's lot. The riots and devastation common during those
years forced them to keep the gift money beneath the floor tiles under the

counter of Bocabella's bookstore on Carrer Princesa. Before the temple's crypt was built, the Asociación used to worship in the Church of the Congregation for Hope on the Carrer Palma de Sant Just.

At five in the afternoon on March 19, 1882, the first stone of the new temple was set and blessed by Bishop Urquinaona in front of the local authorities, a hefty crowd, and the band of the Regiment of Engineers. Since the location was quite far from downtown, many attended the ceremony on horseback or in all kinds of carriages; among the crowd many were drivers, lackeys, and servants of all kinds. From the outset, Pope Pius IX, Queen Cristina, the boy who would later reign as Alfonso XIII, and Father Antoni Maria Claret, later canonized, formed the honor roster of the Asociación Josefina.

The first architect for the temple was Senyor Villar—or Del Villar—a diocesan architect who has left an uneven record. In 1883, a year after the first stone, Villar resigned his post. In 1884, the architect Antoni Gaudí was commissioned the construction of the apse chapel for the altar of Saint Joseph; worship on that altar began on March 19, 1885. This is the real starting date for the Sagrada Família.

During its early years the Asociación had a lot of drive. Its *Propagador*, which began its long life (it was published until 1936) with two hundred subscribers, after seven years had many thousands. Josephine functions spread. The pope was aided during that time with 92,500 pesetas; many pamphlets were printed; 572,000 medallions were disseminated; 392,000 certificates of membership; 16,000 copies of the *Devotion of the Seven Sundays;* and 71,000 of *The Court of Saint Joseph*. When the dogma of the Immaculate Conception was officially adopted, the pope received a silver model of the temple costing 150,000 pesetas. The laying of the first stone gave Josephinism a boost. The improvisational nature of the first few years came to an end with the building of a number of subsidiary structures. The society was showing a great will to persist. By July 1882 fifty masons were working on the crypt, with eight horse carts at their disposal. The intention was to employ three hundred workers.

The building of the chapel and of the apse altar of Saint Joseph, Gaudí's first work in what was to be the Sagrada Família, represented the integration of the architect into the small but growing world of the Josephines. How was that possible? How was it possible that that little world of fundamentalist Catholics moved from the recognized and proclaimed mediocrity of architect Villar to the architectural leadership of Senyor Gaudí? Our country's tradition shows very few precedents for such a phenomenon. Generally speaking, Barcelona architecture represents the

almost permanent victory of the client over the architect—supposing that
the architect had had any say in it at all. The fact is that given the authority
for the work barely begun, Gaudí will at once turn his back on the traditional taste, the pious complexes and tendencies of the Barcelona petty
bourgeoisie, and impose his own criteria. He will impose his ideas of religious architecture on that little world of extreme mediocrity. Villar should
have been the architect. But he was not. It was Gaudí. How can this be
explained? One might like Gaudí's work a lot, a little, or not at all. But
that is not the point. The point lies in explaining for what reasons Gaudí
became the Josephine architect. Take a look—I would not dare ask for
more—at the volumes of *El Propagador de la Devoción a San José*. You will
find, taking the inevitable tone of the times into consideration, one of the
vastest and most important concentrations of inanities, of clichés, and apol-
ogetic trash this country has ever produced! But facts are facts: it was the
world of the *Propagador* that allowed Gaudí to take to fruition what he
intended to do. It is literally astounding.

In the last years of his long life, Josep Pijoan was still unable to
understand these facts, in spite of all his reflecting on them and on the
documents he had.

"What was Bocabella like?" I asked him one day in Switzerland, two years before his death.

"He was a typical merchant; he sold books, but that does not
matter. He was a petty merchant. This is not to criticize him! I mean to
say, simply, that Bocabella was, in sensibility, in ideas, in his view of
things, and in his religiosity, at the opposite pole from Gaudí."

"And how can you explain the fact that they understood each
other?"

"They understood each other out of supra-real reasons."

"Are you serious?"

"People in Barcelona said at the time, particularly in the world
of Josephines, that a relative of Bocabella had the divine inspiration that
the architect for the projected temple would have blue eyes. When the
leaders of the Asociación found themselves before Gaudí, whose eyes were
blue (this took place in architect Martorell's office, the man who designed
the neo-Gothic façade of the Barcelona cathedral, a gift of Senyor Girona,
who was Gaudí's boss), Bocabella said: 'This young man will be the architect of the Sagrada Família.' And so he was. It is a world difficult to
understand; it cannot be explained by rational models, which are always
precarious and fall short. People are people. If you ignore this explanation,
what can you find? I know of no other. Gaudí was neither a flatterer nor

self-infatuated. He had the noble pride of superior men, as is perfectly natural. Little things had no influence on him. When we have the documented and authentic book on the Sagrada Família and Gaudí, then we shall know something. In any case, one thing appears certain: what Gaudí did with the Josephines once he was placed at the head of the works he would have been unable to do in Paris or London or Berlin, to say nothing of Italy or the United States, at the time, and that is because of the critical faculties of the distinguished Catholics in the corporation with whom he would have had to deal. When the Barcelona Josephines were convinced that Gaudí was the God-anointed person to direct the Sagrada Família's construction, they gave him carte blanche and set no unsurpassable obstacle to his prodigious creativity. And that is how the temple was started and slowly began to rise. At times I have wondered if some medieval cathedrals did not have the same beginnings. . . . "

The progress of the work was slow. During the early years the Josephines were very active. In truth, there was never enough money to give the work a rapid pace. Bocabella's death—at a young age—had a definitely ill effect. The money they spent was seldom given spontaneously; it was money they scraped together. Gaudí spent his life making calls and asking for alms. This sad story has two exceptions. At a given moment, as a consequence of some articles published in the *Diario de Barcelona* by Senyor Martí Mateu, a great friend of Gaudí, the architect received an anonymous check for 800,000 pesetas. Not much later, he received a second, smaller one. These were duly cashed and delivered to the temple's Diocesan Junta. In 1905 Maragall published his great article "Una gràcia de caritat." Its title, "Alms, please," is clear enough. In 1906 he published, as usual in the *Diario de Barcelona,* "En la Sagrada Família," to the same end. Maragall and Pijoan raised money from all social classes but mostly from humble folk. Some years later Joaquim Ruyra published an "appeal" printed on a broadsheet and distributed widely. The goal: always the same, to ask for donations. At a given moment the Barcelona City Hall voted a certain allowance for the continuation of construction. The decision was later attacked by leftist councilpersons, and City Hall reached a compromise: the money would be spent for the making of a model but not for the continuation of the work. Gaudí, when he died, left to the project all his capital: fifty or sixty thousand pesetas.

All the observers, witnesses, and scholiasts of the mess around the Sagrada Família agree that the history of the temple is inseparable from economic scarcity and lack of money. The fact that the money available at every occasion never met the budget but was rather an amount gathered by irregular solicitations and beggings, meant that a construction plan for a determinate period could only be established in a vague manner, always dependent on unforeseen developments. An almost continuous oscillation ensued between the total or partial halting of the work and the possibility, always chancy, of restarting them. Gaudí spent his life and his blood in those tragic oscillations. Those who hinted or proclaimed that the Sagrada Família was the cathedral of the poor could count that state of affairs among their reasons.

Nevertheless, something was done at all times—though certainly not much. Only long stretches of time made progress visible. In a few years we shall celebrate the centenary of the laying of the first stone. Only the enormous, indescribable will of Gaudí managed to overcome the long period of grayness the work on the temple went through in the course of its existence.

It seems obvious that such overwhelming slowness had specific causes. The process of its construction has been and will be, ultimately, what the citizens of this country, and especially those of Barcelona, have wanted and will want. It is possible, it seems to me, to have certain doubts as to whether the Sagrada Família awakens a visible degree of interest in the human mass, on the main body of the citizenry. The minority which from the outset felt a passion for Gaudí's work has doubtless grown considerably; some embraced it for religious reasons, some for artistic ones, and some for both. The latter was the case with the architect's greatest admirer, my old and respected friend the deceased architect Ràfols, whose memory is for me indelible and most dear. When I went to Barcelona in 1913 to study at the university, I was surprised by the indifference of my fellow students—almost all from bourgeois families—for the project. Later, having established some contacts in intellectual circles, to report I found indifference would be a great understatement. I witnessed an open, deliberate, and conscious opposition. It was the triumph of noucentisme. Gaudí was Eugeni d'Ors's nemesis. I cannot expand on this topic—which is otherwise quite well known. I shall simply recall that the only intellectual who was totally marginal to Catholic society and perfectly free-thinking and who defended Gaudí was Francesc Pujols. He defended him with his pen and with his words, in the midst of a dense hostility. Pujols's position in regard to the great architect is one of the keys to the post-noucentista movement, a movement Pujols helped formulate and maintain, even though his easy-going demeanor was little prone to the formation of those hierarchies intellectuals need to survive. All this is a subject that should be studied and systematized—a job that may be done some day. In any case, the post-noucentista generation looked at Gaudí's work quite differently, much more freely, and without the prejudices of Greek culture filtered through the French-German eighteenth century, that is, of the academicians of plaster. Anyhow, all those debates had little effect on people, and Gaudí's prestige was low. Gaudí received the indifference or the opposition of society and of those intellectuals we could call "distinguished."

But the slowness of the work resulted from other causes. Since the Josephine Association began its worship at the church on Carrer Palma de Sant Just, it had as its spiritual guide the Reverend Doctor Josep Vendrell Porta, the true representative of the bishop during the early years of the construction of the Sagrada Família. By episcopal decree, on July 20, 1895, Bishop Català appointed an administrative committee with Reverend Frederic Millan as president and Senyors Martorell, Monteys, Alvar C. Camín, J. Dalmases i de Riba, Nogués Taulat, Nogués Sagarra, Gil Llopart, and a representative of the Friars Minor, Bocabella-Dalmases, as members. Some of these gentlemen eventually died; Senyor Millan fell ill, and Cardinal Casañas, successor to Bishop Català, appointed a new president, Doctor Cortès, auxiliary bishop, and new members: Senyors Joan and Josep Llimona—great Gaudí admirers, like all the members of the Cercle de Sant Lluc—Senyor Martorell i Bernadí, and Senyor Josep Mundó; he also confirmed the remaining members in their charges. Doctor Cortès and Cardinal Casañas died later, and the bishop who succeeded the latter, Laguarda, named Doctor F. de P. Mas, who would later become the bishop of Girona, president of the committee.

The personalities on those lists show the interest of the episcopal see during the first years of the Sagrada Família. During that period there was no difficulty among those persons who in some way or other were involved with the construction. In 1907, considering the extraordinary volume reached by the parish of Sant Martí de Provençals (thirty thousand souls), Cardinal Casañas had the idea of making the Sagrada Família a branch of the Sant Martí parish, since the temple was being built in its territory. The cardinal dealt with the issue with great delicacy. He sent a document to the committee in which he told them, literally: "The growth [of Sant Martí] has led the Most Excellent Cardinal Casañas, bishop of Barcelona, to request the Asociación's authorization—while we wait for the establishment of a new parish—to set a parish branch in the temple, with the understanding that if such provision would hurt the temple in the very least they should say so freely for he will find another solution." Of course the cardinal's wish, so delicately and objectively stated, was granted.

In 1912, when the bishop of Barcelona was Doctor Laguarda,

there was an attempt to convert the Sagrada Família into one more of the city's parishes. The building committee learned about the existence of a decree to this effect, already signed. Gaudí went to see Senyor Prat de la Riba, president of the Mancomunitat. Prat went to see Laguarda, who not only withdrew the decree but also gave his word that the Sagrada Família would not be made into a parish. Here verbatim under the title "Is Gaudí leaving the works of the Sagrada Família?" is how Prat made the news public in the evening edition of *La Veu de Catalunya* of December 21, 1912:

> There have been hot debates in one of the spots frequented by our country's artists over the news that Gaudí would abandon direction of his genial work, the Expiatory Temple of the Sacred Family, before witnessing the mortal blow that the conversion of the temple into one of the many parish churches of the city would signify. If we never believed that our most worthy prelate would want to belittle this new see that our country, with noble pride, is offering God, we still considered it our sacred duty to discover what truth there may be in this matter which is of transcendent importance, and thus we want to inform our readers.
>
> From people we hold in the most absolute confidence and who are well abreast of the matter, we learned that the temple's committee addressed the issue some time ago, after its illustrious president reported that he had been told by the bishop in a personal interview that the temple would not be made into a parish. Since we cannot question the honesty of the most respectable words from our prelate, we think we may safely state that, for the time being, there is no reason for alarm.

If the 1912 decree of Bishop Laguarda had prospered and the Sagrada Família had become one more parish in Barcelona, not only would the end for which it was created have been betrayed but Gaudí's involvement also would have ended. No one would have continued the expiatory temple, and all monies would have been given to the new parish, bringing about the loss of all grants marked specifically and voluntarily for diverse purposes within the Sagrada Família. It would have represented the transformation, if not the total destruction, of those purposes. More than indifference, the decree would have provoked immediate suspicion. Senyor Prat's intercession meant a literal salvation.

Doctor Laguarda's word was sustained by his successors, Bishops Reig, Miralles, and Guillamet, and everything seemed to indicate that Bishop Irurita would follow suit. But on November 20, 1930, in a letter from the councilar canon and chamber secretary, Doctor Ramon Baucells, to the president of the Junta of the building, Canon Doctor Francesc Parés, the committee was informed that eight days earlier Bishop Irurita had signed a decree converting the Sagrada Família into one of the parishes of the diocese, thus threatening the existence and continuation of the expiatory temple. Gaudí was already dead. The little world of the beginnings of the temple was gone. The bishop's decree gave a strange idea of this bishopric's Catholic unity!

Senyor Josep M. Dalmases-Bocabella, grandson of the founder, tried to enlist several personalities to obtain the derogation of the decree. The lawyer Anguera de Sojo, who was justly considered an authority in canonical law, understood that if a recourse were filed only the Vatican could revoke the decree. When could the revocation take place? Anguera was unable to give a precise date. "In general," the jurist said, "revocations come after the death of the prelate who issued the decree." Anguera was convinced the bishop would come to realize the harm done. But it was all useless. After Irurita's phrase "These are no times for cathedrals," they pointed out to him that the Sagrada Família was a votive temple, an expiatory temple. He replied wearily: "All temples are expiatory and impetratory." The president of the Junta, Doctor Parés, a canon and vicar general, visited the bishop twice. The second visit lasted a minute. A few hours later Doctor Parés resigned. Senyor Dalmases-Bocabella died in 1932, obsessed with the future of the temple. The pressure, however, did not subside.

The committee heard that Canon Baucells said Bishop Irurita "had ordered the new treasurer of the Sagrada Família to try to find a site, and rent or buy it to serve as parish church." Senyor Damià Mateu, a member of the building committee, used this news as a pretext to visit the bishop and offer him a site adequate to serve as a parish church: the old Maristany warehouses, close to the Sagrada Família. Irurita considered the proposal grumpily, and Canon Baucells reported that the bishop had been upset by it. But at least the bishop had not said no. It was a precarious result, but it was a result. Senyor Mateu's proposal had been straightforward and without animus.

In the meanwhile, the Junta's secretary, Senyor Martí Manlleu followed the correct behavior for a great lover of Gaudí's work and especially of the Sagrada Família—a behavior that the gentleman in question explains in his pamphlet "Open letter to the Lord Bishop of Barcelona." This pamphlet—harder and harder to find—is priceless for its information about all this deplorable history. It is a respectful, equanimous, correct, and absolutely objective document. On September 30, 1935, Senyor Martí Manlleu was fired from his post; soon thereafter Canon Baucells asked the journalists in charge of ecclesiastical news not to publish anything about the Sagrada Família without his explicit authorization.

Senyor Martí Manlleu attempted to draw the Barcelona art societies and the architects' congress, gathered by that time in Tarragona, into the affair. The art societies failed to respond. The architects' congress turned a deaf ear to him.

In the meanwhile, donations for the temple were dwindling visibly, and subscriptions to the *Propagador de la Devoción a San José* were lapsing. This trend was accentuated when the bishop gave the review's editorship to a Reverend Rodríguez de Robles, who had lived in Barcelona for only two years and knew nothing about the Sagrada Família or its creator. The publication shrank and, as had been forecast, provoked widespread suspicion. Reverend Rodriguez was replaced as editor of *Propagador* by an editor from the *Correo Catalán* who was also a churchman. The latter, however, managed to publish only two issues because the Civil War of 1936 had begun.

Everyone knows that in the course of those tragic events the Sagrada Família suffered phenomenal damages.

Many things were destroyed, and Gaudí's tomb desecrated. Some people, however, have wondered what would have happened if they could have continued speaking of the temple *as a work of art,* if its *populism* and its authentic *exemplarity* could have been stimulated. It is anyhow unimaginable that such considerations would have been very effective in July 1936. That it was a parish church, that is, ultimately, a bureaucratic ecclesiastical establishment, had no effect on the rioting masses. It is also possible that if the Gaudí Pavilion had been built on the proposed site (a site they had had to give up because the ecclesiastical administrator of the Sagrada Família parish reserved it as the parish dump), then the sketches and blueprints for the temple, Gaudí's professional legacy, or at least the exhibits for the Gaudí Museum planned for the pavilion would have survived. It was all destroyed in a bestial manner. The creative, architectural, and genial legacy of the great architect should have been saved. But who could save it while it was in the care of a neighborhood parish?

The little and the big history of the Sagrada Família, inseparable from Gaudí's life, is a long and not very edifying affair. All the witnesses, observers, and scholiasts of the work agree that the parish period of the Sagrada Família was characterized by the tragic loss of the most elementary serenity in persons who should have been able to maintain it.

Originally Senyor Bocabella had proposed the building of the Josephine temple to the diocesan architect, Senyor Villar Lozano, who designed a perfectly ordinary neo-Gothic structure. Construction of the crypt began at once. At a given moment, however, architect Martorell, who was Bocabella's adviser for the newly started construction, had a disagreement with Villar over some technical matters, and Villar resigned his post. Martorell, having been asked to replace him, declined out of prudence. He thought that, having intervened in Villar's resignation, he ought to stay out. He proposed his collaborator, who was accepted. It was Gaudí.

Once in charge, Gaudí went through a fumbling early phase. That phase was not short. He accepted Villar's project but immediately made incidental modifications to it. He at once abandoned the classical moldings and replaced them with new structures inspired by nature. The architect Quintana described those changes in his book *Les formes guerxes del Temple de la Sagrada Família,* indispensable for the understanding of Gaudí's evolution: "From that process came the project of a *Gothic-Mediterranean* style which we might (following the great master's appropriate terminology) call *dressed Gothic.*" (We shall later see how the word *Gothic* must be understood in reference to Gaudí's work.)

That first phase full of perplexities for the Sagrada Família coincided with the great commissions, both civil and ecclesiastic, offered to Gaudí—by Senyor Eusebi Güell, and at Astorga, León, and so on—some of which were completed, and others not. It was in response to one of Senyor Eusebi Güell's commissions that the prodigious spectacle of the appearance and flowering of Gaudí's contribution to architecture, the demonstration of his genius took place. In 1908 he was commissioned to build the Church of the Colònia Güell at Santa Coloma de Cervelló. Unfortunately, only the crypt was ever completed, but it is evident that in the studies and in the model for the construction of that church we have, *ab ovo,* the Sagrada Família. In Gaudí's evolution, Santa Coloma de Cervelló is the fundamental milestone, the essence of everything to come. In the Sagrada Família such evolution becomes obvious if one compares the crypt with the apse and the apse with the nativity portal. Better than I could do it, the architect Quintana asserts the importance of the Colònia in the essay already quoted:

> In the sketches and designs for the Church of the Colònia Güell, freed from all sorts of encumbrances and prejudices, Gaudí projected, in accord with Count Güell and under his patronage, the commissioned church with the full originality of his powerful genius and in a visually integral manner, since the plans were drawn in relation to the curves of the pressures regulating the stability of the building. Unfortunately, only the crypt was ever built; that part of the study, however, sufficed to determine in a definitive manner the forms that were to give being to the temple of the Sagrada Família.

With his formidable mechanical sense and his wonderful perception of forms in space, with his lopsided forms, Gaudí got such surprising results when he applied them freely to the columns and the vaults of said crypt that he could not resist applying their great ductility and luminous richness to the forms of the great temple, the masterpiece of his powerful fantasy. The Colònia Güell church was, then, a kind of trial for the temple of the Sagrada Família.

And thus Gaudí, leaving aside all Gothic reminiscence, projected a temple exclusively of hyperbolic paraboloids. . . . For the columns, the solution with paraboloids took him at once to the use of helicoids: another lopsided form with great possibilities.

In the copious Gaudí bibliography there are some capital texts, most of them written by immediate collaborators. One of those texts is architect Quintana's study. Other important ones are Puig Boada's *El temple de la Sagrada Família,* Domènec Sugranyes's *Disposició estàtica del temple de la Sagrada Família,* and the writings and lectures of Senyor Bonet Garí. In Senyor Sugranyes's essay there are elements that may complement Senyor Quintana's.

The present layout of the Sagrada Família resulted from a series of coincidences. To begin with, Gaudí's freedom. If, as Bishop Morgades had requested, the complete plans for the work had been presented early on, Gaudí's freedom would have been curtailed. The bishop's death prevented this. Second, the languor and poverty of the construction allowed for thorough studies. The Santa Coloma de Cervelló work became a concrete essay of great efficacy.

Senyor Sugranyes has written:

The evolution of Gaudí's ideas on the Sagrada Família shows the gradual avoidance of the techniques of the Gothic cathedral. From his earliest attempts he wanted to modify the Gothic disposition. In the first complete study of the temple's structure, made around 1898—at the time of the Santa Coloma commission—the structure was Gothic, since the columns were vertical; there were no buttresses, however, and the edges of the nave and aisles were elevated in order to diminish their horizontal reactions and, mostly, to ensure that the pressure curve of the nave would add to that of the aisles without help from the buttresses at the baseline of their arches. Some twenty years later that study was revised into the one presently projected, which returns the temple to basilical simplicity, although with radical differences: whereas the basilica was roofed in wood, the Sagrada Família, both inside and out, is to be roofed in stone.

In the Sagrada Família each column supports its corresponding canopy independently of the others, so that the enormous weight of the nave, like that of the aisles, goes directly onto the ground without resorting to the complicated route of buttresses and abutments, which characterizes Gothic, and which may now be suppressed.

The elimination of buttresses and abutments has been achieved in the Sagrada Família simply by giving the columns the inclination that results from the composition of weights which gravitate on it; this is exactly what a big tree trunk does when it bends in accordance with the masses of foliage the branches must sustain. All architectural styles have related the columns to the idea of trees, and Gothic cathedrals have been compared to forests with interlaced branches; these comparisons have only a literary value, however, because Gothic columns and vaults have nothing to do with trees. Each tree has an individuality independent of surrounding trees; each tree has at its disposal all the balancing elements it needs, and requires no help or support. That is the opposite of what happens with the columns and vaults of a Gothic cathedral.

The true, real, and individual tree appears for the first time in architecture in the buildings of Gaudí.

In the Sagrada Família the column is an independent entity that brings together and balances the elements above it. The tree, as a column, holds its true reality. The disposition adopted here is new in architecture, although not in nature, since nature—Sugranyes writes—"has existed since the third day of creation."

"In Gothic disposition," the architect goes on,

the complex play of actions and reactions that constitutes its essence makes the resultant forces rest on the columns supporting the nave and aisles. Gravity is vertical, but the resultant forces are angled to a greater or lesser degree, which means that the centers of percussion do not coincide with the center of gravity of the columns. Consequently, the distribution of compressions on these sections is done unevenly and taxes the strength of the materials. This weakness is solved by Gaudí's disposition in which the axis of the column, with its resultant weight composition, spreads the compression uniformly and thus uses the strength of the column's materials optimally, as it sets on these only the section strictly necessary to support the load they have been assigned.

If we compare a diagram of the Sagrada Família with a diagram of a Gothic cathedral we shall immediately see the superiority of the temple's static disposition. The diagram gives a sensation of repose and calm that satisfies the spirit. On the other hand, when we look at the section diagram of a Gothic cathedral, the sensation of repose fades away, as the simplicity of the temple's equilibrium of forces is here a complexity of actions and reactions; naturalness has turned to artifice. The play of forces is an ingenious and belabored combination, but the spirit derives little satisfaction from it. More: it is quite frightening to consider that the permanence of such a majestic edifice is based on the resistance of every single thread of the complex fabric of forms that make up its organism, even more so when we consider that most of that fabric sits outdoors, unprotected.

Senyor Sugranyes's text ought to be read in its entirety if one is to have an idea of Gaudí's constructive mechanics. We have attempted to give a minimal but clear idea. His text can be found in the *Anuario de la Asociación de Arquitectos de Cataluña* (Barcelona, 1923). Ràfols reproduces it in his book. It is a decisive document.

Gaudí's undertaking with total dedication of the direction of the temple coincided with his busiest period and with far-flung commissions. He managed to accomplish his work on all fronts thanks to the help he got from Senyor Berenguer with the Sagrada Família. This Senyor Berenguer, who was not an architect, understood completely Gaudí's ideas and was an example of his most active followers. It has been said many times that Gaudí was one of the first persons in our country to work in a team. In truth there are many kinds of teams. By itself a team is nothing, but under a permanent leadership teams become indispensable, important to the highest degree. Gaudí's team, his successive teams, were excellent because Gaudí was heading them. He not only had a global understanding of his projects; he also intervened in the smallest details. For example, the architect had a prodigious understanding of the sonority of bells.

As all direct testimonials to Gaudí's work are supremely interesting, I shall refer to a letter from Senyor Vilaplana in which he writes to me about a vacation the architect took in the house of Senyors Rocafiguera in Vic in 1910. During his sojourn, Senyor Vilaplana showed him Vic and its environs.

"During our walks," Senyor Vilaplana tells me, "we conversed about many things, including matters of art and archaeology. I thought Gaudí's ideas on those topics most singular. Speaking of Gothic architecture he told me it was a lame and imperfect architecture, because a Gothic form, to sustain itself, needs the crutches that are the abutments and buttresses. 'The Sagrada Família,' he added, 'is held without crutches, for I am not in favor of any crutches or artificial perambulators.' "

I find this other note, a notably enigmatic one, in his letter: "One day he told me," says Senyor Vilaplana, "that years before he had purchased a book by a French author on the curious and varied curved and wavy forms wood takes as it dries: on the glitches of wood, so to say. I thought he gave great importance to that book, to the point that I imagine the most singular shapes Gaudí gives his arches and walls derive from the tumefactions and undulations of bent wood."

Given the modesty of my literary abilities and the complexity of the topic, the memory of some episodes in his life may serve to fill in the outline of the great architect.

On the road to Portugal by way of Galicia I have stopped a few times at León and Astorga to see the works erected in these towns under Gaudí's direction. His first commission was the episcopal palace of Astorga; Astorga, capital of *maragato* country, has a bishop even though it is a very small town. The natives say it quite well when they state that "in Astorga, if there were no bishop, there would be nothing." This building project took place between 1889 and 1890. Born in 1852, Gaudí was nearing his fortieth birthday.

The See of Astorga seems to have been prone to having Catalan bishops. The present prelate (1962) is one. Félix Torres Amat, the author of the *Diccionario de Autores Catalanes,* was also bishop of Astorga. In Gaudí's time, J. B. Grau Vallespinós headed that diocese; he was not only Catalan but also a Reus native, like the architect himself. I doubt, however, that their relationship was influenced by their native landscape. They did not know each other. Gaudí was the architect of Senyor Eusebi Güell i Bacigalupi, the son of Senyor Güell i Ferrer, the great protectionist, one of the people who worked hardest for the industrialization of our country. Senyor Güell was the brother-in-law of the first Marquis of Comillas. Among many other activities, the first Marquises of Comillas had great influence on the pious and diplomatic art of making bishops. They made some highly celebrated ones. Given this panorama, who better than Gaudí to build the episcopal palace in Astorga? To round things off, it turned out the bishop was from Reus. One could not imagine a better conjunction. This explains how it was that the architect had a piece of work in Astorga and an apartment house in nearby León, which, in truth, was the tail of the ecclesiastical building.

My modest information here is not born of fantasy. In Astorga I once went into a pastry shop to purchase some *mantecadas,* that area's most famous sweet. Not a bad pastry, for a local product. The baker in the pastry shop, a rather unlaconic man, informed me that his establishment is the one patronized by the miter for all unavoidable occasions. An unavoidable occasion is that which results from limitations in production at the nuns' convent, the usual provider of the sweet delicacies for the social needs of the house. This fact, insignificant in itself, has provoked its inevitable consequence: the owner of the pastry shop is a permanent source of local information and, concretely, of ecclesiastical gossip, the only matter of weight and positive dimensions in the little city. The baker is a news sponge.

To what extent may we say the episcopal palace in Astorga, as we see it today, is a genuine product of Gaudí's spirit? The plan to build a residence for the prelate and some bureaucratic offices went through hard times. First it had to be approved by the Academia de San Fernando, and as it notoriously did not please, it suffered its first modifications. Once these early difficulties were resolved, the work began and everything went smoothly until the unfortunate day when, the work half completed, Bishop Grau died. Gaudí's project fell into disgrace with Grau's successors, first the administrator of the curia and later the new bishop. For a number of years the work was stuck: for twenty years, to be exact. In Barcelona Gaudí would say somberly: "They will be unable to finish it, and all will be interrupted and bastardized." After many lengthy attempts, the palace was finished, but reluctantly, with reticence if not hostility. It is one of Gaudí's works and carries his mark, but it is a cheated, diminished, precarious work—a skeleton of balancing bones—and ultimately bastardized. All the same, some edges of that construction, particularly under a favorable light, show a spiritual energy.

The Astorga adventure is important in Gaudí's life not so much because of the episcopal palace itself but because of his own religious process. It seems safe to state that his contacts with Bishop Grau consolidated Gaudí in the dogmas of the Catholic, apostolic, and Roman faith. Senyor Dalamses-Bocabella, one of the founders of the Sagrada Família, wrote in *El Propagador de la Devoción a San José,* which for many years was the official organ of the house, that "Astorga opened wider horizons for his soul."

The solidification of Gaudí's religious feelings and thoughts, begun sometime earlier, reaffirmed through the contacts with Bishop Grau, came to a close as a consequence of his later friendship, by 1904, with Bishop Campins, who commissioned some works of restoration for the Majorca cathedral.

León is an important provincial capital, quite a large city, enjoying a cool climate, bustle, and thirst for life. The traditional levitic images of León are a thing of the past. It is a kind, open town that has overcome in part its provinciality without too much confusion or chaos in its rise. The whole town, however, is under the effects of its immense, impressive, prodigious Gothic cathedral. Its volume is so considerable that it affects the totality of the urban layout. After the cathedral—which, let us say in passing, offers some great windows that are a dream of wonder—the rest of León appears secondary. The cathedral erases everything and puts everything at its feet.

Given these conditions, it must not be very amusing to work as an architect in León. The city contains, in effect, an overabundance of architectural messes that are extremely thin.

Gaudí was commissioned to build a house very near the cathedral by Senyors Fernández-Andrés. And thus rose the Casa de los Botines, as it is called there. It is not one of the most Gaudinian of the architect's works, but it has his personality. If we compare it with contemporary architecture in León, we must recognize that he did very well. The architect's tendency to build in stone whenever possible gave him at once, in León, a personality. It is a house that looks like no other house in León, nor in all of the old kingdom of León, nor in Old Castile. It is a solid house made of a whitish stone (the material is not too pleasant) with a sui generis design. Gaudí was never a catalog architect, whether ancient or modern, as are many important architects. He was always most particular, even when he was commissioned to build an apartment house in León.

It was summer, late in July; it was a great day, the sky was clear, and as I admired the Casa de los Botines from the terrace of a café, I thought I was in a different country, with a different climate, much farther to the north, a great deal farther. The house has a very northern look and was built thinking of a hard climate with low temperatures and abundant and persistent snowfalls. The León area is certainly cold, and the owners of the future house must have insisted that the architect not forget this condition in his project. In Astorga Bishop Grau, who commissioned the construction of the episcopal palace, also insisted on the need, for the love of God, not to overlook the heating systems (see J. F. Ràfols's biography of Gaudí). The architect, of course, kept it in mind and designed it thinking of winter. When the weather is bad—one only needs to see the postcards of the house—it appears at its best. Covered with snow, it makes one think of some building in Finland, not from the time when the Russians built following Italian or French models but of more modern buildings subjected to the pathos of the winter climate in a country of forests and livid waters.

"If you saw that house in winter, when the weather is bad, your insides would shiver," the waiter in the café tells me.

It is the natural reaction; being the only house built in León with winter in mind—or one of the few—its singularity accentuates, in a way, in a kind of theatrical way, the frigidity of the climate. Gaudí, for the Casa de los Botines, became a winter architect—which is, I would think, not to his discredit.

In Senyor Vilaplana's letter from Vic, which I mentioned before, one finds the following lines:

I want to add to these remarks an episode of this architect's life which is unknown by many—at any rate I have not read any reference to it in the more current biographies available. In the lives of people, all things have their meaning, the successes as well as the failures. Now that Gaudí's name is in full glorious rise, this episode must be remembered, among other reasons because it was a great mishap.

At the time of the World's Fair in Paris, at the end of the century, he had the curious idea of exhibiting there a display of what he considered his decisive work, the Sagrada Família. With the financial help of his patron and admirer Senyor Eusebi Güell, he had a number of voluminous models of the temple built. The manufacturing of those artifacts, their conveyance to Paris in enormous boxes, the inherent hullabaloo, cost a bunch of thousands of pesetas. In Paris, they had to rent a large hall in one of the fair's palaces, which was no easy thing, nor cheap either. But what would Senyor Güell not have done for his architect and great friend? At the moment to which we refer, Gaudí was getting over his youthful phase, totally given over now and fully adherent (not without a struggle) to Catholic dogma. That man who had cultivated, with perhaps a childish passion, all forms of external life, who had been such a smart dresser, who had eaten like a gourmet, who loved to raise his head as he promenaded by car on the Passeig de Gràcia, who had devoted so many hours to conversation and socializing, was becoming day by day more unkempt, marginal, and crusty. The last tie to hold him to his old world was Senyor Güell. . . ."

Well, the idea for the World's Fair was a complete failure. Neither the public that visited the hall nor technicians nor critics showed the least interest in the architect's exhibit. He felt a great disappointment, and subsequently went through a long phase during which he stated with hammer blows and an expression of sour grapes that the French were a drove of ignoramuses and did not know what architecture was, or art, or anything. The French would be the last to feel an interest for Gaudí's work, just as in our country the last would be Eugeni d'Ors and the noucentistes. In the latter case not only because Ors's architect was Palladio but because they were gallicized to the marrow of their bones, because they liked their Palladio with a French label and with the spirit of the French eighteenth century, which was what tickled Ors—concretely the after-dinner chats and salons of eighteenth-century Paris. The strict French, what interest could they feel for Gaudí's work? Soaked to the bones in rationalism, in frozen neoclassicism, in symmetrism, and with their sensual tendencies stylized to rococo and *mignardise,* they could not appreciate Gaudí in any way. And in fact, all notable French Catholics who visit Barcelona are never interested in the Sagrada Família.

At any rate, the Paris fair episode was a mistake in timing: half a century before its time. Had the materials been sent today, now that the French have begun to like (as the papers claim, although I have my doubts) the functional architecture of the day, those models would have had, out of snobbishness if nothing else, what is normally called a *succès d'estime*.

In 1905 Gaudí, was asked to undertake some architectural and liturgical restorations for the Palma de Mallorca cathedral—a restoration that was never completed. The proposal put him in touch with Bishop Campins, in whom he found an active religious sensitivity. Their meeting probably marks the final point in the religious process initiated perhaps with his contacts with Bishop Grau of Astorga: the total, absolute, active acceptance of the dogmas of Catholicism. In 1905 Senyors Milà commissioned him to build their house on the Passeig de Gràcia, the one to be called La Pedrera.

After that project Gaudí devoted himself completely to the Sagrada Família. We cannot give the turn an exact date. We must put it after 1906. Until that time Gaudí derived a salary—certainly meager, but real—from all he did as an architect, perhaps with the exception of the Sagrada Família. In 1906 he bought the land on which he was to build his house on Park Güell, made a payment to Senyor Güell, the owner of the park, and moved there with his father, very old then, and his niece Rosa Egea. His father, the boilermaker from Riudoms, died soon thereafter. His niece took care of Gaudí's personal matters, but that woman—who lived somewhat influenced by alcoholism—did not last long, so that at a given moment the architect found himself completely alone, with no family ties, either close or distant. And since in practical matters he had always been a helpless inept, that isolation weighed on him. When his father died, Gaudí was fifty-four.

Gaudí's total, absolute dedication to the Sagrada Família lent his economic situation a heavy languor. The work sustained itself from public alms, and even though at times it received some important gifts—always sporadic and intermittent—its permanent state was that anguished one in between bankruptcy and making do, day by day, dripping along precariously.

On the other hand, the slowness of construction gave Gaudí and his main collaborators time to study, enlarge, and enrich the project—for the visual imagination of the architect had no limits. And so the scantier the means, the more enormous, fascinating, and rich the conception of the Sagrada Família would become. Blindly subject to the designs of divine providence, Gaudí believed always that those setbacks were perfectly normal and obeyed a superior order, an order which the normal means of human reason would have been unable to elucidate. Ultimately, then, those setbacks favored the good progress of the temple.

In general one may state—in general and with the necessary but few exceptions—that rich Catalans have felt a rather anemic interest in the Sagrada Família. Gaudí turned this fact inside out and claimed that our country has no rich. He considered the external signs of wealth in Barcelona, those things that impress foreigners, shows of ingeniousness more than of substantial wealth. The architect Cèsar Martinell relates that once a Dutchman who came to Barcelona to sell strongboxes told the architect how impressed he was with the luxury in dress, on the streets, of Barcelona ladies. "Such luxury," Gaudí replied, "is no proof of a greater wealth. The climate here is good; we have light and sunshine that encourage strolls. Women have the opportunity to spend and to dress for the outdoors. In cloudy countries, however, one is forced to stay at home, and by asking some friends to dinner one day, may spend as much as an elegant lady here does all season. Where is the money, here or abroad?" Gaudí's group tried to prod the reluctant bourgeoisie by awakening the generosity of the more modest, not to say humble, folk. That initiative pleased Maragall and Pijoan. It was brought to practice, but it was—by no means—a definitive solution. Gaudí declared once—in the presence of Martinell—that in times of abundance, when they could spend all they needed in the works, they spent 200,000 pesetas in a year. He added that 175,000 would have sufficed. When Gaudí spoke that way, their capital amounted to 50,000 pesetas, and their deficit was . . . (Martinell does not supply the amount).

Gaudí's finances became indescribably precarious. He was never paid for his work, a situation he found perfectly natural. It is even conceivable that he contributed money of his own. After a certain point he did not want to own anything at all. He gave what he had (from an inheritance) to Riudoms, his town, and the soccer field of the place occupies a lot that had belonged to the architect. He donated his house on Park Güell to the works of the Sagrada Família. So he was all alone and poor besides, a solemn, absolute, and definitive poor.

After the death of his niece Rosa, his little house on Park Güell was cared for by some Carmelite sisters who showed up once a week to clean. Once a week! It seems that one of those good women is still alive—may she live much longer. Gaudí was a very clean, neat man, but of course the air of carelessness and negligence his life understandably took influenced his person, and consequently, not only was he an authentic pauper but he also looked like one; it was apparent he was poor. A time came when he considered it not worthwhile worrying about the hair on his head and face, and so he let it grow with a total indifference. Still there would be a day, after a long spell, when he decided he would have to trim it some. After the operation Gaudí appeared transformed; he was another man. Such a phenomenon, however, was quite sporadic.

Gaudí, who as a young man had light hair with overtones the color of clay, became with the years intensely white-haired, after having gone through a red color that turned gray. Maragall mentions his reddish beard. Even in his advanced maturity he was a hefty man, not to say portly; then he lost a lot of weight and seemed to grow smaller. This transformation was unaffected by the change in dress. During the years of his corpulence one may say he was a careful dresser; later, as he became poor, he also dressed like the poor. The shrinking of his figure was due to his weight loss rather than to the clothes he wore with great listlessness—his pants were quite baggy. In speaking of the external elements of Gaudí's figure we must insist, because these are the facts, that in their adoption there was never the slightest element of deliberation or will or desire to impress, for whatever reason. They obeyed the obsession of his spirit and the unconventional taste for simplicity and modesty the architect took to the limit.

Of his face, of average features within the peasant (Roman) norm of the Tarragona area, his eyes caused the greatest impression. They were blue. Gaudí's eyes! His blue eyes were almost devoid of nervous movement, but their calm showed a singular intensity; it was not a calm tending toward ecstasy and whiteness, but a calm full of force, passion, and life. All who met Gaudí remember his eyes as the impressive, fascinating element of the image they keep of him. He seemed to transport things and people with his eyes; his eyes gave him a constant presence. This presence excluded all physical possibilities for human buffoonery, the most generic characteristic of human beings we all sooner or later manifest. His was not the kind of seriousness upheld by dint of stiffness and perseverance which in the long run makes one laugh. It was rather an unfathomable candor fused with a very visible tenacity—a virile humanity with no external underscoring, but at once tender, dreamy, floating on a vast inner life, full of sensible elements and a clear, precise intelligence. His eyes' presence was so decisive that even if he had made more of an effort to despise his person, he would only have managed to augment it, and impose it. His voice suited him: absolutely atonal and polite in his habitual affairs, at times it showed a clear and cutting strength.

We said, a moment ago, that, totally devoted to the Sagrada Família, his work never received the slightest remuneration. But this may not be quite exact. Out of the work's precarious economy the architect derived his miserable subsistence. While, his niece Rosa still alive, he kept his home on Park Güell, he was in charge of it. To minimize commuting from his home to the workshop, he preferred to take his meals nearer his work, and thus Gaudí became an intermittent guest of the temple's concierge, an intermittence that turned to fixity when his niece passed away. He ended up sleeping in a corner of the workshop because as he grew older he thought it necessary, at first when the weather was bad and later every day, to remain there at night. These successive adaptations to his needs were in truth not directed by any anticipating deliberation or with any effect in mind. They were created by life itself. In fact, however, Gaudí's sustenance ended up as an invisible, microscopic line in the general budget of the works.

His upkeep did not exceed the limits of the most absolute paucity, among other reasons because he practiced the dietary and hygienic doctrines of the German priest Kneipp. He slept with his window open. He walked a lot. He was a vegetarian. One day the architect Bonet Garí found him eating lettuce dipped in milk. A strange recipe! We need not say that any form of alcohol or tobacco was excluded from his diet. Enjoying—as I suspect—hypotension, he survived very well Barcelona winters, which may be frightful for those who have no means of defense. Gaudí never had any. He bandaged his legs to keep his feet warm. Ultimately he was a hearty man who with no major difficulties nearly reached the age of seventy-four. His physical vitality allowed him to work, literally, like a giant. When one thinks, leaving aside the other transcendental commissions he saw to, that he created the structure of the Sagrada Família heedless of the formulas of traditional architecture and particularly evading those of the Gothic cathedral—creating, in a word, the cathedral without crutches and dressing its structure, an enormously rich and complicated one, in all the splendor of liturgical symbolism, and taking care even of the smallest details—Gaudí's work produces a unique, forbidding, sensational impression. Since every person is a world, it is clear that the ascetic life was good for Gaudí. It was, in any case, no hindrance to his work—rather the opposite. One may imagine that his conception of the world was at no time incompatible with the forms of extreme poverty.

When one speaks of Gaudí's total dedication to the Sagrada Família one should take this word in the literal sense. He was not only its author; he even did fund raising for it. "Once," architect Martinell writes, "asking for a gift, he told the would-be donor: 'Make this sacrifice.' As the patron answered 'It's my pleasure; it's no sacrifice,' Gaudí insisted that the gift be raised until it was a sacrifice, because charity that does not have sacrifice as its base is not true charity, but rather vanity."

His devotion to the work made Gaudí renounce all social life. He concentrated exclusively on his work. The person who walked with him daily from the house on Park Güell to the Sagrada Família was one of the temple's modelers, Matamala by name, who lived in his neighborhood. Matamala's death surely contributed to Gaudí's abandoning of his house on the park. "In his ripe age," architect Ràfols writes, "if one does not count a few gatherings at the Ateneu, one cannot imagine him going to any meetings; as for intimate friends, he probably had no more than Doctor Pere Santaló, his lifelong companion with whom he went on a stroll on Sundays, even down to the seaside, which is not easily reached in Barcelona." It seems Gaudí would have preferred to see Tarragona's coast rather than the Barcelona wharf, but this was all he had. He said the sea unites people and mountains separate them. In this sense he considered our country much more tied to Italy than to France.

Almost daily, at sundown, he went, normally on foot, from the Sagrada Família workshop to the Church of Sant Sever, in the heart of old Barcelona, his habitual church. On his way back home—to the house on the park or to the bed he had in the middle of the tools of his trade in the workshop—he would sometimes take the streetcar. This long walk to Sant Sever and his Sunday walk to the port with Doctor Santaló may have been the only amusements of his mature life. Needless to say, no one ever saw him in a theater.

I do not know if one may state that Gaudí was an optimist. He was too intelligent to hold cheerful, obvious, and dreamy positions. He was no scatterbrain; he was obsessed. On the other hand, he was an absolute, total Christian and thus showed an explicit and clear conformity to providence. If we limit ourselves now to material life, Gaudí's ideas were admirably positive. With a certain daring these ideas could be summarized in three comprehensive slogans. Whenever he meant to signify that he was a man with deep roots in his land, he said: "The Catalans are all one people." Whenever he wanted to manifest the faith he had in his country, he formulated this axiom: "The prime of a people is the moment of the temple." Whenever he spoke about art, he held that its essence and reality came from the Mediterranean basin. He said: "Do not go north to find art and beauty; this is found on the Mediterranean, from whose shores— Egypt, Assyria, Greece, Rome, Spain, North Africa—have come all works of art." Enlarging on this concept, he told architect Martinell: "The north and the tropics do not have light hitting them at forty-five degrees, the best light for the perfect vision of objects; where there is not enough light, or light is too zenithal, the objects, inadequately lit, appear deformed; more than the object, they see the ghost of the object; their heads fill with ghosts, and fantasy overtakes them. In the north, literature is fantastic, and so is Gothic architecture; the same is true of the art and poems of India. We Mediterraneans have eyes unaccustomed to ghosts, only used to images; we are more imaginative than fantastic and therefore better gifted for the visual arts."

During the spring of 1910 Gaudí lived for three weeks in Vic. The architect was going through one of the most intense, overworked, feverish periods in the construction process of the Sagrada Família. His fame was already established. His work progressed amid a great polemic. In many sectors of Barcelona intellectual life, this work was the object of a permanent criticism. But it would be a mistake to believe that everybody was against it. In general the libertines, the so-called "strong spirits," mostly artists, almost all of them in love with Parisian life, were against Gaudí.

Senyor Vilaplana i Pujolar, a Vic pharmacist who was a member of the museum committee of that town, sent me a report on Gaudí's sojourn. People who knew Gaudí in person are fewer every day. Time goes by and people grow old, and leave no written trace. That is why when we have a direct testimonial we must record it, so as at least to contribute to the biography that some day will be written of Gaudí.

During the winter of 1910, Senyor Gaudí fell ill. His body could not sustain him; his head felt faint. Upon learning the news and being a man of action, Father Ignasi Casanovas of the Company of Jesus, a great friend of the architect, decided to do something. He took Gaudí to the office of a specialist, who prescribed a restful spell at some quiet place outside Barcelona, a more substantial diet, and abstention from all intellectual work. If a doctor alone, no matter how eminent, had recommended the above, Gaudí would have paid no attention, because he never listened to doctors or to any recommendations for the well-being of his person. But as Father Casanovas was the intermediary, he obeyed.

"Senyor Gaudí must take care of himself, he is too thin, undernourished," said the reverend Jesuit.

The burning of convents during 1909 had heated some heads, and had manifested to some that things were not going well. Those are the times of Father Casanovas's influence on the most intelligently conservative sector of the leading class. All in all, Gaudí was part of that class.

Father Casanovas had a great friendship with the Rocafiguera family of Vic, and he thought it best for Gaudí to go to that city, which the priest deemed ideal for the architect's rest, and for him to gain a few kilos. He knew that Senyora Concepció Vila, the widow of Senyor Josep Rocafiguera, had opened with magnificent hospitality the doors to her own house for however long it would take to put Senyor Gaudí back on his feet. To arrange the matter, some letters were exchanged between Father Casanovas and Senyora Concepció, full of compliments and exhalations of generosity, and indicative of the excellent reception the Rocafiguera family gave to Father Casanovas's proposal. In all those arrangements, Senyor Gaudí played an absolutely passive role.

"Senyor Gaudí must be taken care of, he is too thin," the reverend Jesuit repeated.

One good day Father Casanovas and the architect arrived in Vic. The first did not stay long, only long enough to make the introductions and to leave Gaudí at the Rocafigueras. Gaudí was a gruff man, closed, obsessed, alienated from all possible social life. The widow Rocafiguera and her children treated him like a member of the family and did all they could to make his stay pleasant and amusing. "The main thing is to keep him entertained," Father Casanovas had told the hospitable family when he took his leave.

"Two days after the arrival of the architect," Senyor Vilaplana continues, "Senyora Concepció, who was my relative, came to see me and said:

" 'Quimet, we don't know what to do with this good man. He speaks very little, seems very sad, and, even though we do everything to please him, I think he is bored. He is not costing us much money, though: he's never hungry, eats nothing, we are at a loss to find things that may please him. I thought you could help us out in this situation. What will Father Casanovas say if Gaudí does not improve a little? You must be the best person to take him out on a walk, to show him Vic and the countryside. Walking may amuse him, awaken his appetite, and his anemia might go away.'

" 'My pleasure!' I told my relative. 'I'll pick him up today and we'll go for a walk.'

"That afternoon I went to the Rocafigueras, they introduced me to Gaudí, and we went out. He walked very slowly, seemed deflated, and his face had a sickly and broken color.

"During that and other outings we visited the cathedral, the museum, and what is most notable in the city. We also got out; I took him to see the Romanesque churches of Sant Sixt and Sant Fructuós, which are close to Vic, and we even stopped at some farm houses of the vicinity, those I thought for some reason or other deserved a visit.

"We spoke of many things. One of his obsessions—and I say obsessions because he insisted on it many times—was to affirm that true art had been produced around the Mediterranean and nowhere else. I timidly objected that something had also been done in other parts and that, to limit ourselves to Europe, we could not forget the magnificent cathedrals of the European west, the urban medieval architecture of Flanders, Holland, and Germany, the magnificent palaces of the French and English nobility. He replied, curtly, angrily, that what I said had nothing to do with true art, that all that had been derived from older and more authentic models the origins of which were Mediterranean. I countered that in any case such figures as Rembrandt, Van Eyck, and Van Dyck, among so many others, had been great artists, and that northern Europe had produced glass, furniture, tapestry, and ceramic makers of the first order. Hearing those opinions he became ostensibly frazzled.

" 'You refer,' he said, 'to bourgeois living-room artists, third-rate decorators who cannot be in any way compared with the artists working in Mediterranean countries.'

"I soon realized my statements, even though I presented them as kindly as I could, upset him greatly in a morbid and bitter way. Because of this—in order to prevent an attack—I decided not to bring the subject up again and eliminate from my conversation whatever, in my modest understanding, could bother him. To argue with Gaudí was not pleasant, and not exactly because he would hit you with a profusion of points. It was not pleasant because he argued by dint of hammer blows.

"In the course of our conversations we spoke only a few times about the Sagrada Família, and in general of his architecture. If Gaudí, whenever he argued, was proud and haughty, his discretion vis-à-vis his own work proved to me he was a man with no vanity.

"Once I asked him if he had traveled much. He answered he had not traveled at all, that his very few trips had been short, and that he had never felt the desire to travel. He added that once in a while he looked at photographs of some art object and that practically—according to him—that was all he had seen in that respect. At times he gave the impression of being a snob of humbleness, scarcity, and precariousness. Some people say they know all and know nothing; they claim having seen all and have seen nothing. Gaudí functioned in the opposite sense, but I never quite believed him about that.

"One day, walking down the road to Vilatorta, he discovered next to the lower window of a mill a naive sculpture of a calvary, the work of some rustic artisan, quite rough in his knowledge of drawing. For this exact reason, he said, the work appealed to him.

       " 'What a pity that our friend Pujol would not see this calvary!' he said with a sorrowful expression. 'He would like it so much!' "

       "I think Senyor Gaudí," the pharmacist Vilaplana writes as a conclusion, "was a good man, incapable of hurting anyone, stubborn as a pig, a simple Christian of impressive sobriety."

       Hit by a streetcar—no one realized the victim was Gaudí—he died in the hospital like a pauper, which is exactly what he wanted. His will, in any case, was always so.

       Gaudí is one of the Catalans of greatest stature in our history. The whole world is pouring such interest, such curiosity, such an enormous mass of bibliography on his figure and his work that his case tends to be a repetition of that of Ramon Llull. As Gaudí's universal dimension expands, however, his Catalan roots appear more clearly; the man from this country is made more manifest.

       From the viewpoint of our habitual mediocrity, Gaudí seems an inflamed man, carried away by his ideas of grandeur, an unabashed fool, but this fool and this inflamed one is at once a calculator, a sharp mathematician, a builder of pure rationality. It is the same case as with Ramon Llull in a different field. He is not inflamed by nothing, a fool of inanity, as many Catalans may be; he is the man who, fleeing from the (empirical) formulas of the Gothic cathedral, calculates rationally, micrographically, and brings to life an immense production. This sensational, unique fact reveals the man's greatness. And just like Llull, he gives his sublime obsession a total focus, lending it the last drops of his own human misery—within a country of superficial people blinded by money.

       But besides being a great builder, Gaudí was a great artist, a nerve of visual beauty, a permanent meditative, hypersensitive to the forms and colors of life. And so he dressed his principal monuments with the symbolism of Catholic liturgy—a prodigious, immense world—but he did so following his earthly roots, transforming symbolic abstractions into realized, that is to say, real, realistic, even naturalistic symbols.

A Note on Palau's
"Picasso and Catalonia"

 Barcelona, a vibrant artistic center during the period straddling the turn of the century, had a great influence on Pablo Ruiz Picasso. The artist resided in Barcelona during his early formative period and in this city had his first one-man show; later, a convalescence in Horta de Sant Joan signified a turning point in his style. His celebrated *Les demoiselles d'Avignon*, for example, was inspired by the professionals of a certain whorehouse on Barcelona's Carrer Avinyó; Picasso's irony gallicized both the title of the painting and the name of the street. Yet Barcelona was at the same time a city where an increasing flow of migrant workers and a deep economic cleavage were provoking the tragic social clashes that characterized it during the first third of this century. These immigrants, for whom the Catalans had coined the derogatory term *xarnego*, were in the most part Andalusians like Picasso himself. Born in Málaga, the artist moved to Barcelona with his family when his father obtained a position as an art teacher in the city's most prestigious art school. Picasso, although no *xarnego* himself, must have felt included in the Catalan middle- or upper-class disdain and hostility toward those poor unskilled laborers from his native region. Perhaps his later membership in the French Communist party had something to do with this. Picasso's friendship with the Catalan painter Isidre Nonell, who

often chose the destitute as the subject matter of his canvases, may have been strengthened by the torn feelings of Picasso's social self.

In Barcelona, Picasso found a haven for his art in the café opened by Pere Romeu and baptized Els Quatre Gats. The phrase echoes the common Catalan expression *quatre gats,* "four cats," used to signify a notoriously poorly attended gathering: only "four cats" showed up, Catalans will say. "Els Quatre Gats" is an eminently Bohemian name for a coffeehouse where Pere Romeu gathered painters and poets for shows and readings. Despite its name, it soon became the hub of the progressive artistic life in Barcelona, the last bastion of *modernisme.*

Josep Palau i Fabre, a poet, dramatist, and essayist born in Barcelona in 1917, has devoted a number of pages to Picasso. The present essay was originally published as an "Interlude" in his *Doble Assaig sobre Picasso* (Barcelona: Selecta, 1964), which received the Josep Yxart prize. His piece, written ten years before Picasso's death, illustrates not only an important period in Picasso's artistic development and the artistic milieu of early twentieth-century Barcelona, but also the ambiguity with which Catalans view their great figures.

My translation follows the first edition.

JOSEP PALAU I FABRE

Picasso and Catalonia

We have often claimed Picasso to be one of us Catalans. People from Málaga are now beginning to do the same, in part thanks to a Catalan, since it was Jaume Sabartés who, some years ago, donated all his Picasso papers to Málaga's Municipal Library and awakened the somewhat sleepy local pride by digging in the archives of that city for documents referring to Picasso or relating to him. After the Malagueños, he is now claimed by all Castilian-speaking Spaniards. The French find it hard to think that Picasso was not French; the School of Paris, for all its cosmopolitan character, provides French chauvinism with a good springboard for its claims. And there are even some Italians who, invoking the artist's family name, defend a supposed Italian origin for Picasso.

What may we think of all this? Whose side shall we take? It would be ridiculous by now to hold to any fanaticism or narrow particularism of whatever kind. Picasso's case is quite complex and cannot be resolved axiomatically or bluntly. Lacking clear and direct statements from the man himself, we nevertheless have his life story, his career, his actions; all these may help us clarify the issue. And while we are at it, is it not as good as a formal statement that he never gave up his Spanish nationality, refusing to change it even when it was to his advantage to do so? (About 1945, to be precise, he wanted to remarry and possession of French citizenship would have simplified his divorce.) Earlier Picasso accepted the post of curator of the Prado Museum and contributed, as a Spaniard, to the

Spanish Pavilion of the 1937 Paris International Fair. On the other hand, he did participate in the demonstrations of the School of Paris, and he appears in books and shows of modern French painting without deigning to deny or deauthorize such affiliation, even when those paintings belong to museums or private collections and seldom have been submitted directly by him. This French designation has not prevented him from participating in group shows of Spanish, Iberian, or simply Catalan painters. Surely Picasso feels no contradiction between these diverse manifestations and thinks in his heart that people will be able to see the partial truth in each of them. Perhaps the most obvious anomaly, speaking of this, is the fact that he joined a "French" political party, not because of the party's ideology but because it was French. We could spill a lot of ink on this topic as well.

Let us now return to our starting theme: up to what point is Picasso a Catalan and up to what point may we Catalans claim him as one of our own? As in El Greco's case, the problem is thorny. Let us remember that in the latter case we have, it seems, Jewish origins, a Greek—Cretan—birth and childhood, a Venetian formative period (often overlooked but obvious whenever one visits Venice and sees its Tintorettos), and a maturity in Toledo. Picasso's case seems to have at least three layers: an Andalusian birth and childhood, a Catalan formative period, and a Parisian flowering. Surely this will be the overall pattern that will survive for Picasso, but it still does not tell us in what proportion or measure these three stages or ingredients balance out. Let us advance, as a confession of principles, our general criterion on the matter before we apply it to Picasso.

All human identity is made up of three strata: what I am, what I think I am, and what I want to be. "What I am" refers to that part of one's identity we may consider vital; it is shaped by birth and race (and to a lesser degree religion). "What I think I am" refers to those situations that were adopted by individuals because of their environment or history but that could have been different. For example, nineteenth-century Flemings and Algerians may very likely have believed themselves and called themselves, respectively, Belgian and French. Or, to give another example, many Spaniards of Jewish or Arabic descent may have completely lost their notion of race, and believe themselves fully Catholic without the faintest notion that their ancestors practiced a different religion with the same faith or fanaticism. Or similarly, many who consider themselves perfect French citizens might be called Shaeffer or Schumann and even be Germanophobes. "What I want to be" refers to the voluntary bent of one's personality. One may be Catholic and want to be Protestant, another may be

Turkish and want to become French, and so on. There is a region clearly incompatible with our will, and that is race and birth. One cannot be Caucasian or native American if one is not born that way. One cannot be from Paris or London if one was born in Barcelona or Constantinople.

Clearly those countries and individuals who overvalue the first of these strata may fall easy victims to racism. But to those who believe that their freedom is what differentiates human beings, no matter how light that freedom, the belief in it, or even their will to freedom, the third of the above factors becomes cardinal. One is mostly what one wants to be: Protestant or Catholic, Greek, Turkish, or North American.

In Picasso's case, his will to remain a Spaniard is remarkable, but such a title is somewhat loose and may contradict others. To be precise: would Picasso have chosen the Catalan nationality if this had been possible? We do not think so. Not because he despised that nationality, but because its adoption would have meant renouncing the Spanish one, and we have said that Picasso never appears ready to renounce anything peculiarly his. It would be more prudent to say, therefore, that Picasso reiterated his Catalanness within the Iberian complex and without ever renouncing his Andalusianism. Picasso in effect iterated his love and faithfulness for our country with some important gifts to the Barcelona Museum of Modern Art (*Harlequin, Minotauromachy*) before the Civil War; now—at the height of his glory—his wish to illustrate two Catalan short stories by his deceased friend Ramon Raventós, his murals for the College of Architects in Barcelona, his recent homage to the Father Abbot of Montserrat with its reference to the Virgin of Montserrat, Patroness of Catalonia, and his help in the founding of the Picasso Museum in Barcelona leave no doubts as to the existence of a sentiment of predilection toward our country. On what does this sentiment rest? To what is that predilection due? Or, more exactly, what are Picasso's feelings for Catalonia? What nexus unites him to our country and how large and deep are his roots in our land?

We must consider Picasso an extremely gifted man, a genius on whom life has smiled, as we say colloquially; he has been a favorite of fortune. Saying this we are not ignoring his adversities, his privations, his suffering; those seem to have been sufficient to stimulate but not to drown him. Picasso could make his that maxim of Goethe's: "What does not kill me makes me stronger." Clearly we are now entering a high-risk zone in his consciousness, for he is the only one who knows what has befallen him and how he has fared. But in so far as we may judge from the outside, it would seem that the plan of his life—as we understand it—is the one we have just outlined.

When we speak of his good fortune we have in mind a number of things. His early formation at the side of his father gave him, from a tender age, what others acquire much later. His sojourn in Barcelona coincided with years bursting with the most turbulent vitality in our city's history. His journey to Paris took place during the relatively sweet beginning of the century. During the war of 1914–1918, Picasso, being a Spaniard, was not drafted, as were some of his fellow painters. By the time of the Spanish Civil War, which affected him so much, his age allowed him to go on painting, undrafted again. During the German occupation of France his prestige was already so great that he commanded respect. We also have in mind his powerful physical energy that allowed him to reach an advanced age and continue working tirelessly, and even remarry, and so on.

But all this takes us away from our topic, which was an analysis of his time among us. His debt to Barcelona, what his prolonged sojourns in our city have meant for his work, has been admirably stated by Rafael Benet (*Art,* no. 1, October 1933):

The great anarchist inside Picasso's spirit was shaped by that raggedy, crazed, and heroic Barcelona of the time of the bombs in the Liceu and Canvis Nous. In the Barcelona that had, atop its Montjuïc, the military fortress to avenge but also to increase its crimes. In that conspiratorial and revolutionary Barcelona that had grown too fast and absorbed too many people from all over the world while it kept its allogeneous and patriarchal politics, based mainly on big sticks.

Many of the artists of the time had shaped their minds amidst all kinds of civil monstrosities. To be a Bohemian was then fashionable; it was fashionable to be miles away from the bourgeois and the petty bourgeois who were considered ordinary and egoistic. Some Catalan intellectuals, of refined bourgeois background for the most part, bet their honor on the card of those persecuted for their crimes against society. There was a reigning atmosphere of anarchistic dilettantism; not even Maragall was free from its influence.

From such eccentric atmosphere came many monstrous personalities. Gaudí, the man of the New Cathedral, enthroned with his genius a new lyrical style in architecture. Manolo [Hugué], the sculptor of degenerates, invented the first "expressionismus" before the Germans.

From all that anarchistic art we now have, as a supreme sample, the Barcelona *eixample,* a graceless monument crowned by the so-called apple of discord on the Passeig de Gràcia.

Pablo Ruiz Picasso was formed in that *fin de siècle* Barcelona whose motto was "fend for yourself." Surely his keen and enormously contradictory mind was deformed forever in that atmosphere. But Picasso had as his first formative element his Andalusian blood: a great irony rounded out by Oriental mysticism. The *pícaro* in him has, time and again, strangled the Italian—the artist of pure form—who cohabits the conscious and the subconscious mind of the great Malagan. The Florentine may have decisively triumphed over the Gypsy had Picasso not experienced our *fin de siècle* Barcelona.

But his greatness as much as his weakness also rests on this Barcelona formation. All of Picasso's strange experiments that have revolutionized the art world have an anarchistic and very Barcelonese root: his mutilations, his abstractions, his new concept of volume and rhythm, and his calligraphies that have altogether led a legion of artists—some with positive talent—to take intricate paths or dead-end corridors. All this had its moment of fecundation in our Barcelona. It does not matter that Picasso, when he went to Paris, acquired—up to a point—a typically French taste and sense of measure; nevertheless the formation or deformation of the artist was carried out in his early youth in our Barcelona, a city full of all sorts of follies.

The above study, from which we have quoted extensively because we deem it pivotal, is not exhaustive, however; nor does it pretend to be. We must consider and evaluate the ambivalence Picasso must have felt for Barcelona: on one hand, we cannot delude ourselves and ignore that, having been born in Málaga, he must have felt like a foreigner. Picasso must have sensed quite acutely the social difference that generally separates the *crème de la crème* from the immigrant workers. More than once—principally during the period of adaptation—Picasso must have experienced the alienation that Barcelona society imposes on the marginalized, native or alien. Picasso must have considered himself disdained from the outset by that bourgeoisie. On the other hand, this feeling must have been compensated, in his inner being, by the immediate camaraderie that normally reigns in youthful art circles. In those, he must have felt at home and among his own people. The Quatre Gats represents the happy times of that exhilaration and creative medley that disregard frontiers and races. This was Picasso's true entry gate into Barcelona.

But still, in saying this we have not come to the heart of the issue, which lies in a much more intimate and, in so far as we know, unexplored zone. Two basic facts—one positive, the other negative—mark Picasso's time in Catalonia. They are worthy of consideration.

One revolves around the exhibition organized by his friends from Els Quatre Gats, which was Picasso's first, and his subsequent trips to Paris and, later, Madrid. Let us say that the trip to Paris was almost a duty; probably all the young artists of the time dreamed of doing the same. But why, upon returning from Paris, did Picasso go to Madrid instead of remaining in Barcelona? What was he seeking in the Castilian capital? Picasso must have known perfectly well, after a first incursion two years before, that the artistic atmosphere that predominated there was by no means as alive and up-to-date as in our city. Why then leave this one for that one where he is an unknown, where he must start from scratch? Perhaps because of the success of his *Ciencia y caridad* of three years before? This must have weighed on the scales, but it was not the decisive element.

His Quatre Gats exhibition, as Sabartés comments in his memoirs (*Portraits et souvenirs,* 60–63), is a poor man's show, a kind of marginal exhibition. Picasso presented it with the help and encouragement of some friends who had faith in this Andalusian whom they viewed as their leader. The exhibition's portraits, as opposed to those in the more or less official or recognized shows, did not present well-known personalities of the Barcelona bourgeoisie. The bourgeoisie, then, did not flock to visit the show. The only success and echo that Picasso could aspire to could only be of an artistic order: critics, collectors, artists. In reality, Picasso's exhibition in the Quatre Gats cannot be understood—in its historical and psychological context—if we do not consider it as a challenge to Ramon Casas, the official painter who was the favorite of Barcelona society. Why this challenge? The questions we should really ask about that exhibition are: did it have the success it deserved? Was there a conspiracy against Picasso? Here we find dissenting opinions.

We read, for example, in Sabartés's book:

> What must have attracted the public to the Quatre Gats exhibition? The subjects of the portraits? Unthinkable. We are simply a bunch of unknowns, most of us poorly dressed, and all of us badly thought of as we agree little with the established taste: those of us who managed to penetrate the newspapers' gates are barely read; those who draw or paint or sculpt are still in workshops or in school. The others are neither writers nor musicians nor sculptors nor painters nor poets; at most they are apprentices in journalism or followers of artists.
>
> And, all told, who is the author? An Andalusian? A young man who, as they say, is making waves; but for the moment this is all. Perhaps he exhibits elsewhere? Who talks about him? His friends cannot extend their admiration beyond their own circle, which is limited to ne'er-do-wells with no credit. On the other hand those who have a well-recognized capacity to speak ignore him; if they deal with him, it is to criticize him; if they detect his worth, they do not say so, or they do so in a hidden way, with a superior smile; and so you may well believe that if they were to write what they think, they would succeed, with a wily twist of their pens, only in leaving their readers ignorant as to whether their judgment expresses doubt or affirmation.

A few pages before, Sabartés had written: "The visitors are few and poorly chosen. The great public does not come; we are the most assiduous, because we all find, more or less, the time to drop by, to go for coffee and chat with our comrades gathered around a table."

In contrast with this opinion we have the words by Miquel Utrillo written one year after the exhibition (*Pèl i Ploma,* Barcelona, June 1901):

> The talent of the young Andalusian painter, who speaks Spanish with a Barcelona accent (as was reported in the only issue of the Madrid journal *Mercurio*), revealed himself a pioneer among his fellow artists, a jury deserving of higher credit than those who grant medals to paintings as if they were chocolate products. Some "half exhibited" works in the Quatre Gats were quickly acquired by those who seek Art's early fruits, and the Catalanist journal *Joventut* published Picasso's first drawing.

This text by Miquel Utrillo, under the pen name Pinzell, "brush," reveals that Picasso was held in admiration by his fellow artists, the kind of admiration that is almost always provoked in those co-religionists or comrades-in-calling when they see markedly superior talent. Such implicit recognition is not always trailed by explicit or manifest success; there is no lack of reluctance among certain folk, and these may even form an antagonistic cabal. But the second part of this text makes something very important clear: whether there was a cabal against Picasso or not, the secret recognition of his talent was arresting or unconcealable enough, his worth obvious, and the admiration he awakened ample enough to ensure that the gallery which, according to Sabartés, had no visitors, quickly sold the exhibited works. Who bought them? Not his comrades, who, Sabartés informs us, hadn't a penny, but rather, as Miquel Utrillo says, some Barcelona *amateurs.* Considering Picasso's age (he was eighteen) and the fact that it was a first exhibition, this result is by no means negligible. It may not have been a roaring success, but it was closer to that than to a failure.

But we still have not found the core of the problem. The true center of the problem is, as Jaume Sabartés hints, the fight with Ramon Casas and with established values, for reasons Sabartés does not analyze or develop.

The true center of the problem lies, as we understand it, in a law as old as the world itself, the law that we commonly formulate when we say there cannot be two cocks in a henhouse. When a man is born to reign, in whatever field, and his due position is denied him, his reaction usually is the one Picasso had at the time. "Aut Caesar aut nihil." Picasso knows he has been made to reign, his heart bursts with this feeling, he knows he can prove it at any time, feels the impatience of his youth. His reaction is normal. An inscription at the foot of one of his self-portraits, dated precisely on the eve of his departure for Paris, seems to confirm our assertion: *Yo el Rey, Yo el Rey.*

But why should Picasso, after his first show and his relative success, not keep on fighting to get the place that was due him? Why did he rush off to Paris, and above all, why did he then go to Madrid instead of continuing to grub and hustle in Barcelona?

The answer, as we see things, is very simple: even though his talent was recognized by his fellow artists and by other persons with higher authority, and even though the sale of works exhibited in the Quatre Gats may be considered a legitimate success, Picasso knew there was an insurmountable obstacle preventing his ascension to the first rank of Catalan painters, and that obstacle was Ramon Casas. Not because Casas was the enthroned and almost official painter of Barcelona society, nor because he was a good painter and an excellent portraitist. These qualities did not scare Picasso. In any case this was a field in which he felt capable of battling. What frightened him, what irritated him, was that the main art magazine of the city, the publication that could have done him justice and promoted him, was *Pèl i Ploma,* and this magazine was practically owned by Ramon Casas. Ramon Casas reigned as the despotic monarch in *Pèl i Ploma.* The covers were almost all invariably his, and the contents were strewn with his drawings and reproductions of his works, often accompanied by articles on his personality. Picasso knew very well that no matter how much he tried, no matter how much others conceded, he would never be granted that place of honor, that privileged position; he would never be able to supplant Ramon Casas in his domain, in his home. For Picasso, Ramon Casas's strength was based on a weapon he did not have, the economic. His journey to Madrid confirms what we are saying. In Madrid, helped by Soler, Picasso rushed to found *Arte Joven,* a magazine in which he would hold a role equivalent to that of Ramon Casas in *Pèl i Ploma.* But the mood in Madrid was not receptive to artistic innovation, and his friend Soler's purse was not fat enough to continue this venture indefinitely.

Miquel Utrillo astutely realized all this, as we deduce from his article, and it must have been at his initiative that a year later *Pèl i Ploma,* the magazine owned by Ramon Casas, organized an exhibition of Picasso's pastels at Parés, Barcelona's premier gallery and Ramon Casas's outlet. But it was too late to turn back the clock. Some things, such as Ramon Casas's supremacy in *Pèl i Ploma* and over Barcelona society, were irreversible; in addition, Picasso had already made his first trip to Paris and, by the time Utrillo's article, an article with a clearly "expiatory" nature, was published in *Pèl i Ploma* (June 1901), Picasso was again in Paris. At that stage of Picasso's life, one week, one day, one hour may have been incalculably long.

The memory of those events might well have given someone else a decisive feeling of frustration toward Catalans and Catalonia. Had Picasso, instead of being who he is, been a failed or embittered man, that is the feeling that would have prevailed. But Picasso is an eminently healthy man, and in his mind, next to those events, other more positive factors come to counterbalance and even tilt the scales in our favor. The most important of all these factors would be (and this is the second fact we wanted to point out, even though it is an earlier event) his friendship with Manuel Pallarès, who, after Picasso's first trip to Madrid from which he came back sick, housed him in his estate in Horta de Sant Joan for almost a year, allowing him to regain his health and work to his heart's content. The importance of that sojourn and the feelings it provoked are attested to by a well-known phrase of Picasso's: "All I know I have learned at Horta de Sant Joan." Perhaps his serene image of the world is completed by the vision of that youthful friend (we are still referring to Pallarès) who, even though he was a Catalan and belonged to a comfortable social class and had, therefore, a certain influence in Barcelona society, has remained an obscure painter, forgotten by his very own co-religionists and compatriots, much more so than Picasso ever was by the Barcelonese of the Quatre Gats period. That society was not especially unjust to him, and perhaps even a little less so than are many societies toward their own children.

Later, on his way through the world, Picasso must have remembered that it was a Catalan, Soler, who helped him financially to publish *Arte Joven* in Madrid; that our great Isidre Nonell freely offered him a studio in Paris during his first visit to that city; and that, once there, his first agent, Manyac, was a Catalan. And we should have no need to add to this list the names of Vidal i Ventosa and Jaume Sabartés, his lifelong friends.

Picasso, on his way through the world, has surely come to understand that what happened to him in Barcelona was no worse than what would have happened to him in any other part of the world, and that our people are, more or less, a little like people everywhere, no better, no worse.

A Note on Foix's
"Three Painters and Four Colors"

Josep Vicenç Foix i Mas (the first surname pronounced *Foshe*), who signed all his writings with what he termed the "false pseudonym" J. V. Foix, is probably the most illustrious poet of twentieth-century Catalonia. Born in the little town of Sarrià (incorporated today into Barcelona) in 1893, he died there the day after his ninety-fourth birthday, on January 29, 1987. His contributions to poetry won him a number of awards, among them the Premi d'Honor de les Lletres Catalanes (1973), gold medals from the Generalitat (1981) and the City of Barcelona (1980), and the Spanish government's Premio de las Letras Españolas in 1984, the same year he was made doctor honoris causa by the University of Barcelona.

During 1918 Foix kept a diary of dream-based prose that was to be one of the main sources for his writing for the rest of his life. Those early writings, never published in their original form, established his private universe, the oneiric world he called *ultrason,* "ultra-sleep."

As opposed to more socially minded poets such as Maragall and Espriu, Foix is aggressively lyrical; his many political writings were mostly contributions to newspapers, as were his critical reviews. As a poet Foix has been termed a surrealist, a label he always refused (preferring to call himself an investigator in poetry), perhaps because of the associations of surrealism with communism. Foix, a Catalan nationalist, dreamed of a strong state for his country and admired the political ideas of the French proto-fascist Charles Maurras. Foix's poetry, however, limits itself to the realm of the intimate and, more than an exploitation of communal themes, is an exploration of the language. Foix is the supreme master of modern Catalan, at once an innovator and a conservative who went to medieval texts to create the richest idiom in modern Catalan. His most famous book is a collection of sonnets, *Sol, i de dol* (Alone, and in sorrow) an avant-garde exploration of a futuristic world within the demanding forms of late-medieval metrics. The juxtaposition of old and new—"the old museum and its faded madonnas / and the extreme painting of today"—imbues both the expression and the content of this book. The conjunction of medieval artistic traditions and the technological advances of his day gives Foix one of his favorite thematic resources. Another favored theme is art; he had an interest in painting all his life, cultivated the friendship of many artists—in particular Joan Miró, Salvador Dalí, and Joan Ponç—and produced a poetry that is the verbal equivalent of the great visual innovations of his contemporaries.

I have chosen for this anthology not essays on painting or painters but typically Foixian prose poems; these pieces show an important aspect of his poetic universe and give an idea of the excitement avant-garde art could awaken in Barcelona in the 1930s and later. Foix's work on painting goes beyond critical evaluation and interpretation, for it is at once a poetic creation and a document of the creative act itself. The pieces on the four colors also reveal Miró, who inspired them, as a painter rooted in the Catalan landscape, particularly the stony coastlines of the Costa Brava and Majorca.

The pieces on these three painters appeared as introductions to their first one-person exhibitions and were later incorporated into Foix's *KRTU* (1932). I have followed the recent critical edition by Jaume VallcorbaPlana (Barcelona: Edicions dels Quaderns Crema, 1983). The rest of the selection was written by Foix in 1969 under the title *Quatre colors aparien el món* . . . (Four colors couple the world . . .) from a line in one of Foix's own *Sol, i de dol* sonnets. It was first published by Gustau Gili (Barcelona, 1975) along with four etchings by Miró. For my translation I have followed volume 2 of Foix's *Obres completes* (Barcelona: Edicions 62, 1979), 459–469.

J. V. FOIX

Three Painters and Four Colors

SALVADOR DALÍ

Not many days ago down the street from my home a clever adolescent carrying a bag full of books offered me, in a low voice, some beautiful editions: herbals with chromo-lithographed plates, biology prolegomena, nature formularies, and celestial charts and historical atlases with the processes of the mysterious formation and disappearance of the Atlantic continent. He also had, in reproduction, the most singular images collected at the platforms of the subterranean avenues of pre-sleep. Determined to turn down his offer, I was surprised by his sudden disappearance after he left in my hands an invitation to the opening of the Dalí exhibit at the Galeries Dalmau and a blank catalog.

From six to seven in the evening these winter days, on the streets of the city and in the great mansions' gates, the witches spread their wide and colorful kerchiefs; before they abandon themselves to their cotillion in suburban squares, they flow invisible among the crowd with low chime sounds, deep breathing, and furtive kisses, and as they pass they spread their characteristic scent of baked apples. On Passeig de Gràcia last Friday at that hour as I headed toward Dalmau's, I did not realize that the adolescent from the previous day bore a rare semblance to the painter

Dalí, and it had doubtless been he, only with his tie camouflaged and his eyebrows ingeniously elongated.

But when I was about to go into the gallery I lost heart, seeing that the doorman was the same one as in the Equestrian Club. Discouraged, I turned around, and at that moment the car with the school girls stopped right in front of me, the one that each evening disappears down the Carrer Diputació amidst clouds of luster and incense, leaving a wake of luminous carmine. They got out of the car two by two, carefully folded their large fake wings, and tightened the broad knot of their ties over their lips. At the very end, the smallest, to ensure that she would find her way back, dropped mothballs. As if penetrating a virgin forest, they disappeared cautiously into the penumbra of the hallway.

Then I realized that the doorman from the Equestrian Club had been replaced by a long-bearded gnome who was now kindly signaling to me, and I followed him. Down the long corridor we heard our steps as if lost in the vast rooms of the floor above. At both sides of the corridor, long display cases, also filled with books and more books, showed the rarest specimens of stuffed birds.

"Then, my dear Dalmau, you continue remodeling your gallery?"

Once I was in the exhibition room, Dalí was caressing a big multicolored bird perched on his left shoulder.

"Superrealism?"

"No, no."

"Cubism?"

"No, not that either: painting, painting, if you please."

And he showed me the windows of the wonderful palace he had built at Dalmau's. I had the precise awareness of witnessing the exact moments of the birth of a painter. The vivisection classroom showed lean and limitless physiological landscapes; beautiful bleeding groves lent their shade to the brief ponds where fish struggle from noon till night to get rid of their shadows. And at the bottom of the painter's, the harlequin's, and the mannequin's pupils there appeared black shooting stars over a silver sky. I thought I would remain there, but then from the bottom of each canvas, at the stroke of seven, came the famous ghosts.

It is a beautiful spectacle: subtle, they cover you with their veils and infect you with their immateriality. If only many Barcelonese knew, the spectacle of ghosts filling the rooms at Dalmau's every evening would give them an opening to the "other" world.

When I left the gallery, a deserted, treeless, lampless Passeig de Gràcia was an immense avenue alienated by hundreds of *Shell*, their luminous heads reflecting sweetly on the asphalt. A will superior to mine made me, instead of heading home along Carrer Provença, seek refuge in the *Service Station* of Carrer Aragó.

JOAN MIRÓ

In the middle of April 1928 I was surprised to see the mouth of the Sant Gervasi tunnel obstructed by the presence of a group of ladies dressed in green, with hats and shoes of the same color, and in the fashion of 1890. I was also surprised that each one of them, while contemplating it with undecipherable gestures, would ostentatiously show a lithograph reproducing, life-sized, the Gioconda. ("Mona Lisa! Mona Lisa!" shouted a conductor from the Ferrocarrils de Catalunya. "No, the Gioconda! The Gioconda!" I replied desperately. We almost came to blows.)

That conductor seemed very muscular to me. He donned an excessive mustache, a replica of typographic "mustaches." ("I know you: I saw a painting of you, in 1918, on the walls of the Dalmau Gallery on Carrer Portaferrissa. Joaquim Folguera assured me then you were the husband of a lady always dressed in green. You're an impostor! You are no more than the husband of each of these ladies—now counting 30, 38, 49, 97, 100—and you have grown a mustache like Joan Miró's. You're neither a conductor nor Miró. But, oh God, could you be the painter Miró, the husband of each one of these ladies? But Miró shaved his mustache some time ago. If you didn't wear that big mustache, I'd swear you were Miró. You're not wearing a 1898 mustache nor a 1928 one; you're not clean-shaven, conductor; you're not the husband of each of these ladies. You're Miró, true, Joan Miró, the painter Joan Miró. How goes it, Miró, how are you, excuse me, and how is each one of your wives; how come you've let so many mustaches grow right and left on your face, so that you can multiply as the husband of each one of your wives?")

The convoy, a two-car going to Sarrià, went nonstop behind the tunnel. I continued my dialogue all alone, then I saw that Miró sat next to me, asleep in an eternal sleep. As I tried to wake him, his head disappeared mysteriously through the window, in the form of a phosphorescent ovule; from his decapitated body a flock of birds emerged forming a column, and an enormous, gelatinous hand, like the hypnotic materialization of M. A. Cassanyes's hand, fell on my lap.

When I thought I had reached the provisional station downtown, I verified the presence of thousands of phosphorescent ovules ascending and descending along the coastline of an unknown sea and floating uneasily in the atmosphere. I was about to crack some in my hands and give birth to the beautiful unprecedented worlds they carry in germ, but my arms were the fallen branches of a dead bole, projecting a choked shadow on the landscape.

ARTUR CARBONELL

I met him in the middle of a quicklimy March at the very beach of Sant Sebastià. He was dressed as an angel with a white silk tunic, excessively long, adorned with unreproducible gold filigree. His head was covered with a most exquisite blond wig girded by a diadem of daisies, and his lips were painted in the same magnificent sky blue that oozes from his eyes. An angel all alone on a deserted morning by the sea had to exalt, inevitably, my curiosity. I left the gonfalon with the effigy of Saint Bartholomew, which I had carried all day from the center of town to the parish church, leaning against a crumbling wall, straightened the bow of my surplice, and approached the unknown boy. I had never before addressed anyone suddenly, using the sweet Ab slang from school: "Abisabn't yabour nabame Abartabur Cabarbabonabell?" He folded both wings to his chest and in great reverence answered, "Yabes!" We shook hands and, down the beach, began to shift sand with our fingers laced. And I asked him, "What will you do when you grow up?" For an answer he simply puffed out both his cheeks. Later he said, "And you?" Ashamed of my barren thirty years, I unbuttoned the collar of my cassock and pointed, wordless, at my Adam's apple, which moved vertiginously up and down. We have not spoken since. From time to time I show him the fourteenth line of a sonnet. He only comments by puffing out his cheeks. Then he draws and paints for me, on the canvas, a breast (Matilde's, Enriqueta's, Josefina's). I answer simply by showing him my prominent larynx. Only when from time to time we meet in Sitges, I walking Saint Bartholomew's gonfalon and he dressed as an angel gathering seashells and snails, we repeat with cordial joy our names. "Cabarbabonabell!" I start. And he answers, "Faboix!" Then once again we lace the fingers of our left hands and shift sand.

BLACK

I have never denied how much I enjoy the smell of pitch. As a boy I liked to be taken to fishing villages so I could come close to the boats as they were being caulked. And the fishermen and boat carpenters made me very happy whenever they let me dip the scoop in the pitch caldron. Then I would fill it level, raise it, tilt it, and enjoy seeing the thick tar falling slowly into the viscid blackness of the liquid in the caldron. If they let me, I'd do it again, each time raising the scoop higher and dripping more slowly. As the caulking of the boats and yawls was done at any time of day whenever necessary, I chose the mornings so that to the wonder of seeing that black thickness as it was mixed and smelling it voluptuously, on sunny days in the sun I added the joy of my eyes discovering the colors of the rainbow on the bituminous lumps. Not long ago Miró found me engrossed in that game, whiling away the time in great amusement. Not next to the sea but rather in a boreal city where I was helping a group of girls who had decided to tar all walls, all façades, all monuments with a lumpy surface.

"Have you seen, Miró? These girls claim, in their enthusiasm, that bituminous black ought to cover almost half the buildings in a modern city. In their judgment not only does pitch make our eyesight stronger, but its smell, against the opinion of some experts, also has great invigorating properties and augments one's virile energy. Thousands of tarred ropes ought to hang everywhere, as decorative elements, and it wouldn't be a bad idea if urban planners were to project and enlarge public fountains and jets from which the most pure tars would spew forth with their dense and voluptuous consistency."

Miró was looking at me and listening to me motionless, I'd even say harshly, as if I were a specter sputtering by the grace of the unabashed will of an ancient god, half shirtless and hopeless. I understood then that it was he, Miró, Joan Miró from the Passatge del Crèdit, who was organizing that risky tarring operation with a clear subversive tendency.

"Then it is you, Miró, the head and the planner behind this general tarring."

"*Of course, what do you think!*" he answered, I don't know why, in Balearic Catalan.

"See here . . . "

"*Listen. Foix. To promote black everywhere is our duty in these times of universal melancholy. Not a shadowy and marmoreal black, to be sure, nor a fuliginous one. The black I propose and try to evoke is organic, articulated, and vigorous; a black, I hope to make myself clear, as of burnt ivory, a black with latent whites. For the time being, and I don't think I'll need to rectify as I paint, pitch helps me discover and vindicate its opulent potentials. Remember, Foix. and you most noble and expert damsels who help me in my task, that of the four preferred colors—white and black. red and yellow—I maintain, against the opinion of many, that black virtually holds them all. Because—and if this happens to me, it must also happen to others—over a background of warm, caressing black, the most fulminant reds, the yellows you call "celibate," the hopeful or decadent blues, and all kinds of greens, both catalogued and delinquent, appear, dance, flirt, fecundate, and proliferate with vital warmth.*"

Miró exchanges my brush for one of a larger size that is almost never found in hardware stores; he passes on to me a bucket of bubbling pitch and like the vintner in a hurry to spray the vines with quicklime so they'll heat up, disappears behind the first corner, to my right, where I have never been and where I probably shall never go.

RED

One day, it was an August full of solar licences, I found myself at Port d'Andratx at the time when pirates play their game of *morra*. Someone told me about Sa Dragonera and of the possibility of a brief sojourn there since the lighthouse keeper's boat ferried across twice a week. I had a nocturnal image of that islet and remembered it as a haughty rock where, at night, stone characters looked like old chiefs of all races, illustrious ladies telling their stories under the cloak of shadows, warriors with mace and spear rustling through creamy heaths, and strange ancient birds spying the passage of ships with fiery and frightful eyes. Every time I went to Majorca I hurried to be on deck early to check if the vessel would go near the lighthouse rock and, if the weather were bad, if I could hear the wailing of castaways who are said to float on the crests of big waves. The thing is that I found out I was already at Port d'Andratx and did not know how I had gotten there or who had brought me. Normally, and I have already explained this, on the far side of the walls of ultrasleep there are no distances, and traversing ranges and frontiers or crossing seas is the easiest thing. Where we think we are going, there we are already, and our eagerness shortens all shortcuts. So I was at the Port, and to reach Sa Dragonera I needed neither launch nor guide. The very lighthouse keeper told me: *"I know you well, and I know you know the other way. We shall meet there. Today I am transporting military men and their girlfriends, and smugglers, and there would be no room for you."* So I found myself on the islet and, breathless and waiting for nobody, I climbed the hilltop. Halfway up I felt I could touch the sun with my hands. All was burning, and trees, grasses, and rocks were splitting. I was beginning to have second thoughts about the excursion, as I felt thirsty and feverish and wanted to return and dive in the water. And for some reason I was striving to remember lines from Italian pre-Renaissance poets. But I kept climbing on my way to the old Elizabethan lighthouse. Suddenly I realize Joan Miró is in front of me, smiling and satisfied, fresh and alert, and indifferent to the heat and August mugginess firing up rocks and bodies, and I would say he wore a wide poppy-red cloak and was ready to set fire to a rope tied around a patch of bushes and reeds as goatherds do to prepare, they say, the terrain for pasture. I wanted to convince him to give up his ill-advised burning; but he, Miró, stubborn and smiling, started the fire. The flames soon took hold, and the dry twigs and baked weeds simulated a purgatory. I ran to the top for air and to escape the heat; but Miró, with his thick red cloak and hood, chased after me while exalting the virtues of reds and extreme heat. I asked him what he was doing there and how he'd gotten there and if he planned to stop at the inn and spend the night. He answered, with the certainty of the enlightened, that *"I was waiting for the lightning."* "What lightning?" said I. *"Foix, man, what are you telling me, now: the Lightning!"* "But the sky is a pure crystal, and there is no cloud, nor approaching storm, nor cloud head, nor little storm!" *"I can see that. But here on top of Sa Dragonera a lightning strikes no matter how calm the weather and clean the sky, 'the Lightning' only I and those of us who love pure, red-hot red can see, enjoy, honor, and serve."*

YELLOW

I had never heard from any of those who loiter around the ghosts' granary or the warlocks' vat that Joan Miró practiced water skiing "in

yellow." It was through a sign planted in an herbalist's window that I found
this out. I was roaming, I vaguely recall, the lower part of Plaça Reial in
Barcelona (or Amsterdam?) when I was surprised by a radiant yellow, neither too saffrony nor not fulvescent enough, provoked by the looming darkness of an herbalist's. I stepped back to take a good look. Yes, it was real: a
wide poster the yellow of broom before it is pulled from its bush, a warm
yellow with secret blood veins that only painters find when they need to feed
their hues with intravascular injections. Floating in it, so to say, lemonlike,
some letters at full sail, announcing to the winds: MIRÓ, A WATER-SKI
MASTER IN NEW YELLOWS. The sign was somewhat in the baroque
and elegant style of the painter, and it was not difficult for me to confirm
that it referred to him, Joan. I asked a passerby, the first person to walk by
that spot—the streets to both sides of the ramparts are normally deserted—
and he dodged my question while muttering some words I interpreted as
meaning "Ask Sebastià Gasch." But I couldn't find Gasch, even in the
barber shops. I went straight into the herbalist's, and—oh, beautiful surprise!—in its interior a long corridor with a dry scent of violets led me to the
sea, a sea with tender yellows of dawn and corrosive yellows of dusk. And—
oh, still more beautiful surprise!—Miró, Joan Miró was moving on the water, at once light and fishlike, on his skis, dominating the others, all of them
Mirólike, by which I mean that, tall or short, thin or big-bellied, hairy or
beardless, the skiers, imitators or disciples, and all ill-intentioned—as befits
the followers of futurizing painting—all reproduced the physical traits of our
trailblazer. Dozens of Mirós, therefore, on the wavy surface, with skis tossed
from latter-day outboards: shiny, roaring, and sparkling. I put on my skis,
adjusted them tight in order to hit the water, and looked for a learned and
sensible volunteer to take me where, sure and confident, the master was
gliding. I thought at the time that it was a good idea for me to take water-
skiing lessons directly from Miró himself. Then a bather tugged at me and
said, *"Are you also Miró? Good grief, how much you look like him! You may be the
decisive one, the uncontested."* I told him my name, and he fled as if I had
spoken Zulu to him. But Miró had caught sight of me and came over to tell
me it was all a pretense. And stroking his head with his hand, he went on:
*"Listen, Foix, and believe me. You're wearing too hard a collar and too stiff a hat,
and you are not commanding enough. You look way too far and pay too little
attention to the others. As for myself, as you can see, I pretend to see nothing and no
one, but on the sly I eye and spy them all. I know what they do, what they invent,
what they copy, and what they botch, being often wrong, and I take all I can use.
And I hold myself as straight as you do practically without wetting my feet or the
skis."* In a more confidential tone, picking up and throwing stones, he added,
"In yellow, in red, or in black, I prefer dry skiing." And wrapping himself in a

bathrobe from the good old days, he opened a door I thought led nowhere, and in a few seconds I lost sight of him. I didn't know what to do with my diving suit, and had lost my gloves.

WHITE

If you asked me to tell you precisely, concisely, and laconically how it happened, I wouldn't feel up to it. Therefore I don't know whether it was in the mountains, near the pass where we ache to arrive and discover the other face of the country with its thick forest and dry gorges, where secret trails and paths, on which you never run into anyone, are born, or lost, or die. Or perhaps at the bend of a trough, next to the sea, on the side of a pine grove with far too many clearings. Or perhaps at the four corners of an urban crossroads with asymmetrical skyscrapers, and I myself diminished, overcome, and almost eliminated by the opulence of shops and distilleries, and of vehicles. I don't know. I don't have the vaguest recollection. Yet I can assure you that I recall everything from the moment when—a mountaineer, a sailor, or a pedestrian—a pallid and tender glow (which by its rarity was adverse to that hour's daylight) burst all of a sudden. So much so that the rocky, coastal, or urban landscape was all light and splendor. My eyes closed, as if fogged up and useless. But, singularly and without peer, the clarity, fed by floods of solid and massive whiteness with alabaster lumps, ivory islets, and snow fallows, was more intense to my dead eyes. The more I recognized that I was blind, the more light I caught. I was like a submerged diver sailing through the mirage of a milky way with the joy and fear of those who are lost in the fog of mountaintops or crawl on a sea studded with gigantic reefs and landheads. All my efforts to open my eyes were in vain. The whiteness, like a cascade of silence, exceeded the limits of my comprehension. I had truly gone blind, but I could not understand what had happened to me. I was ready to give in to the temptation of surrendering, by immersion, to the impetuous torrent of disquieted whites when a firm hand, warm, confident, and assured, grasped mine and a candent voice said, *"Do not be afraid, I am with you."* We advanced surely through that abyss of whiteness. I would have sworn they were less hard, those whites, and that we slid on them as on snow. We advanced firmly and straight as on a royal and well-known road. I would say we took long hours, in beatitude and contentment. But where was the finish, the goal, the ending? I interrupted our august silence to ask my generous guide who he was. *"I am Miró."* "Joan Miró, the painter?" I asked. "You must have realized, Miró: I am blind, and my eyes are closed forever; but I can guess it all immensely luminous." *"Fear not,"* Miró answered. *"I know the way all too well. I am also blind, like you. And you see how I trek. Wasn't that you, Foix, who told me one day that only when your eyes were closed did the real became divinely concrete for you?"* And more joyful and happier than ever, we continued together along pathways of resplendent nickel and squares of fresh linen.

A Note on Calders's
"Two Stories"

Pere Calders i Rossinyol was born in Barcelona in 1912 and worked there as an illustrator and journalist. His first literary publications appeared in 1936. Soon thereafter, toward the end of the Civil War, Calders, who had fought on the Republic's side, went into exile, first in France, then in Mexico, where he lived until his return to Catalonia in 1963.

"Subtle Invasion," the title story of *Invasió subtil i altres contes,* was first published in Barcelona by Edicions 62 in 1978; this book received the Lletra d'Or prize the following year. "Catalans around the World" first appeared in Calders's *Cròniques de la veritat oculta* (Barcelona: Editorial Selecta, 1955). That collection of short stories was awarded the Víctor Català prize. I have used the recent editions in Calders's *Obres completes* (Barcelona: Edicions 62): from volumes 3 (1987), 233–235, and 1 (1984), 230–231, respectively.

Calders, the author of several novels and a considerable collection of short—oftentimes very short—fiction, is not only the most popular of living Catalan writers; he has also exerted the greatest influence on the new generation of narrators. If Pla is a master of mordant irony, often intent on debunking established notions, Calders is an outstanding example of an ironic amiability, a writer who has captured a sense of humor many Catalans would feel somehow essentially their own. His fictions of-

ten combine the unexpected with references to archetypical Catalan icons.
Two such icons in these stories are the references to the polychrome
wooden sculptures of saints, carved traditionally in the town of Olot, and
the mention of the folkloric dances associated with the town of Castellterçol; these emblems would represent Catalonia at its most provincial.

PERE CALDERS

Two Stories

SUBTLE INVASION

At the Hostal Punta Marina in Tossa I met a disconcerting Japanese who in no way fit the idea I had of that type of Oriental.

At dinnertime he sat at my table after asking for my permission without much ceremony. I was struck by the fact that he had no slanting eyes nor yellowish skin. On the contrary: as color goes, he was rather rosy-cheeked and red-haired.

I was curious to see what dishes he would order. I confess mine was a childish attitude, imagining he would order uncommon dishes or exotic combinations. The truth is he surprised me by requesting a salad—"with lots of onion," he said—pig's feet, grilled sardines, and toasted almonds. After all that, coffee, a glass of brandy, and a cigar.

I had imagined the Japanese would eat with exaggerated, even irritating neatness, picking his morsels as if they were the pieces of a watch. But it wasn't that way: the man used his knife and fork with great ease and chewed with his mouth full, without any esthetic complications. To tell the truth, he was shaking the foundations of my ideas.

Besides, he spoke Catalan just like any of us, without even the shadow of a foreign accent. This was not too surprising if one keeps in mind that those people are very studious and smart to a high degree. But he made me feel inferior, because I don't know a single word of Japanese. It is curious to note that I was the one who brought a foreign touch to the interview, as I conditioned my behavior—my gestures, words, conversation openings—to the concrete fact that my interlocutor was Japanese. He, on the other hand, was fresh as a rose.

I thought that man would be a salesman for photographic equipment or transistor radios. Or perhaps cultured pearls. I touched on all those subjects, but he rejected them with a broad gesture of his arm. "As for me," he said, "I sell religious objects made in Olot." "Is there still a market for that?" I asked him. And he told me yes, that it was going through hard times but that he himself was doing well. He worked the southern zone of the peninsula, and he added that as soon as he had some time or there was a holiday, he headed straight for home.

"There's nothing like home!" he concluded with a satisfied air.

"You live in your country?"

"Of course. Where would you want me to live?"

Yes, of course; they are all globe trotters and go everywhere. I took another look at him and I may assure you that no detail, either in his clothing or in his person, betrayed his Japanese origin. He even had a pin of the Barcelona Football Club on his lapel.

All together it was highly suspicious, and it worried me. My wife had taken her supper up in the room because she was a little under the weather; I told her about the encounter and adorned my story with my apprehensions: he could well have been a spy.

"And how do you know he was Japanese?" she asked me.

I laughed, perhaps not at all spontaneously, feeling sorry for her naiveté.

"I can smell them an hour away," I replied.

"Are you sure you've seen many of them?"

"No. But I spot them at once!"

"Did he tell you he was Japanese?"

"Not once. They are cagey."

"Did anybody tell you?"

"Nobody told me anything, nor do I need to be told. I have the sharpest instinct!"

We had a row. She is always provoking me and saying I see things and that any day I'll get into real trouble. As if she didn't know me! She seems to enjoy arguing, but she is incredibly credulous.

That night I slept little and poorly. I could not get that Japanese off my mind. Because if they appear as they are, with their little smile, their bows, and those slanting gazes, we shall be able to defend ourselves. I hope so! But if they start coming with so much dissimulation and false circumstance, they're going to give us a hard time.

Once I went to Burma to supervise a sales expedition of plaster of Paris.

The trip went quite well, and when I arrived in Yakri, a local kinglet offered me his trusty hospitality. Since there were few Europeans there,* that gentleman felt an interest in showing off the brilliance of his court and detained me, making my sojourn longer than I had planned.

So that my Western appearance would not dull the palace etiquette, the monarch gave me a mantle all embroidered with pearls and precious stones, with the condition that I only remove it to go to sleep.

The royal apartments in those countries are a kind of park, where animals and people live in common, keeping certain distances. There is a great quantity of birds, garden elephants, felines, sacred and profane tortoises, seasonal insects, and other animals, so rare that they inspire respect.

My stay there was a continuous party. We sang, we danced, and we ate from morning to night, and each craving had its satisfaction. But as I was a person under orders and have never neglected my duties, the day came for me to take my leave, and the kinglet, to regale me, organized a great folklore exhibition.

The sovereign, dressed for a gala, had me sit at his side. He had a panther to his feet and a magnificent parrot on his right shoulder. He clapped and the program began.

After I heard the songs of people from all of his provinces, two hundred dancers started to dance in a monorhythmic manner. The dance lasted long hours, always the same, always to the same cadence. When boredom got the better of me, to let off steam I said out loud, in Catalan:

"For the money, I prefer the dances from Castellterçol."

The parrot let out a guttural cry and, addressing me, said:

"Be careful. If the Great Interpreter hears you, you're a dead man."

He spoke in such correct Catalan that it, at first, left me breathless. Man of the world that I was, I kept my cool before the king, but at night, when everyone was asleep, I looked for the parrot, who told me his

---

*There were none. (Clarification out of conscience.)

story. He was a Catalan parrot from Cadaqués, and fortune had brought
him there.

In spite of all those things that separated us, there was the
language uniting us, and we shared some memories.

We spoke of the Mediterranean and of our hopes to see it
again, and the next morning, when I left Yakri, my heart was much softer
than on my arrival.

Bibliography

This bibliography lists works by authors cited in the introduction and works mentioned in essays that do not have bibliographical notes, works in English on authors translated in the anthology, English translations of works by authors in the anthology, and further readings in English on topics treated in the essays.

INTRODUCTION

Bisson, T. N. *The Medieval Crown of Aragon: A Short History*. Oxford: Clarendon Press, 1986.

Elliott, J[ohn] H[uxtable]. *The Revolt of the Catalans: A Study in the Decline of Spain, 1598–1640*. Cambridge: Cambridge University Press, 1963.

Hillgarth, J[ocelyn] N. *The Problem of a Catalan Mediterranean Empire 1229–1327*. Supplement 8 to *English Historical Review*. London: Longman, 1975.

McDonogh, Gary W., ed. *Conflict in Catalonia: Images of an Urban Society*. Gainesville: University of Florida Press, 1986.

Shneidman, J. Lee. *The Rise of the Aragonese-Catalan Empire: 1200–1350*. 2 vols. New York: New York University Press, 1970.

Ullman, Joan Connelly. *The Tragic Week: A Study of Anticlericalism in Spain, 1875–1912*. Cambridge, Mass.: Harvard University Press, 1968.

Vicens i Vives, Jaume. *Approaches to the History of Spain*. Trans. Joan Connelly Ullman. Berkeley: University of California Press, 1967.

Woolard, Kathryn A. *Double Talk: Bilingualism and the Politics of Ethnicity in Catalonia*. Stanford: Stanford University Press, 1989.

CARLES SOLDEVILA, THE ART OF SHOWING BARCELONA

McCully, Marilyn, and others. *Homage to Barcelona: The City and Its Art 1888–1936*. London: Arts Council of Great Britain, 1985.

MERCÈ RODOREDA, TWO STORIES

Translations

O'Shiel, Eda, trans. *The Pigeon Girl (La Plaça del Diamant)*. London: Deutsch, 1967.
Rosenthal, David H., trans. *The Time of the Doves (La Plaça del Diamant)*. New York: Taplinger, 1981; London: Arena, 1986.
_____. *My Christina, and Other Stories*. Port Townsend, Wash.: Graywolf Press, 1984.
_____. "The Salamander." *Catalan Review*, vol. 2, no. 2 (1987).

Studies

Bieder, Maryellen. "Cataclysm and Rebirth: Journey to the Edge of the Maelstrom: Mercè Rodoreda's *Quanta, quanta guerra . . .*" *Actes del Tercer Colloqui d'Estudis Catalans a Nord-Amèrica*. Barcelona: Montserrat, 1983, 227–237.
_____. "The Woman in the Garden: The Problem of Identity in the Novels of Mercè Rodoreda." *Actes del Segon Colloqui d'Estudis Catalans a Nord-Amèrica*. Barcelona: Montserrat, 1982, 253–264.
Catalan Review, vol. 2, no. 2 (1987), is entirely dedicated to Rodoreda, with articles in English by J. Albrecht, P. Lunn, E. Bergmann, L. Busquets, M. Fayad, K. McGlenn, J. Martí-Olivella, G. Nichols, J. Pérez, and J. R. Resina. Includes up-to-date bibliography.
Clarasó, Mercè. "The Angle of Vision in the Novels of Mercè Rodoreda." *Bulletin of Hispanic Studies* 57 (1980), 143–152.
Nichols, Geraldine C. "Exile, Gender, and Mercè Rodoreda." *Modern Language Notes* 101 (1986).
Wyers, Frances. "A Woman's Voices: Mercè Rodoreda's *La Plaça del Diamant*." *Kentucky Romance Quarterly* 30 (1983).

JOAN FUSTER, MARAGALL AND UNAMUNO, FACE TO FACE

The bibliography on Unamuno is massive. A recent article touches on his relationship with Maragall: Wyers, Frances. "Unamuno and 'The Death of the Author.'" *Hispanic Review* 58 (1990), 325–346.

MONSERRAT ROIG, CATALANS IN NAZI DEATH CAMPS

Roig, Montserrat. "The Everyday Opera." Trans. J. M. Sobrer. In Kathleen McNerney, ed., *On Our Own Behalf: Women's Tales from Catalonia*. Lincoln: University of Nebraska Press, 1988, 207–234.

SALVADOR ESPRIU, TWO PARABLES   223

Espriu, Salvador. *La pell de brau.* Trans. Burton Raffel. Marlboro, Vt.: Marlboro
    Press, 1987. An illuminating afterword by Thomas F. Glick sets Espriu's
    work within the context of Catalan philo-Semitism during the Franco years.
———. *Lord of the Shadow: Poems.* Ed. J. M. Castellet, trans. Kenneth Lyons.
    Oxford: Dolphin, 1975.
———. *Selected Poems of Salvador Espriu.* Trans. Magda Bogin. New York: Norton,
    1989.

JOSEP PLA, ANTONI GAUDÍ (1852–1926)

Bergós, Joan. *Antoni Gaudí, l'home i l'obra.* Barcelona: Ariel, 1954.
Bonner, Anthony, ed. and trans. *Selected Works of Ramon Llull.* 2 vols. Princeton,
    N.J.: Princeton University Press, 1985.
Collins, George R., and Juan Bassegoda Nonell. *The Designs and Drawings of Anto-
    nio Gaudí.* Princeton, N.J.: Princeton University Press, 1983.
Martinell, Cèsar. *Gaudí i la Sagrada Família comentada per ell mateix.* Barcelona:
    Aymà, 1951.
Peers, E[dgar] Allison. *Fool of Love: The Life of Ramon Llull.* London: S.C.M. Press,
    1946.
Puig Boada. *El temple de la Sagrada Família.* Barcelona: Barcino, 1929. Greatly
    expanded edition, 1979.
Quintana, Francesc de Paula. *Les formes guerxes del temple de la Sagrada Família.*
    Barcelona: n.p., n.d.
Ràfols, Josep F., and Francesc Folguera, *Gaudí.* Barcelona: Canosa, 1928.
Sugranyes, Domènech. *Disposició estàtica del temple de la Sagrada Família.* N.p., n.d.

JOSEP PALAU I FABRE, PICASSO AND CATALONIA

McCully, Marilyn. *Els Quatre Gats: Art in Barcelona around 1900.* Princeton, N.J.:
    Princeton University Press, 1978.
———, ed. *A Picasso Anthology: Documents, Ciriticsm, Reminiscences.* London: Arts
    Council of Great Britain, 1981.

J. V. FOIX, THREE PAINTERS AND FOUR COLORS

Catalan Review, first issue (1986), was devoted entirely to Foix; many articles are
    in English.
Foix, J. V. *When I Sleep, Then I See Clearly: Selected Poems of J. V. Foix.* Trans. David
    Rosenthal. New York: Persea Books, 1988.

Index of Proper Names and Terms

(third wife of James II). Founded a monastery for Clarissa nuns in Pedralbes (1326), where, once a widow, she retired. 22.

ern European inspiration and its formal effusiveness drew the criticism of the new generation of *noucentistes* (see *noucentisme*). 5, 9, 11, 16, 22, 60, 90, 91, 161.

Morand, Paul (1889–1976). French poet and novelist. 23.

Moscardó Ituarte, José (1878–1956). Joined Franco's rebellion as a colonel making a heroic stronghold of the Toledo citadel. Later became captain general of Catalonia (1943–1945). 132.

Movimiento, or Movimiento Nacional. The collective name given the political forces united in the July 18, 1936, uprising against the Spanish Republic. After the Civil War it became Franco's political organ. 130, 144.

Muntaner, Ramon (Peralada 1265–Ibiza 1336). Author of a chronicle of contemporary events, completed around 1328. 7, 26, 88.

Narváez, Ramón María (1800–1868). Military leader and a political opponent of Espartero (q.v.). Presided over the Spanish government (1844–1851 and 1856–1867); his authoritarian rule precipitated the revolution of September 1868. 103.

Nicolau i d'Olwer, Lluís (Barcelona 1888–Mexico 1961). Historian, classical scholar, and political journalist. 91.

Nin i Pérez, Andreu (El Vendrell 1892–Madrid 1937). Communist politician associated with the POUM; writer and translator. He was assassinated by Soviet agents. 136.

Nonell i Monturiol, Isidre (Barcelona 1873–1911). Painter, best known for choosing as subject matter for his oils and drawings the downtrodden and outcast. 191, 201.

Noucentisme. A Catalan cultural movement developed mostly by Eugeni d'Ors (q.v.) from 1906 on. The *noucentistes*, who saw themselves at the opposite end from the *modernistes*, sought a return to classical and Mediterranean models. The name derives from *nou cents*, "nine hundred," meaning the new century. 9, 16, 38, 91, 108, 158, 164, 169, 181.

Nova (Nueva) Planta, Decrees of. Dispositions dictated by Philip V between 1707 and 1716. They abolished the old constitutional organization of the Crown of Aragon (q.v.). The decrees established a *chancillería* to administer justice in Catalonia-Aragon; the *chancillería* became the Royal Audience (q.v.) presided over by a captain general and under the jurisdiction of the Council of Castile. 7, 8, 100.

Oliver i Sallarès, Joan (Sabadell 1899). Writer and poet; signed his verses with the pseudonym Pere Quart. 93.

Oliver i Tolrà, Miquel dels Sants (Majorca 1864–Barcelona 1920). Writer. 86.

Oller i Moragas, Narcís (Valls 1846–Barcelona 1930). Novelist. His *La papallona* (1885) earned the praise of Emile Zola. 89.

Orfeó Català. Choral society founded in Barcelona in 1891 by Lluís Millet and Amadeu Vives. 34.

Ors i Rovira, Eugeni d' (Barcelona 1881–Vilanova i la Geltrú 1954). Writer and philosopher. Influential ideologue of *noucentisme* (q.v.). 9, 16, 91, 115, 120, 123, 124, 126, 164, 169, 181.

Ortega y Gasset, José (1883–1955). Spanish philosopher and essayist. 120, 123.

Josep Miquel Sobrer

Associate Professor in the Department of Spanish and Portuguese at Indiana University, is the author of *L'èpica de la realitat*, *La doble soledat d'Ausias March*, and *El llibre dels oracles* and co-editor of *The Singers' Anthology of 20th-Century Spanish Songs*.